Historic Canada

Bridging Saint John Harbour

On the Cover: With the Likely concrete plant on Chelsey Drive in the foreground, work progresses on closing the gap in the bridge. (Courtesy of Heritage Resources.)

Historic Canada

Bridging Saint John Harbour

Harold E. Wright and Joseph Goguen

ARCADIA PUBLISHING

ISBN 978-1-4671-2010-4

Published by Arcadia Publishing
Charleston, South Carolina

Printed in the United States of America

Library of Congress Control Number: 2013931615

For all general information, please contact Arcadia Publishing:
Telephone 843-853-2070
Fax 843-853-0044
E-mail sales@arcadiapublishing.com
For customer service and orders:
Toll-Free 1-888-313-2665

Visit us on the Internet at www.arcadiapublishing.com

We dedicate this book to David Goss, a well-known local storyteller, author, and friend, whose books and walks 'n talks have inspired both of us for years.

Contents

Acknowledgments		6
Introduction		7
1.	The Bay Meets the Wolastoq	9
2.	The Harbour Highway	23
3	The Lost Navy Island	29
4.	Neighbourhoods Destroyed	35
5.	The Suspension Bridge	45
6.	The Cantilever Bridge	59
7.	The Rail Bridges	73
8.	Tourism at the Reversing Falls Rapids	79
9.	The 100-Year Dream Gets Built	89
10.	The Saint John Harbour Bridge Authority	115

ACKNOWLEDGMENTS

There are always many people who help when one undertakes a project like this book. Family and friends are part of that process, and we wish to thank them. Additionally, there are many organizations and individuals who contributed information, photographs, and comments. We would like to thank the following by name: David Goss, Bob Boudreau, Jim Sulis, Cliff Boyer, Bill Thompson, Lois Ellis, Mary Munford, Kelly Honeyman, Member of Parliament Rodney Weston, Michael Wallace, Peter Murphy, Ken Anthony, Bill Flowers, Ashlee Joyce, Donnie Collins, staff at the Information Centre, Saint John Regional Library, and staff at the Provincial Archives of New Brunswick, Fredericton.

Unless otherwise noted, all images appear courtesy of Heritage Resources.

Introduction

For a millennia, the indigenous peoples used the Bay of Fundy and the Saint John River for traveling, fishing, and trading. Some 100 billion tonnes of water flows in and out of the bay on an average tide, twice a day, creating rip currents, swirling whirlpools, and a tidal range reaching 16 metres at the head of the bay. Portuguese explorer Estavan Gomez is believed to be the first European visitor who, in 1535, identified a river on the east coast as the "Rio de la Buelta" (River of the Return). In 1604, Mi'kmaqs gathered on Ouigoudi (Navy Island) where they watched a foreign-looking ship enter the harbour on June 24, St. Jean de Baptiste Day. Aboard was Pierre Dugua, Sieur de Monts, and Samuel de Champlain. After charting the harbour and making note of the Reversible Falls Rapids (this is one of the earliest names of the falls, but for consistency with modern usage, we will use the word Reversing), they sailed down the bay.

This introduction to the white man set up a trading system that lasted well into the 19th century, which included LaTour's and, later, the pre-Loyalist trading posts at Portland Point. In 1783, some 14,000 American Loyalists arrived at the mouth of the Saint John River, founding the towns of Carleton and Parrtown, which amalgamated in 1785 as the City of Saint John. Saint John's North End, then called the City of Portland, amalgamated in 1889. It is in Portland that all of our five harbour bridges are located.

Seaborne commerce became the mainstay of the local economy. Fish, furs, masts for the Royal Navy, livestock, grains, and other foodstuffs were traded, and shipbuilding began. The Saint John River provided the highway into the New Brunswick hinterland.

The city was divided by the harbour and the river, which made all manners of communication difficult. In June 1785, city fathers gave licenses to a Mr. Place and a Mr. Falconer to operate as ferrymen across the harbour. The harbour ferry *Victoria* was built in 1839, and this established a ferry system that carried people, goods, and animals across the harbour until 1954. The only thing missing was a bridge.

Although previous attempts at a bridge were unsuccessful, William K. Reynolds did succeed in the early 1850s at building a suspension bridge at the Reversing Falls Rapids. Later, this was followed by a rail bridge and then the idea to build a second bridge across the harbour over Navy Island. That dream bridge took almost 100 years to realize.

During the 19th century, Saint John became a major immigrant port of entry, with immigrants and mariners passing through the Partridge Island quarantine station during the 19th and 20th centuries. Saint John eventually became known as the "Liverpool of America," as it developed into the fourth largest shipbuilding centre in the world. The shipyards around the harbour launched an average of two ships every week. This was the "golden age" of shipbuilding.

The 1867 Canadian Confederation had a tremendous negative impact on our local economy. The focus of the national economy shifted from the Maritime provinces into the central part of the country. Saint John endured over the next several decades, both from the effect of the national railway system and such catastrophes as the June 20, 1877, great fire. The prophecy that "from these very ashes and ruins a brighter, a more glorious and more prosperous city will arise" came true because, within five years, the city was rebuilt.

Saint John pinned its hopes for continuing prosperity on the port. In the 1880s and 1890s, the Canadian government was using Portland, Maine, as Canada's winter port. This changed in 1896 when Saint John was designated as Canada's winter port. Goods from across the country now went through Saint John's ice-free harbour during the winter port season.

Over the next 20-plus years, harbour facilities improved and were expanded. The increase in grain shipments, due to the development of rail links with western Canada, created a need for a grain elevator. The first grain elevator was built on the west side in 1893, and a second elevator followed on the east side. Port activities were described as "the waterfront was not a pretty place, but it was busy, where ships from all over the world came to load and unload in the winter port . . . [and the] Saint John longshoremen were more honest than those anywhere else, and more efficient." The harbour ferry service continued, but there was still a demand for a second bridge across the harbour.

In 1915, a new bridge was built at the Reversing Falls Rapids. A few years later, a new rail bridge was put in place. In 1923, the country's largest dry dock opened in Courtney Bay. A few years later, in June 1931, a large part of the west side port facilities burned. Quick federal aid to rebuild the port saved the city's economy, and in 1934, the Navy Island Terminal was created. A new coastal ferry, the SS *Saint John*, as well as a new harbour ferry, the *Loyalist*, began their service. Coupled with the new Millidgeville Airport, Saint John could now service its national and international customers by land, sea, and air.

World War II brought economic prosperity, which continued into the 1950s and 1960s. There were many changes in the physical appearance of Saint John. Veterans' housing was built in the Rifle Range and Portland Place areas of the North End, and suburbs emerged in Forest Hills, Champlain Heights, and Millidgeville. A massive urban renewal program replaced slum housing and workers' tenements in the areas around Main Street. In 1968, the look of the harbour was forever changed when the Saint John Harbour Bridge was finally built, a 100-year dream.

The two bridges that service the City of Saint John now, as well as those vehicles passing through the city en route to Nova Scotia to the east and Maine to the west, struggle at times to meet peak vehicle demand. The bridges are old, and being subject to the harsh salt-air marine environment, require constant maintenance. In 2015, the current cantilever bridge at the Reversing Falls will be 100 years old. Maybe it is about time we spoke of finally building that third vehicle bridge.

One

The Bay Meets the Wolastoq

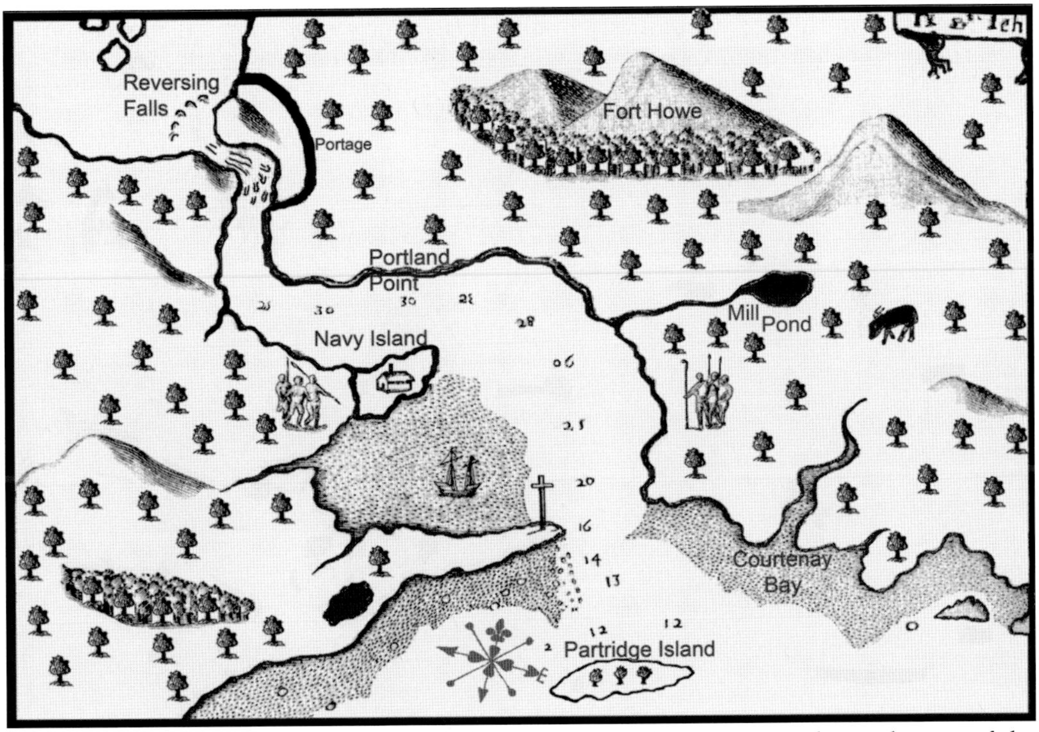

When Champlain arrived at the mouth of the Saint John River in 1604, he made note of the following harbour features: the Reversing Falls Rapids, Navy Island, and the waterway that went from the harbour at the Long Wharf area out along the Great Marsh Road (now Rothesay Avenue) to Glen Falls. His map also made note of the native encampment on Navy Island as well as the native caribou.

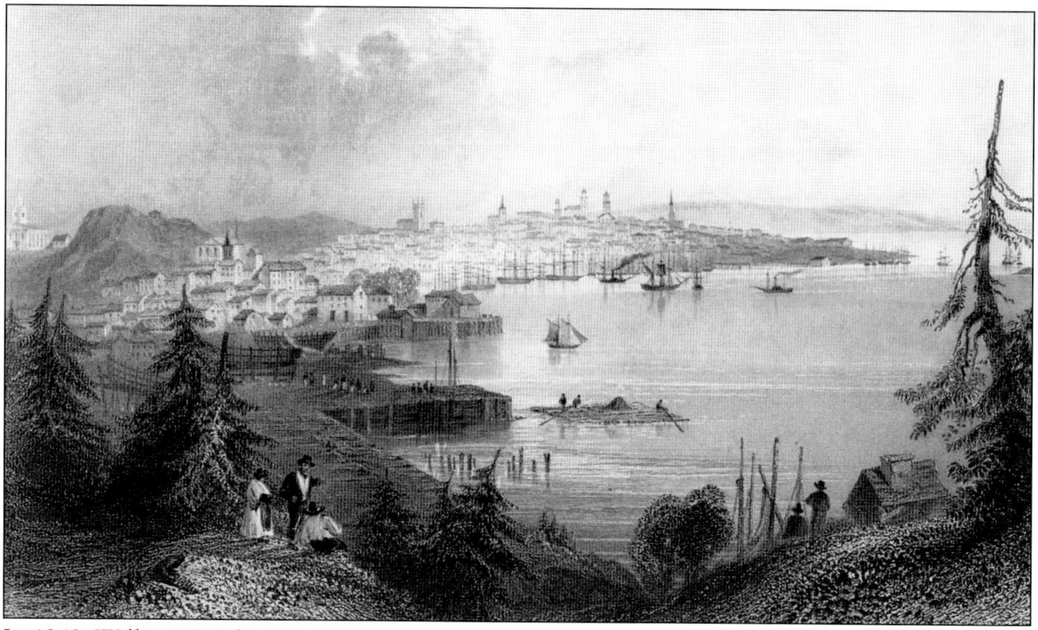

In 1842, William Bartlett printed several images of Saint John. This one shows the harbour from the general area where Douglas Avenue meets Main Street. It shows the shipyard at Hilyards Point, now the site of HMCS *Brunswicker.* In the centre appears to be the first harbour ferry, the steamer *Victoria.* There are over two dozen vessels in the harbour, showing just how significant the waterway was to Saint John's economy, exporting New Brunswick goods around the world.

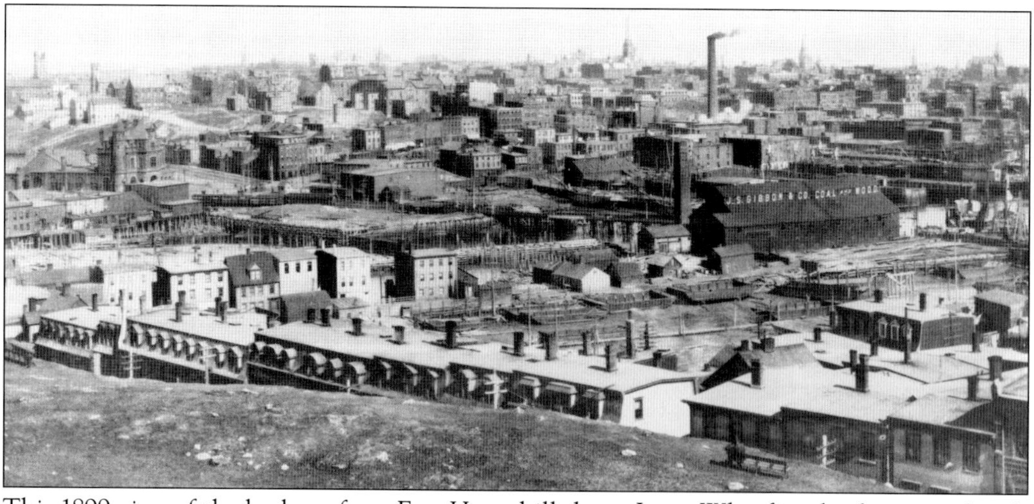

This 1899 view of the harbour from Fort Howe hill shows Long Wharf in the foreground with York Point in the background. At this time, Gibbons's coal and wood warehouse was on Long Wharf. Note the lumber scows in the millponds at low tide. In the background are at least eight church steeples, testament to the importance of religion to the community at this time. Much of what is shown in this image had been destroyed in the Great Fire of 1877.

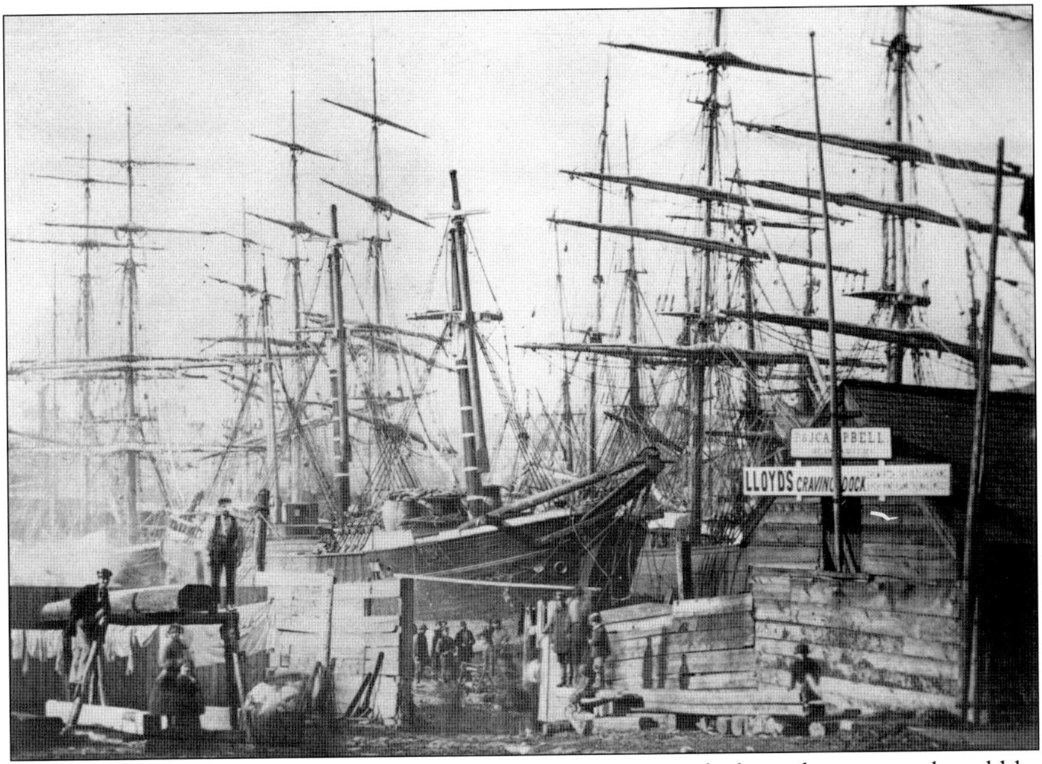

Here is Lloyds Graving Dock, York Point, in 1863. A graving dock is where a vessel could be taken out of the water for maintenance or repair. When harbour tides went out, the vessels were worked on below the waterline, and when the tide returned, work was done above the waterline. The number of masts is misleading as not all these vessels were in the graving dock; some were tied up at Long Wharf. At the left is a large piece of timber that appears to be in the process of being squared, probably to be used for the repair of a ship.

The ship *Edgar Cecil* appears to be unloading guns for the new harbour defences in 1878. The *Edgar Cecil* had at least two voyages into Saint John in the 1860s and 1870s. In 1878, England and Russia were at the brink of war, and the harbour defences on Partridge Island were renewed with new "antiquated" guns.

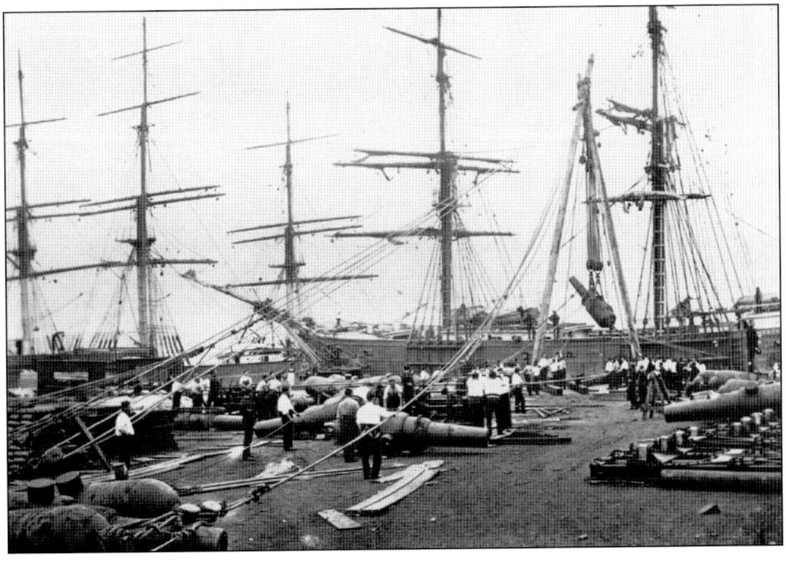

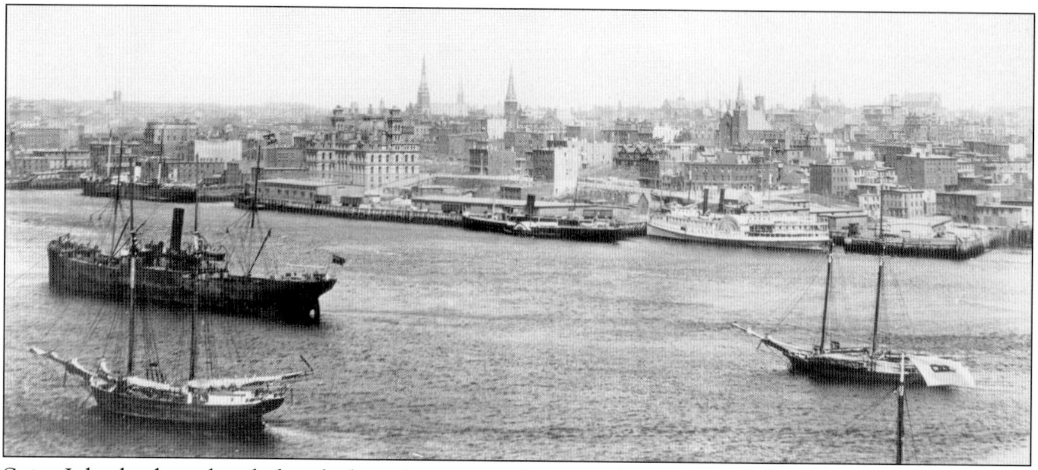

Saint John harbour bustled with ships from around the world for most of the 19th century, carrying finished goods into and from the city and immigrants and passengers from and to countries around the globe. By the end of the 19th century, steam-powered and iron vessels were replacing the wood sailing ships. In the centre of this photograph is the Boston Boat, at the pier at Reeds Point.

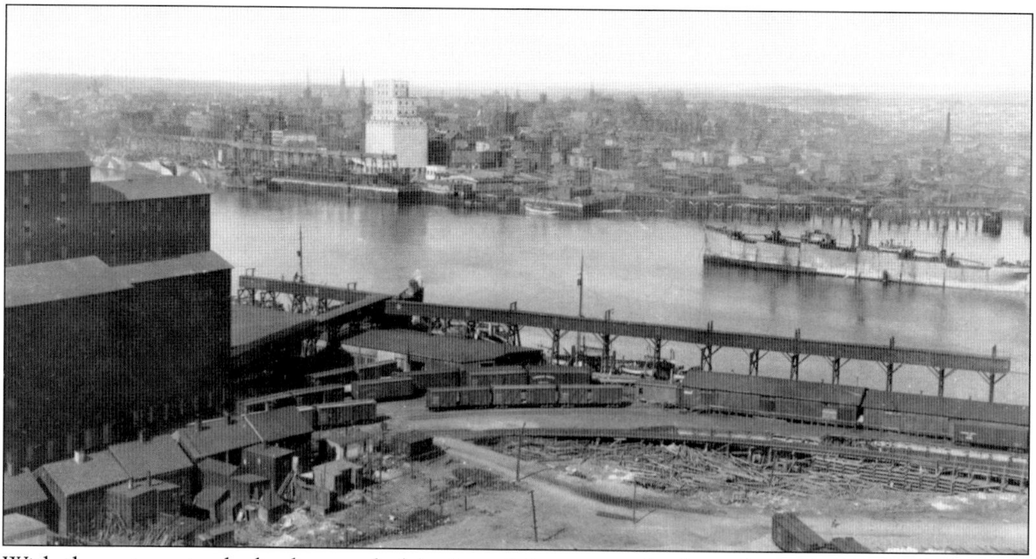

With the uptown in the background, this view of the western harbour front shows just how closely residents lived next to industry. Houses at the lower left are literally feet from the rail lines and boxcars and the overhead gantries from the grain elevators. Much of this section of the port remained like this well into the 1960s.

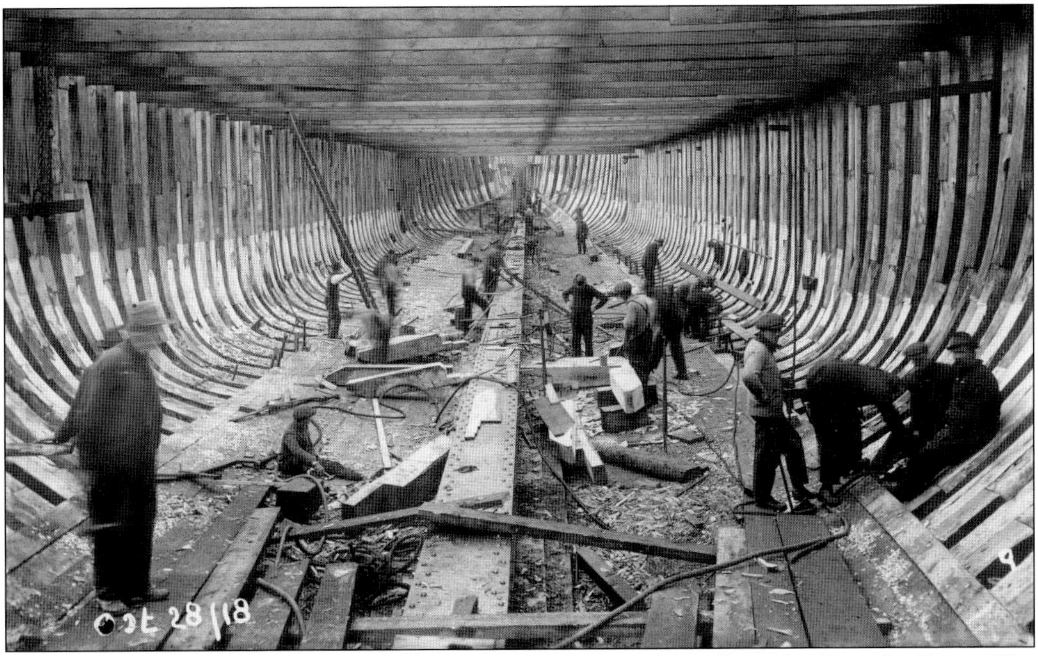

Between 1917 and 1919, the wood boat industry was revived briefly at the Straight Shore. The sister ships *Randfontein* and *Dornfontein* were built using the traditional construction methods of the 19th century. Laid down in 1917 and launched in June 1918, the *Dornfontein* had a short career. In August 1918, she was captured by a German U-boat in the Bay of Fundy and set afire.

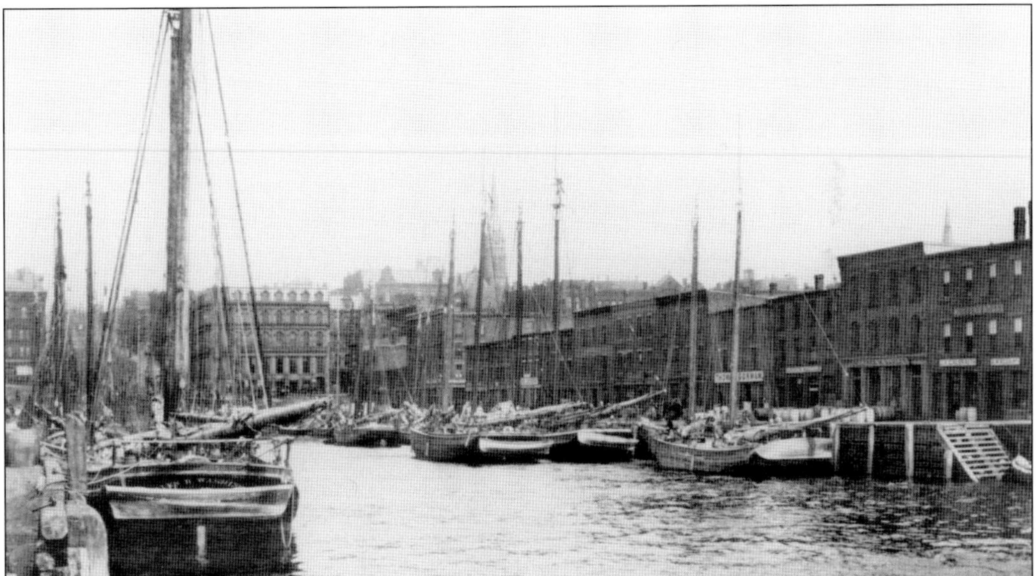

Here is Market Slip facing Market Square at high tide. It is rare to find good views of South Market Wharf. The number of vessels tied here show the importance of this spot. Many of these ships were coastal vessels, carrying goods between Saint John and other communities along the Bay of Fundy. Most of the buildings in the background were wholesale merchants. In the early 1960s, this area was demolished for the Coast Guard base, which, by 2013, was slated for redevelopment as the Fundy Quay retail and hotel space.

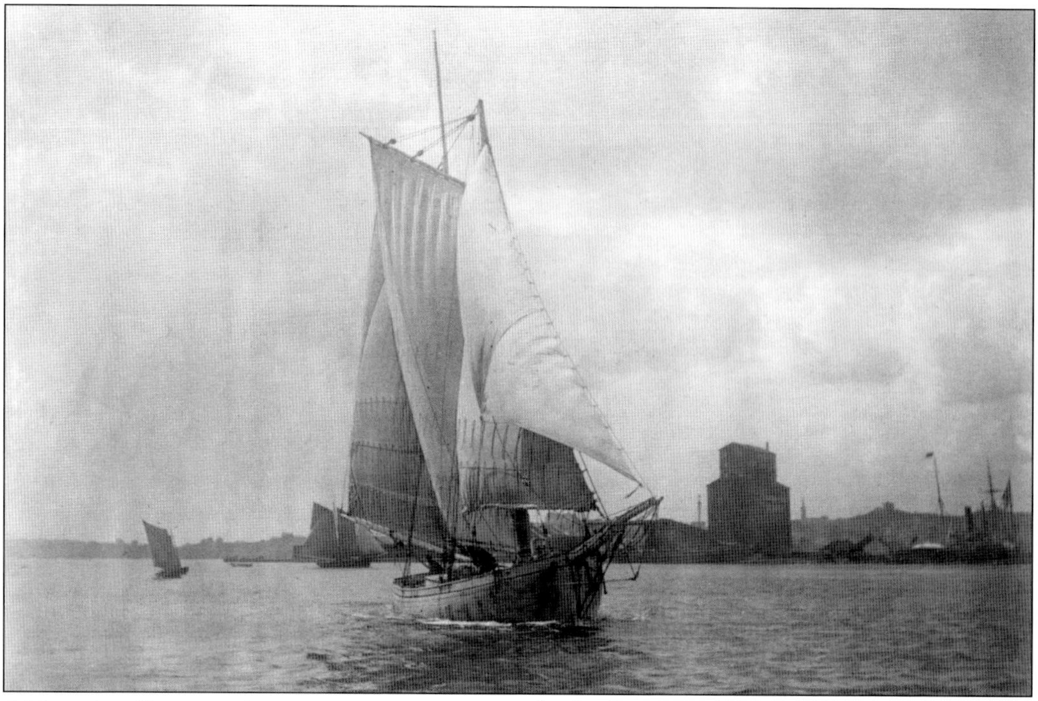

Although sailing vessels were a common site in the harbour until the 1920s, it is not the case today. Today, the only sail vessels would be pleasure craft seeking the calm waters of the Saint John and Kennebecasis Rivers.

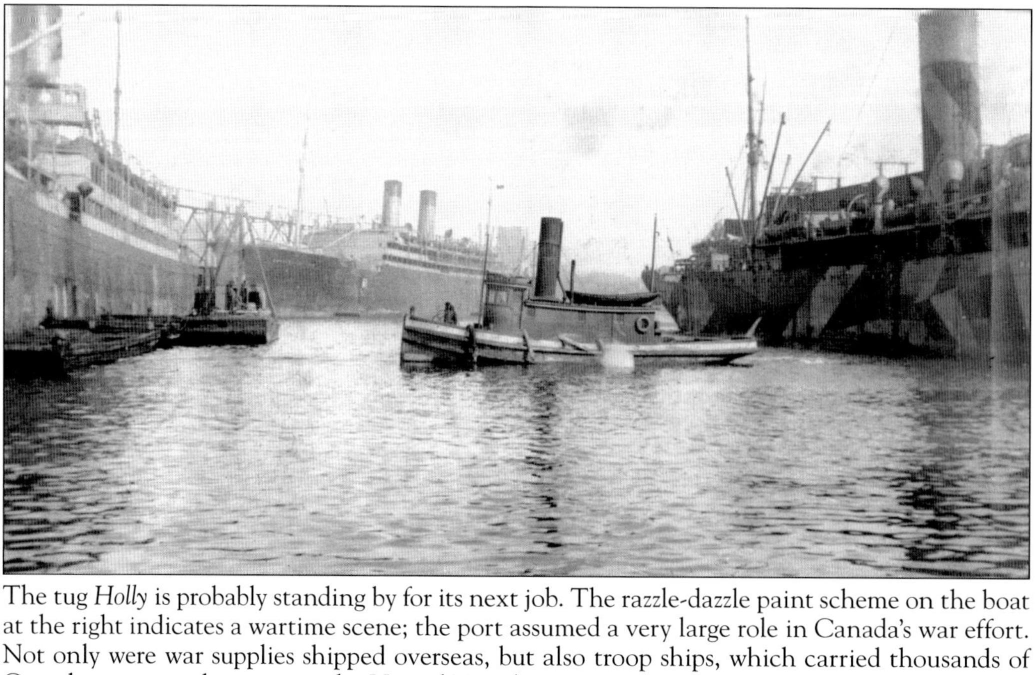

The tug *Holly* is probably standing by for its next job. The razzle-dazzle paint scheme on the boat at the right indicates a wartime scene; the port assumed a very large role in Canada's war effort. Not only were war supplies shipped overseas, but also troop ships, which carried thousands of Canadian men and women to the United Kingdom.

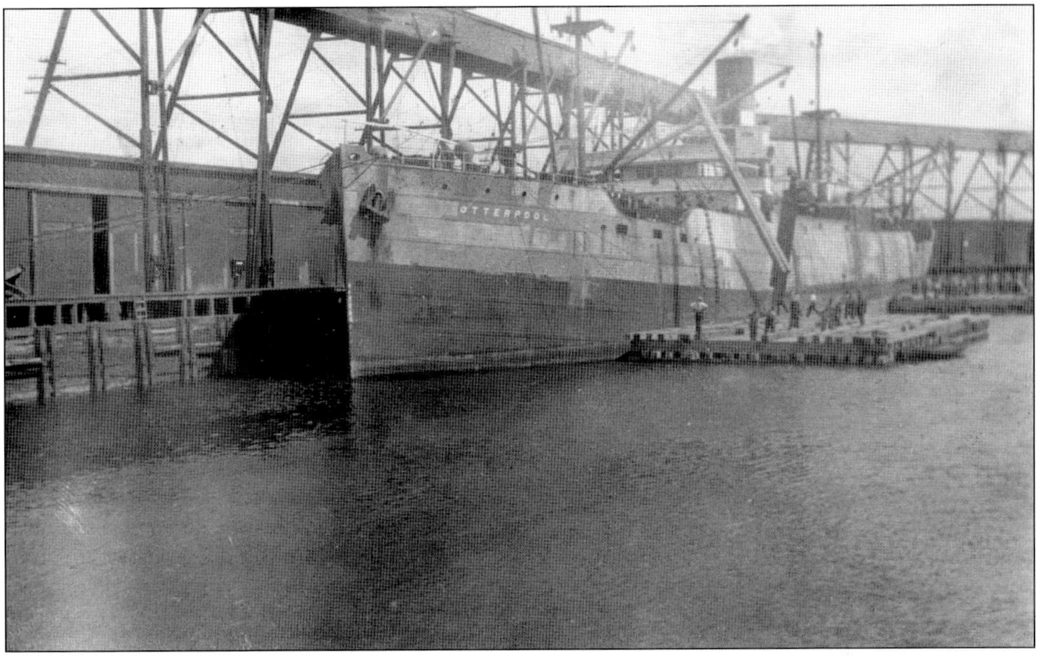

The ship *Otterpool* is loading square timber in August 1929. Timber was brought to the ship by the scow and then loaded using deck derricks. It appears that the second scow at the stern of the ship is also loading timber. Square timber, known in the Maritime provinces as "ton timber," was sticks of hewn timber, squared with axes, and shipped to Great Britain.

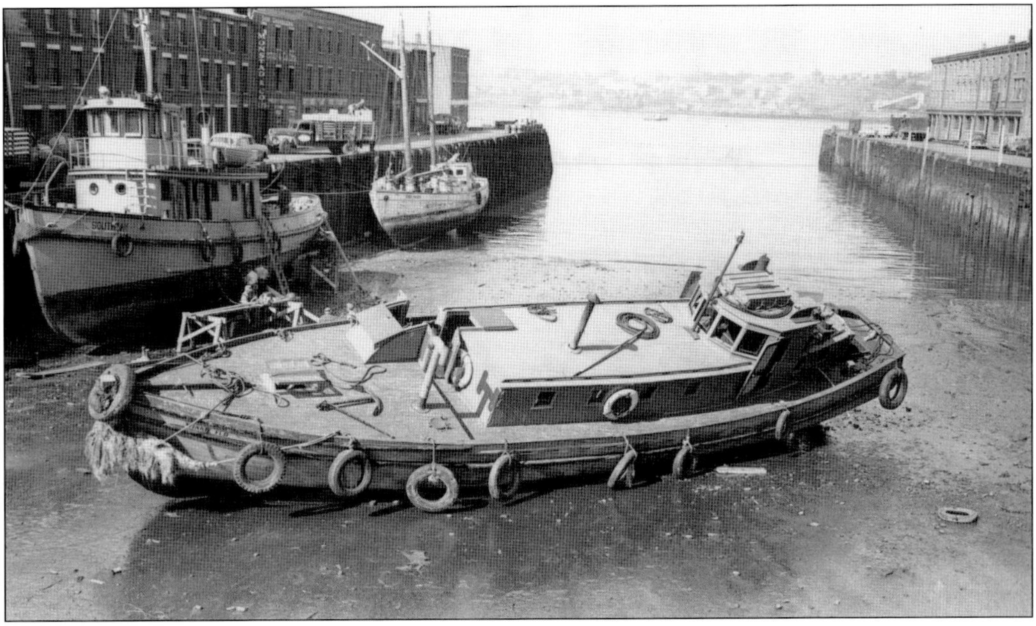

This 1950 image of Market Slip at low tide shows what happens to vessels with no water in the slip. The hull of the tugboat *South Bay* is being repaired. Behind it, the fishing schooner *Snow Maiden* appears to have just finished unloading several boxes of fish. The sign on the side of the truck reads, "Storage and Cartage," but the company name is unclear. The vessel in the foreground is George Cossaboom's diving tender. (Courtesy of Cliff Boyer.)

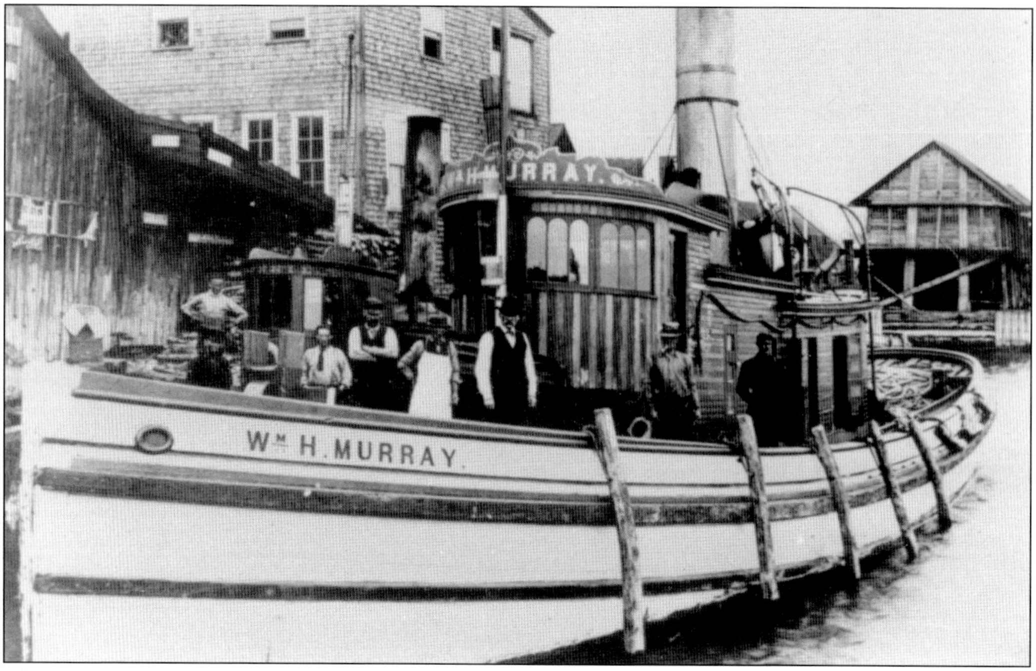

The tug *William H. Murray*, around 1900, was named for one of the owners of the Murray & Gregory lumber mill at Prospect Point just above the Reversing Falls Rapids. Murray was a longtime resident of Douglas Avenue. This tug was owned by the Indiantown firm of J. Holly & Sons. (Courtesy of Cliff Boyer.)

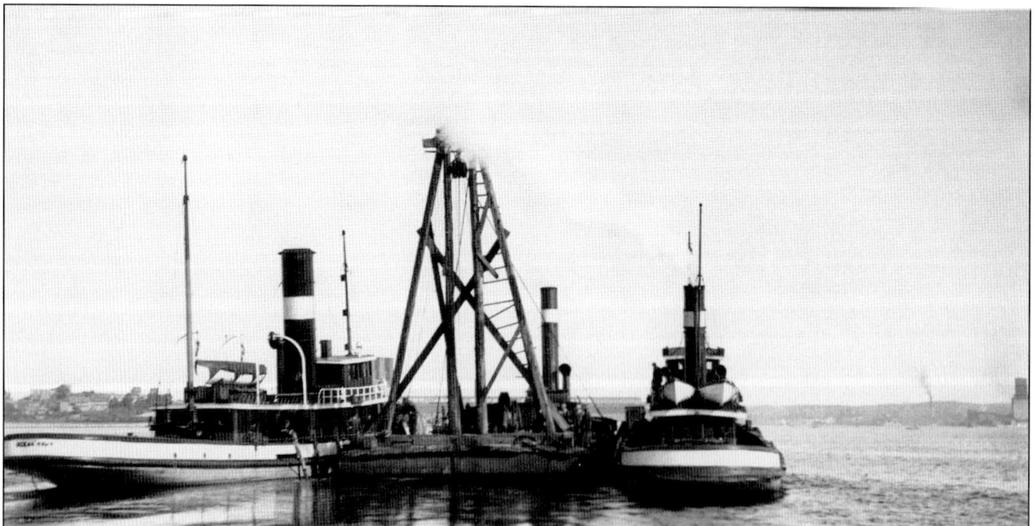

With the tug *Ocean Hawk* at the left and an unidentified tug at the right, the scow in the centre is dredging the silt from the main harbour. The tremendous currents in the bay, combined with the silt washed down river, cause the harbour channel to fill up over time. Every few years, parts of the channel must be dredged to keep enough depth of water for the safe navigation of ships.

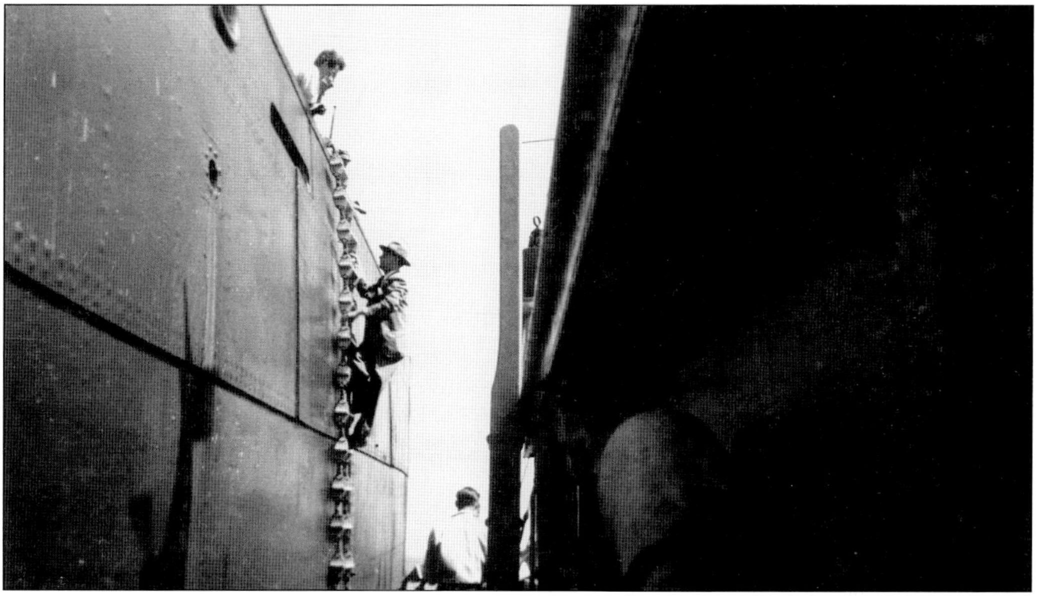

Vessels entering and exiting Saint John Harbour do so under command of a harbour pilot. Pilots have been doing this job for over 200 years. It is a dangerous job, with pilots having to board and depart a ship using a rope and wood ladder, as pilot William B. Alexander is shown doing. Alexander became a pilot in 1921, retired in 1966, and died in 1968.

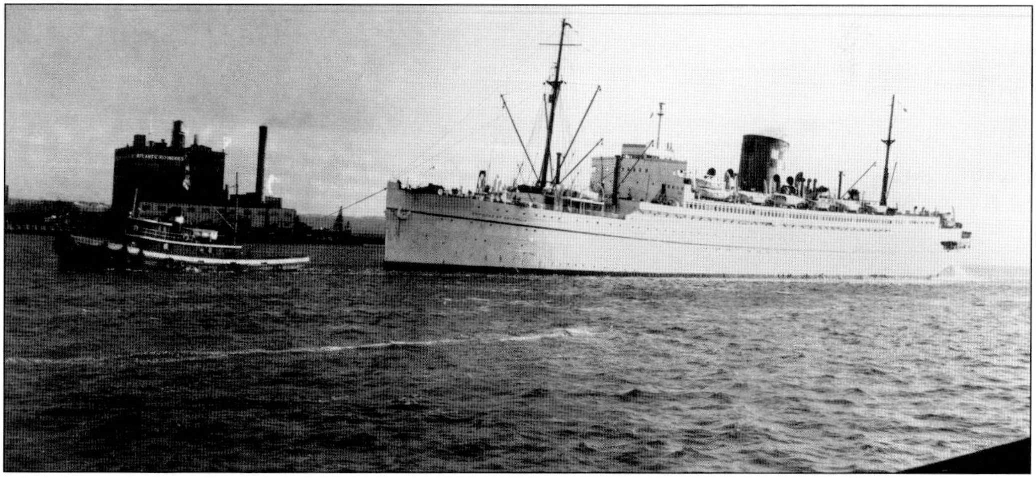

The tug *Ocean Hawk II* is bringing the Canadian Pacific (CP) SS *Empress of Australia* into port. The ship was launched in 1924 as the *De Grasse* but was renamed the *Australia* in 1953. She remained with CP until 1956, when she was sold and renamed the *Venezuela*. The ship was wrecked in 1962. The *Empress* ships brought passengers and immigrants from Europe into Saint John where they were disembarked at the immigration shed at Pier No. 12. (Courtesy of Cliff Boyer.)

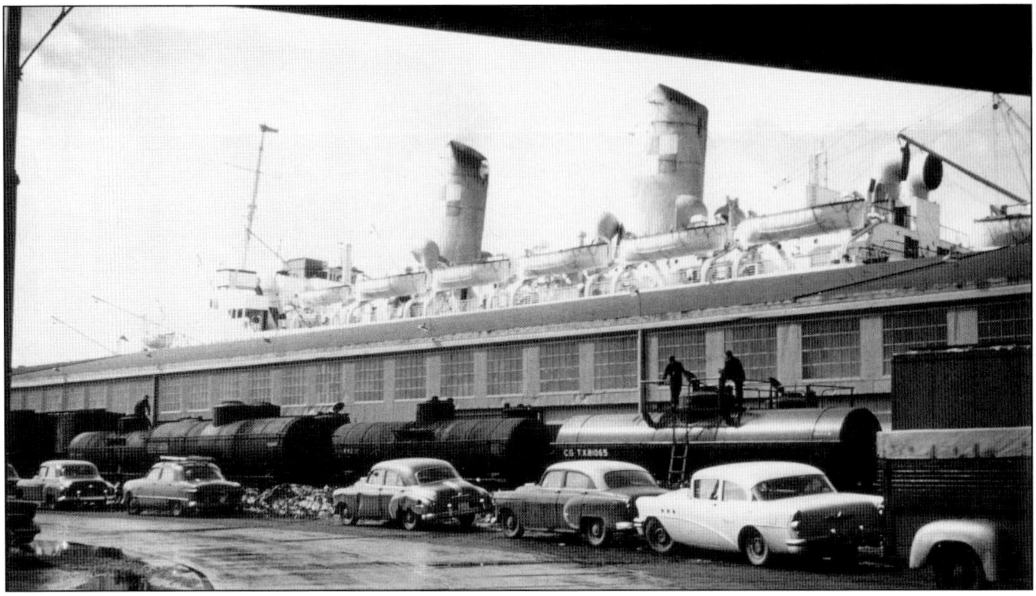

In March 1959, the *Empress of France* arrived at the Saint John immigration shed at Pier No. 12. After disembarking passengers, the 17-car Canadian Pacific Railway (CPR) train departed for western Canada. This CP passenger liner and cargo ship was initially named the SS *Duchess of Bedford* when she was launched in 1928. The *Duchess* served as a troop ship during World War II. During its postwar refit in 1947, she was renamed the *Empress of France*. The ship was taken out of service in 1960.

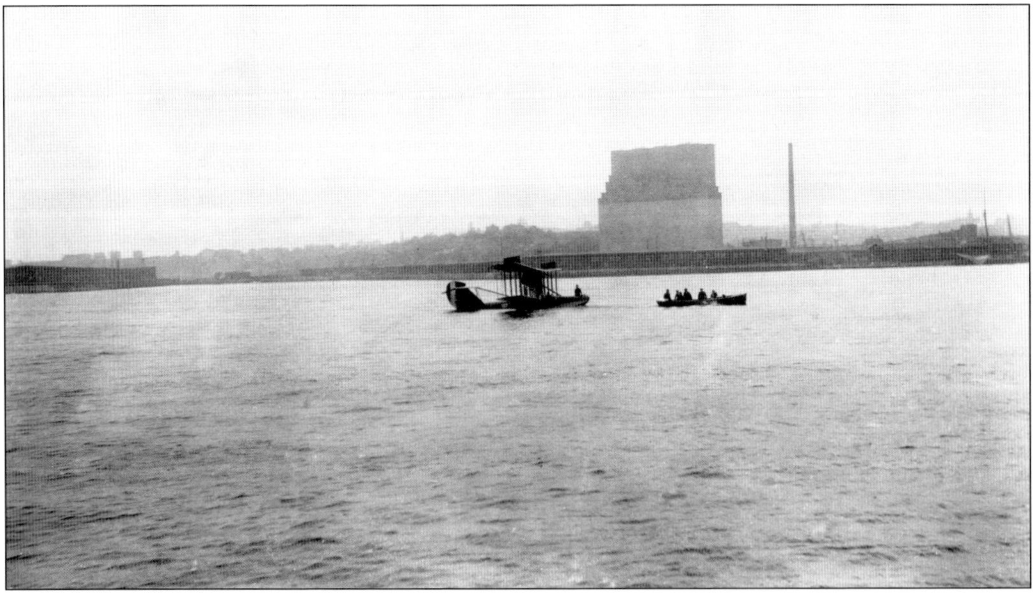

In June 1919, a Curtis H2SL flying boat from Dartmouth, Nova Scotia, landed in the harbour while en route to Quebec. After an overnight stay, it continued to Fredericton and finally landed in Quebec where it was used by the St. Maurice Forestry Protective Association. The pilot was Capt. Stuart Graham, assisted by his wife, Madge, and engineer William Kahre. The flight covered some 645 miles and took 9 hours and 45 minutes of flying time over four days. Graham visited the Millidgeville Airport several times in the 1930s as the inspector of aviation.

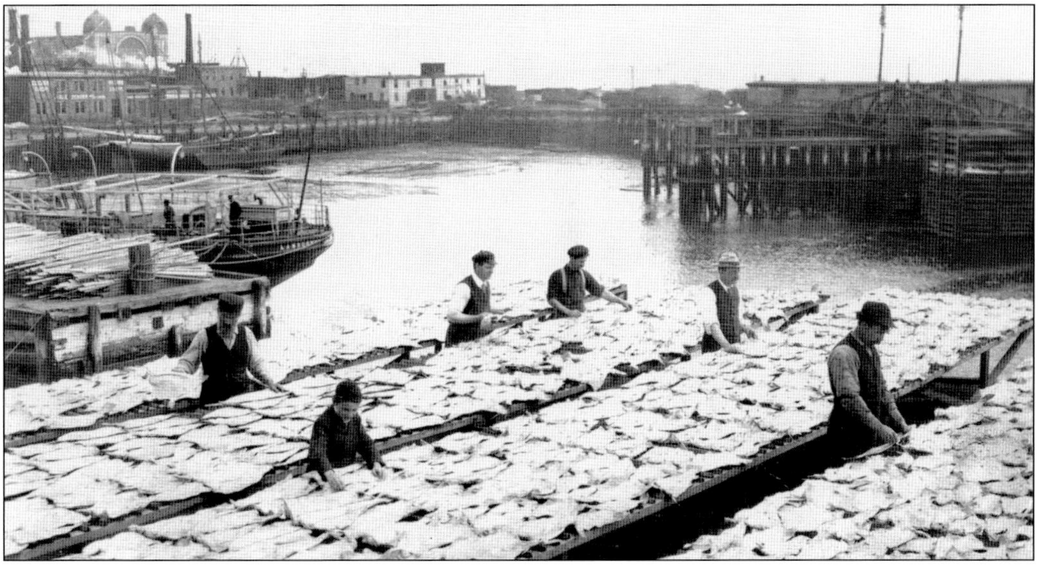

When one thinks of cod fish, it normally is of Newfoundland and its famous cod industry. Few remember when the Bay of Fundy used to be home to a small cod industry, as shown here at Robertson's wharf at the Lower Cove in 1900. There are literally hundreds of dried cod being sorted. The only individual named is Thomas Evans of Britain Street; he is the man with the generous whiskers at left. In the background is the government vessel *Lansdowne*, which was used to patrol the bay. At the rear is the Saint John Exhibition Building, and the area at the rear right is where the Lantic Sugar Refinery was constructed in 1914.

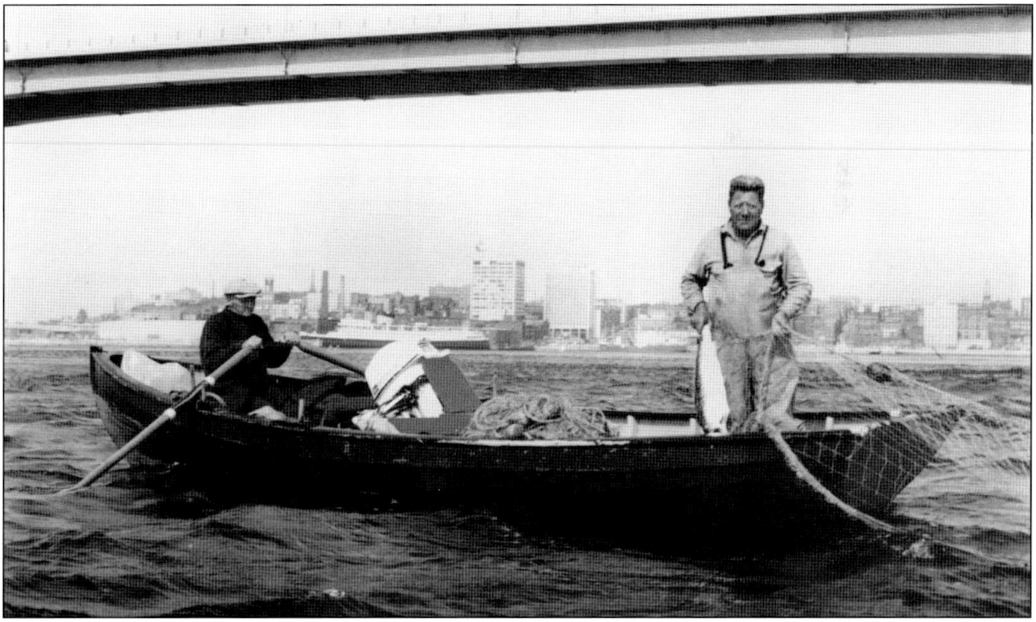

In 1971, the New Brunswick Publishing Company's calendar included this photograph of two harbour fishermen under the Saint John Harbour Bridge. Murray "Mousie" Gray is manning the oars while Walter "Squeeze" McGuire holds up the salmon he appears to have recently caught. The reality is that the fish were not running, so they went to the city market, bought a salmon with its head removed, and posed with their "catch."

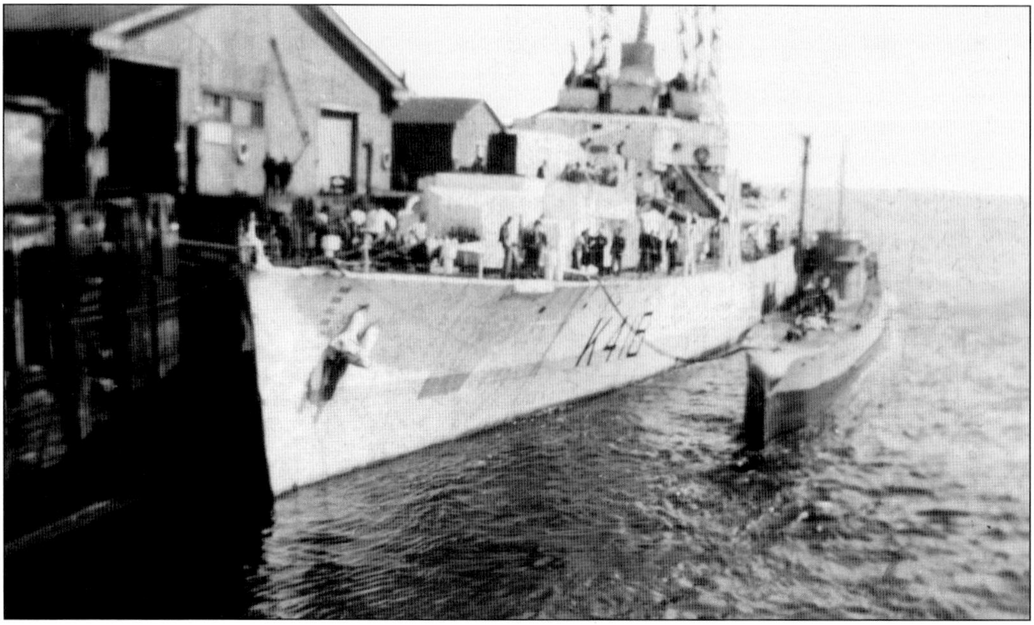

Here are HMCS *Joliette* and U-889. The *Joliette* was a sister ship of HMCS *Saint John*, being launched in December 1943. U-889 was a type IXC/40 submarine, built in 1941. After the German surrender in May 1945, the U-889 surrendered to the Royal Canadian Navy (RCN). Later that month, the U-889 was commissioned into the RCN. Under the sponsorship of the Navy League of Canada, the submarine paid a courtesy call to Saint John in August 1945.

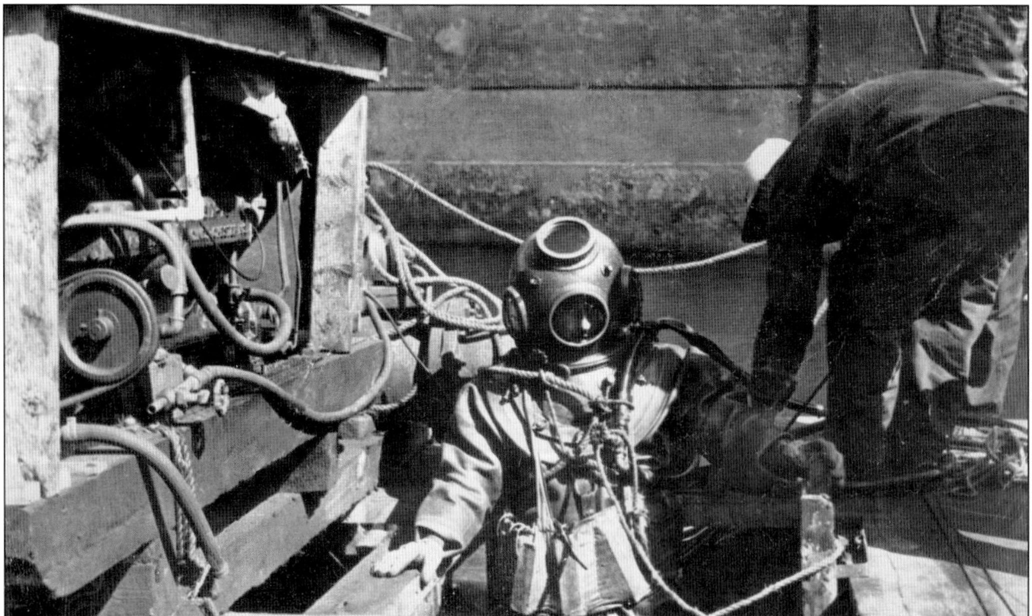

Diver Price Theodore "Spike" Palmer came to Saint John after 1947 to work at the Saint John Drydock. There, he inspected the hulls of vessels requiring repair. He also dove on sunken barges and ships and recovered bodies of drowning victims. Born in 1906, he served in the Royal Canadian Navy as a deep-sea diver during World War II. Spike died in 1968.

Loading grain aboard the SS *Selizh* at Pier No. 9 in 1974 was labour intensive. All bulk cargo required dozens of men to load the ship, and this only gradually changed later in the decade with containerization. Western grain was shipped through three elevators, the National Harbours Board and CPR elevators on the west side and the Canadian National Railway (CNR) elevator at the foot of Water Street. All elevators have been demolished.

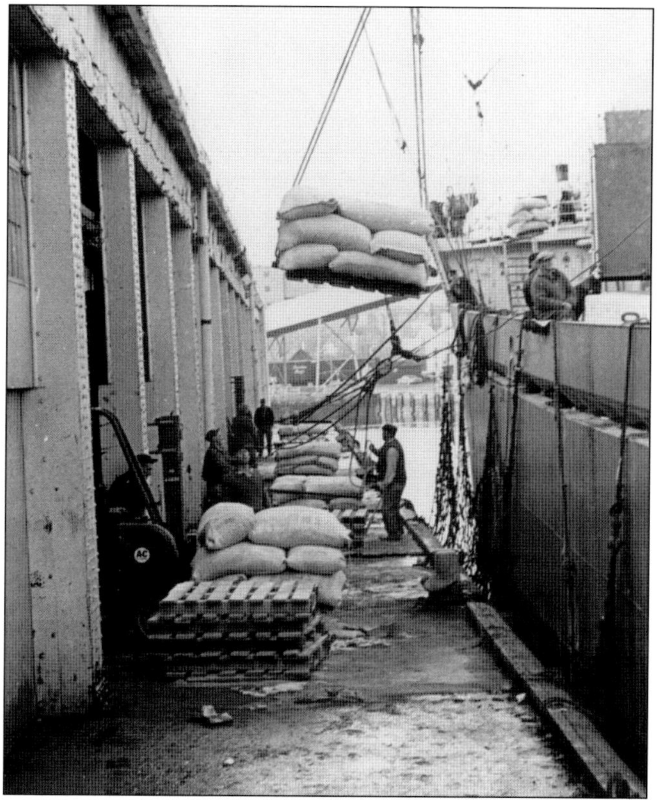

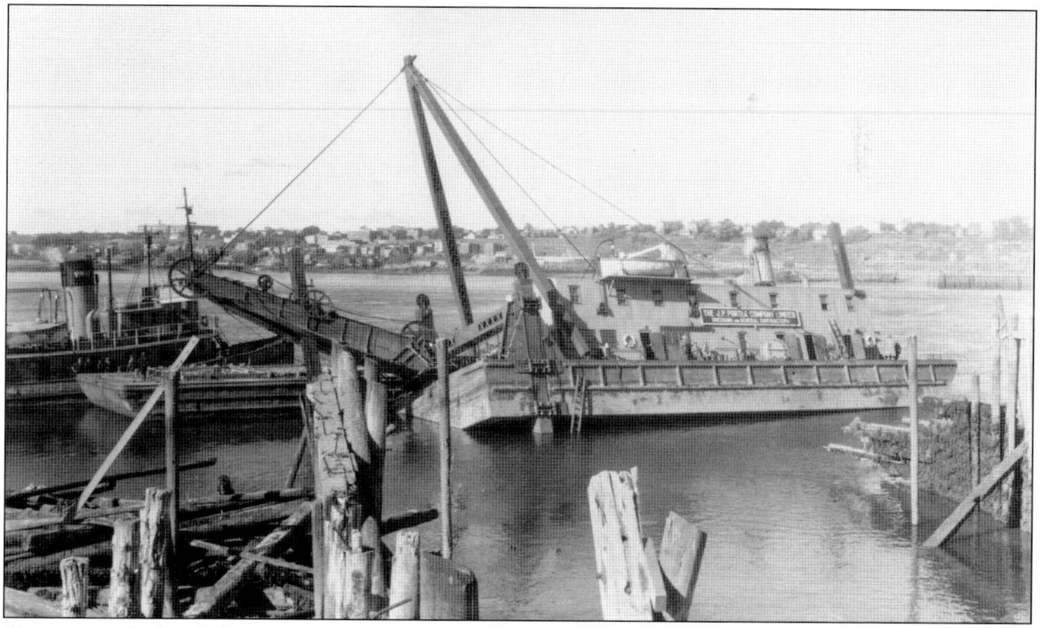

City council decided to remove the ferry *Loyalist* from its run in 1954. The following year, all evidence of its existence was gone. The ferry was towed to Chatham, and the ferry landings on both sides of the harbour were removed by this barge of the J.P. Porter Company. (Courtesy of Cliff Boyer.)

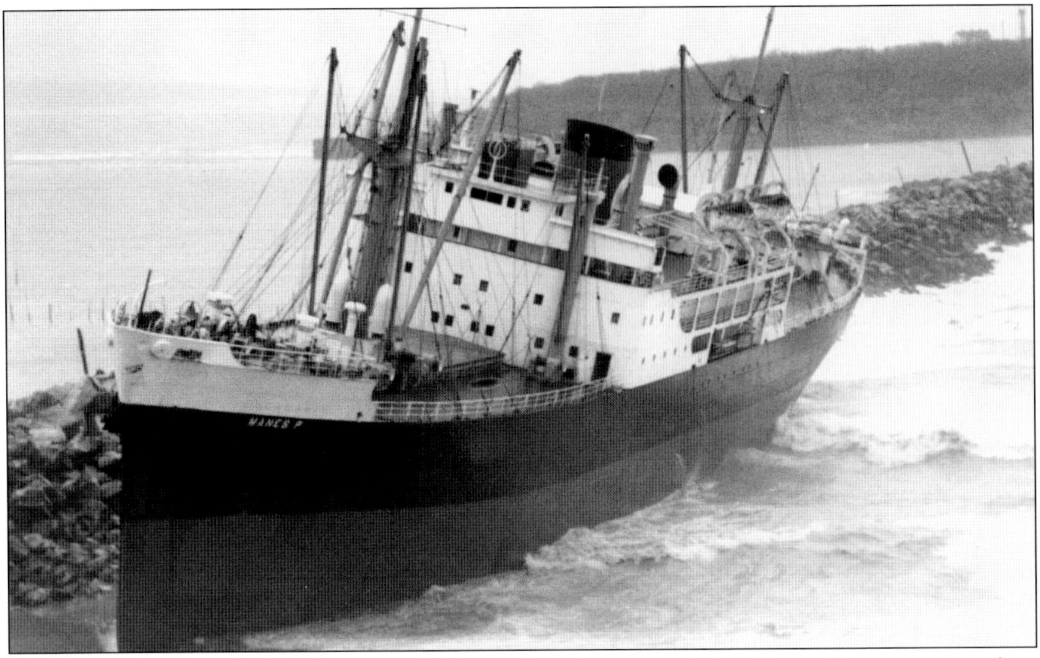

During a violent storm on February 3, 1970, the Greek registered ship *Manes P*, went aground on the Negro Town Point Breakwater at Bayshore Beach. This ship was the former *Escalante*, and with damages over $1 million, the owners decided to scrap the *Manes P* at the breakwater.

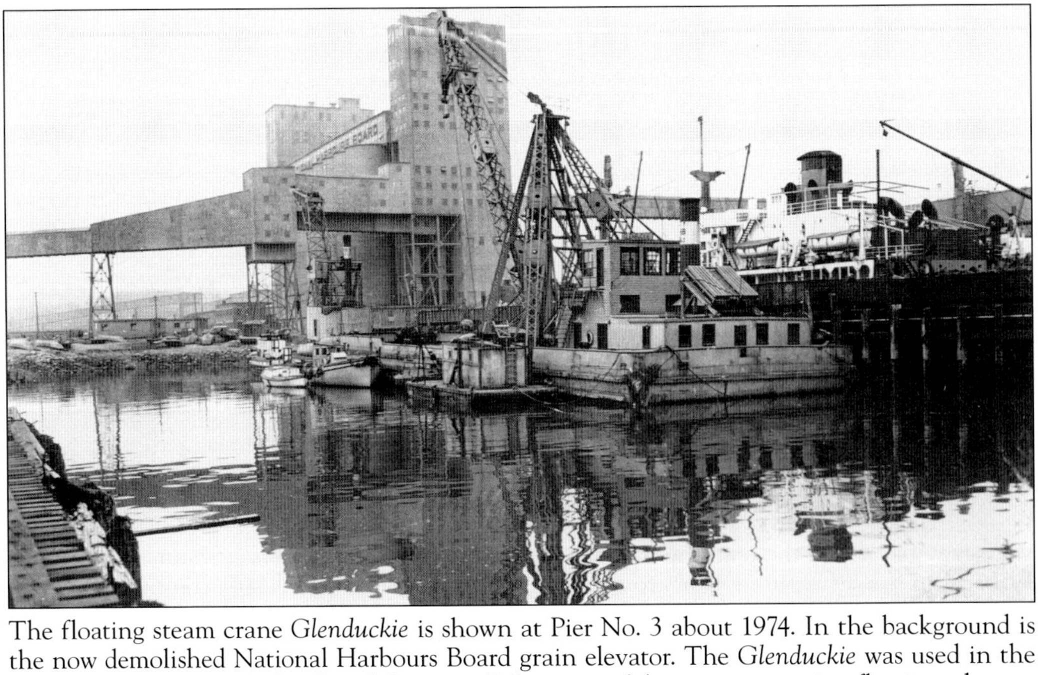

The floating steam crane *Glenduckie* is shown at Pier No. 3 about 1974. In the background is the now demolished National Harbours Board grain elevator. The *Glenduckie* was used in the harbour in a variety of roles, from lifting small ships out of the water to putting floating wharves and gangways in place.

Two

The Harbour Highway

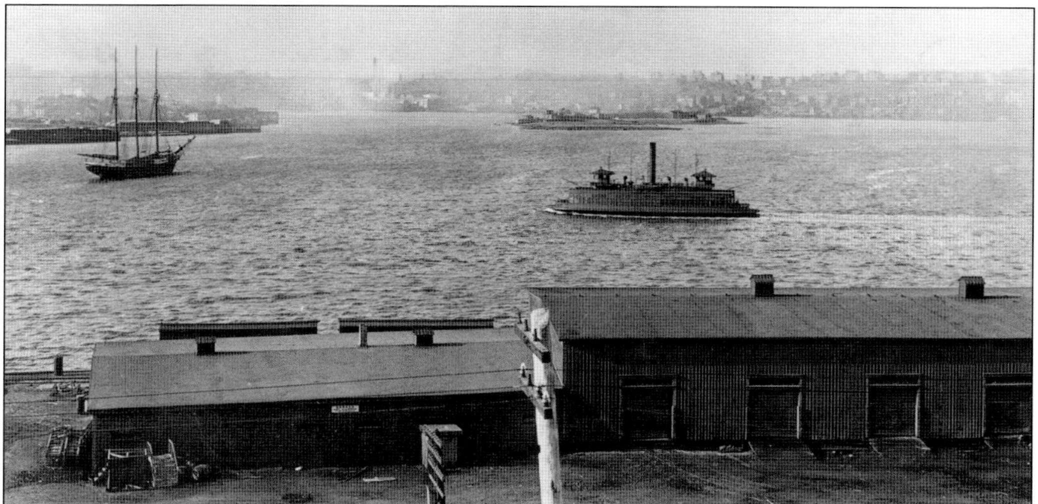

With Navy Island at the rear, the harbour ferry *Ludlow* is crossing to West Saint John around 1910. From the city's first visitors to today's thriving cruise ship industry, the harbour is the lifeblood of Saint John and its surrounding communities. Many types of vessels have used the harbour, from war ships, cruise liners, ferries, and steamers to fishing boats, canoes, rowboats, and pleasure craft. If it floats, it has probably passed through these channels at some point in the harbour's history.

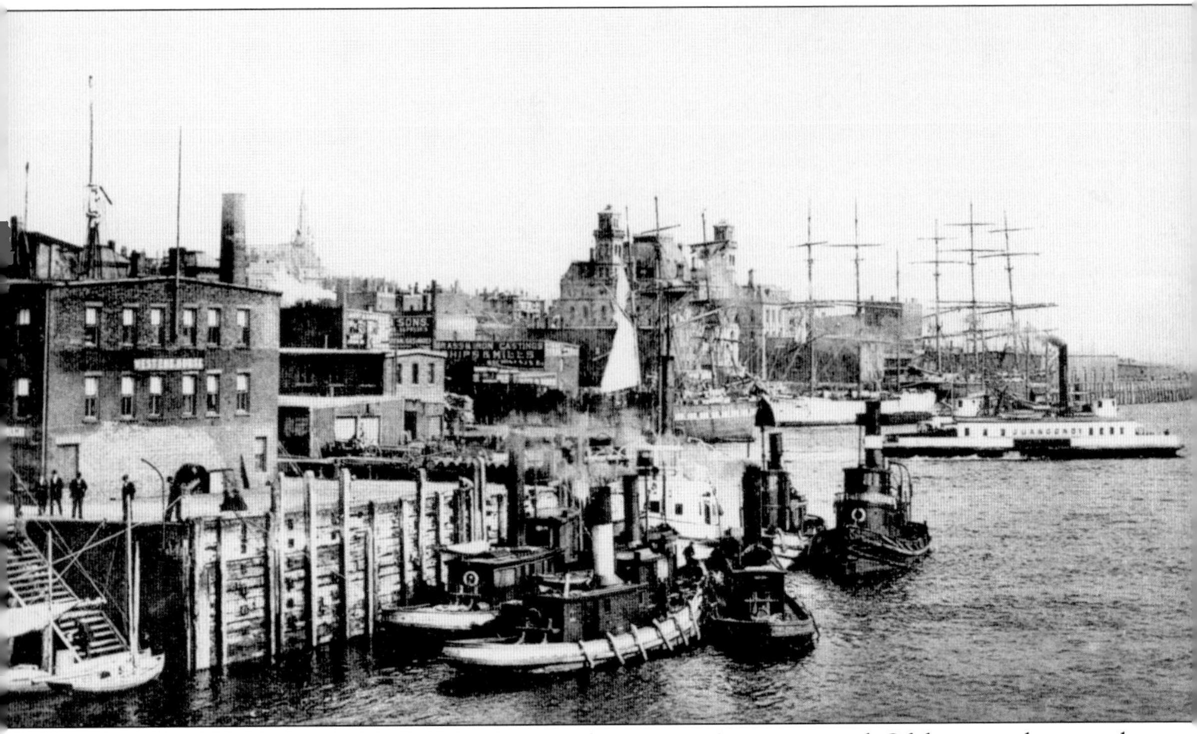

The harbour ferry *Ouangondy* is approaching the Princess Street terminal. Of the six tugboats, only the name of *Lord Roberts* is visible. The *Roberts* was built in Courtney Bay by Edward McGuiggan prior to 1914. The first harbour ferry was the steamer *Victoria*.

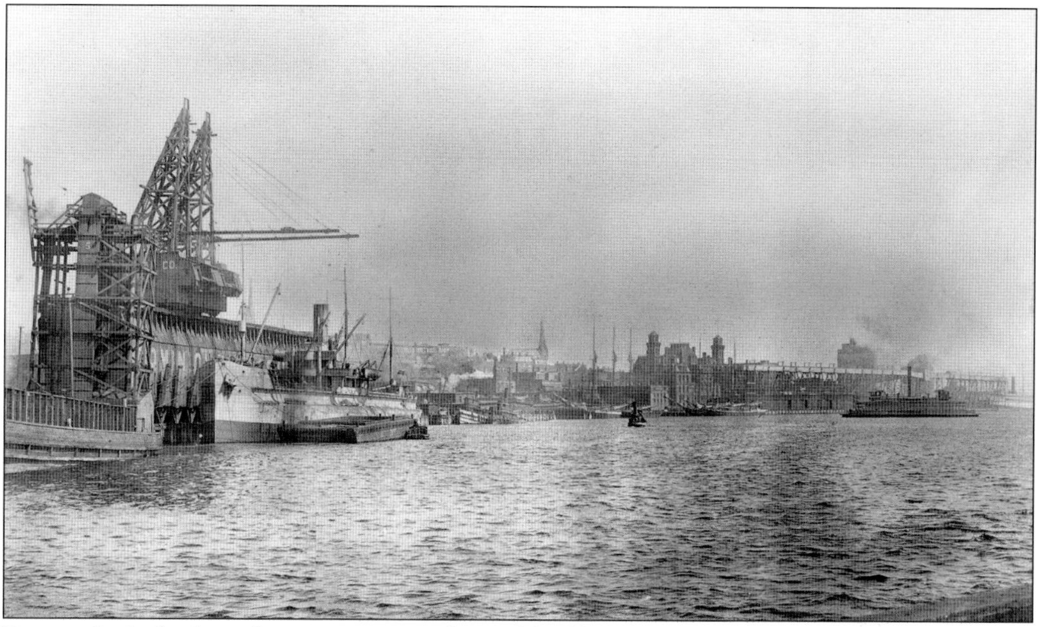

Even with the harbour ferry service, people would still try to navigate the Reversing Falls Rapids themselves. In the summer of 1838, a party of 25 men, women, and children attempted to cross here. The boat got caught in the rapids and capsized, throwing those on board in the whirlpools and eddies. Only 6 of the 25 were rescued.

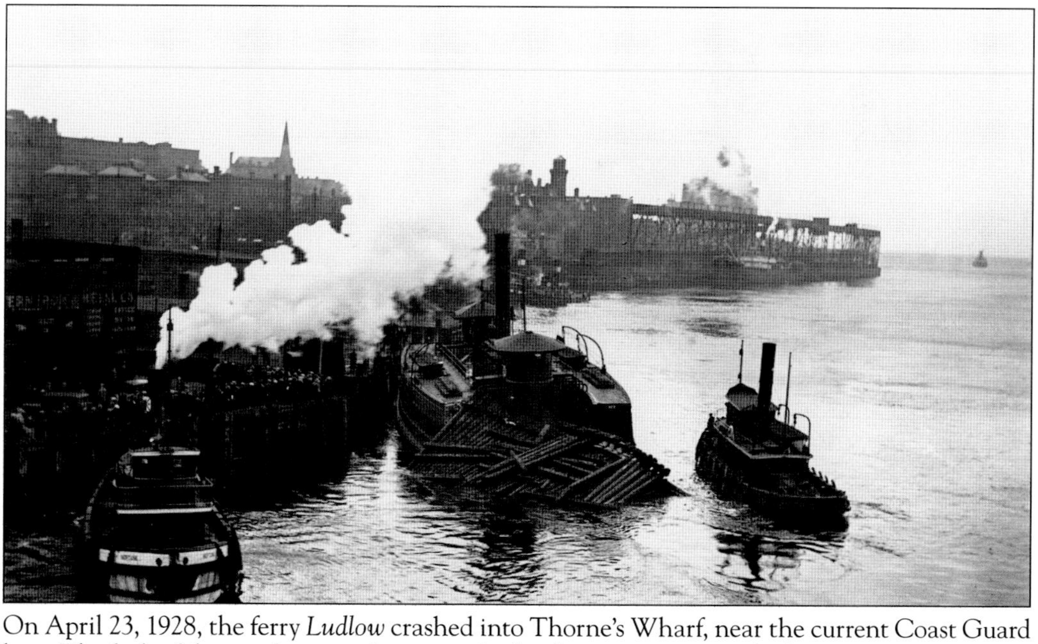

On April 23, 1928, the ferry *Ludlow* crashed into Thorne's Wharf, near the current Coast Guard base. The fault of the accident was determined to be the immense water freshet "swinging the vessel out of position." Over $20,000 in damages was done to the ferry, the pier, and the tug *Neptune*.

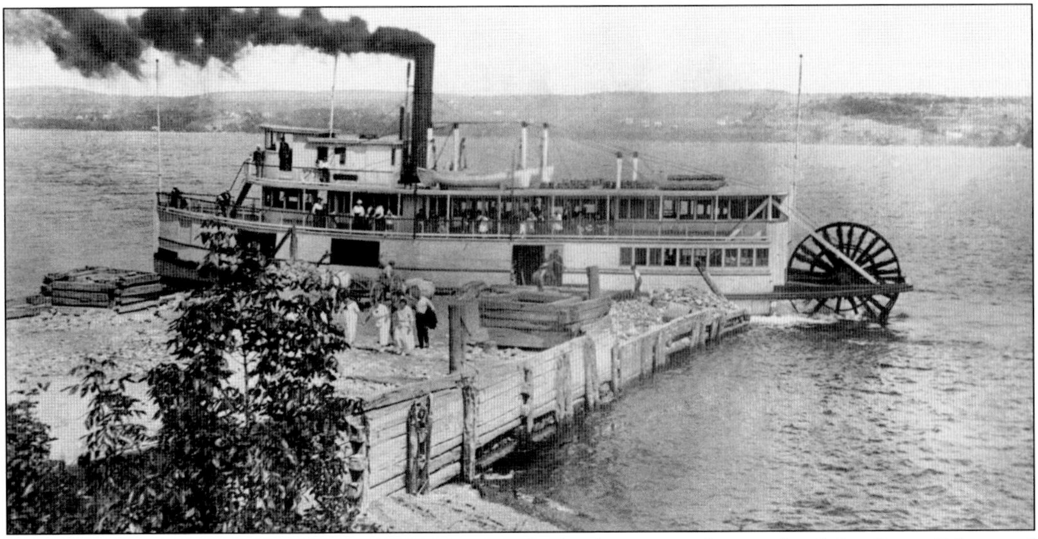

Before there were any bridges or a ferry to cross the harbour, riverboats plied the Saint John and other rivers, carrying commerce to and fro. The first riverboat was the *General Smythe*, launched in 1816. This is the riverboat *Hampton*, which operated between 1906 and 1930.

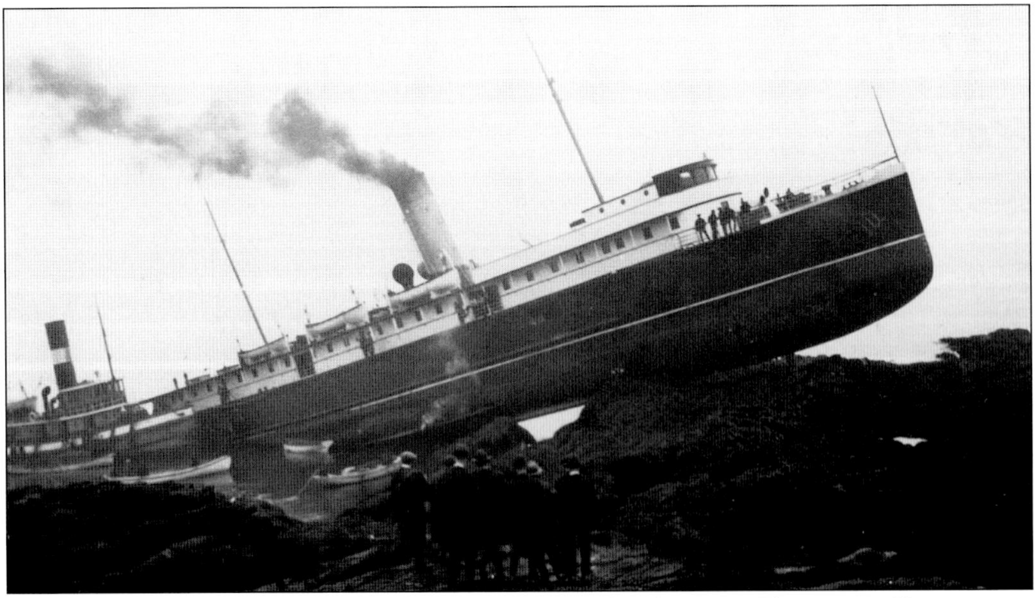

The tremendous tides of the Bay of Fundy can be cruel and unforgiving. The steamer *Empress* went aground at Black Point in Mispec on September 29, 1922. She was later refloated and repaired at the Saint John Drydock. She was destroyed in the 1931 port fire.

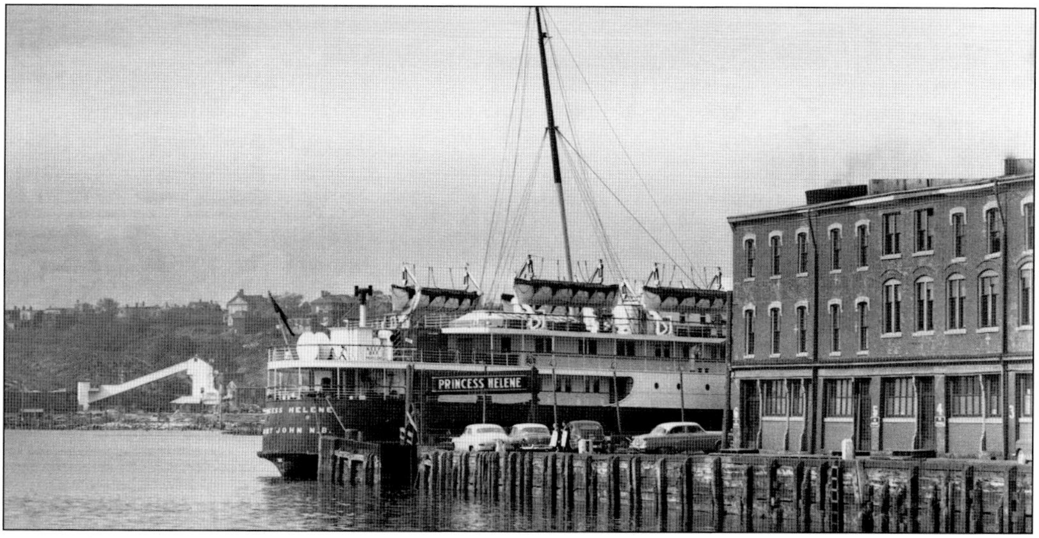

In October, 1955, forty-five crewmen of the Seafarer's International Union went on strike against the Canadian Pacific's *Princess Helene* ferry to Digby. The strike lasted 10 days. Launched in 1930 in Scotland, the *Helene* was both a passenger and freight ferry; she remained on the Bay of Fundy run until 1963. She was then converted for budget cruises in the Mediterranean until 1972; she was scrapped in 1977.

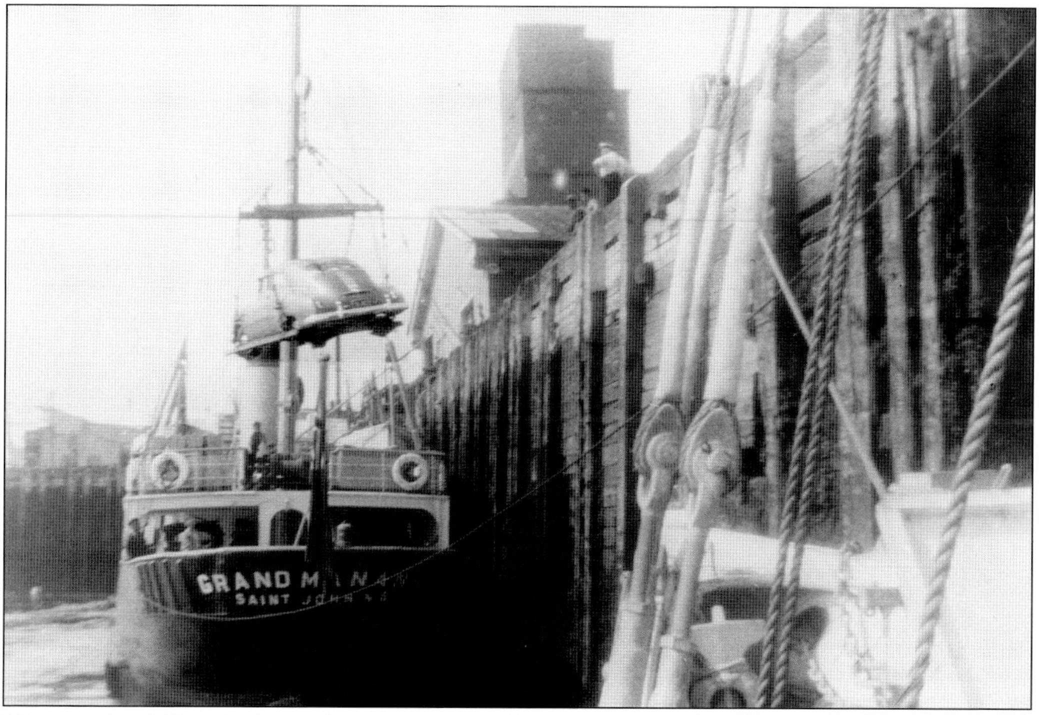

The people of Grand Manan have been served by passenger and car ferries for decades. Today's ferries accommodate more cars than are shown here. There are two year-round ferries that take residents, tourists, cars, and trucks, which keep this island's economy operating all year long. (Courtesy of David Goss.)

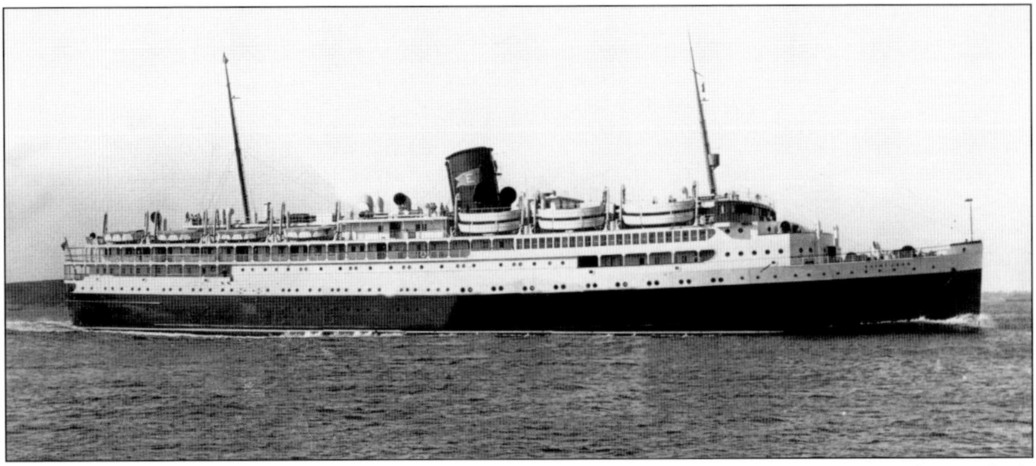

The new coastal ferry SS *Saint John* arrived at its home port on May 3, 1932. Inside its plush interior were paintings and murals depicting Saint John Harbour in 1604 and in 1932. The *Saint John* was purchased by the US Navy in 1941 and served as a submarine tender and a troop ship and became the hospital ship USS *Rescue* (AH-18) in 1945. She was decommissioned in Seattle, Washington, in 1946 and scrapped in 1958.

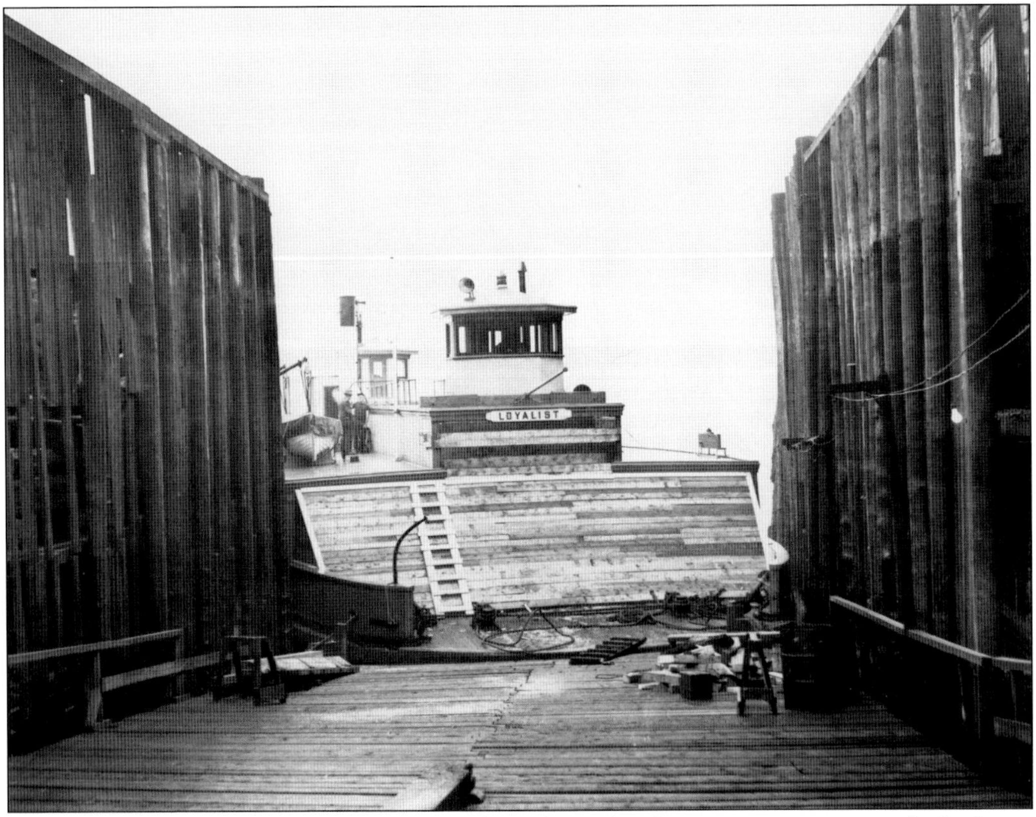

Although the current bridges now serve as the only mode of transportation across the harbour, the legacy of the ferry service is extremely important to the development of the city. It connected people who lived on the west side to employment in the city centre. The ferry *Loyalist I* is shown at the Princess Street slip just prior to its removal to Chatham on the Miramichi River in 1954.

Three

THE LOST NAVY ISLAND

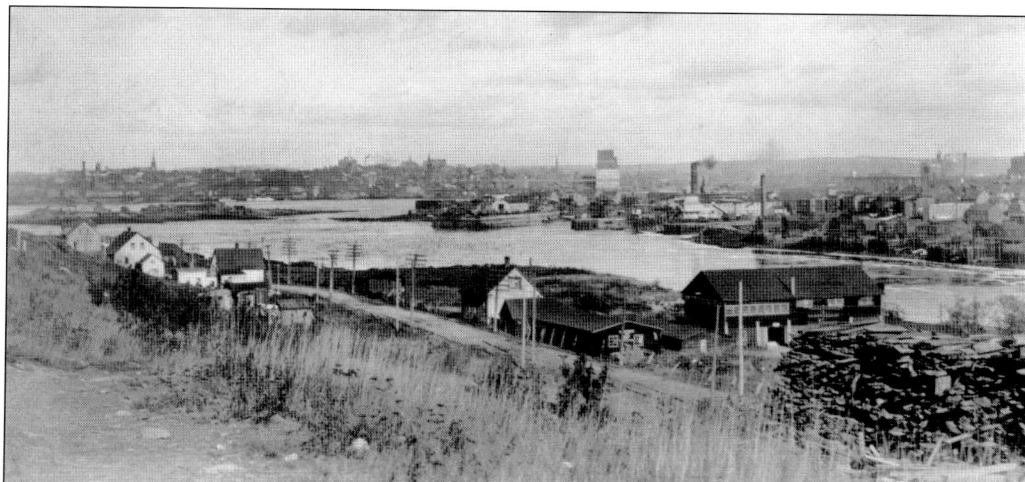

In 1925, the fishing community of Navy Island was thriving, unaware that its destruction was only a few years away. Buttermilk Channel separates the island from the mainland at Fort Neck in the lower west side. Chesley Drive in the foreground shows the last remnants of the various mills and shipyards that once were located here on the Straight Shore.

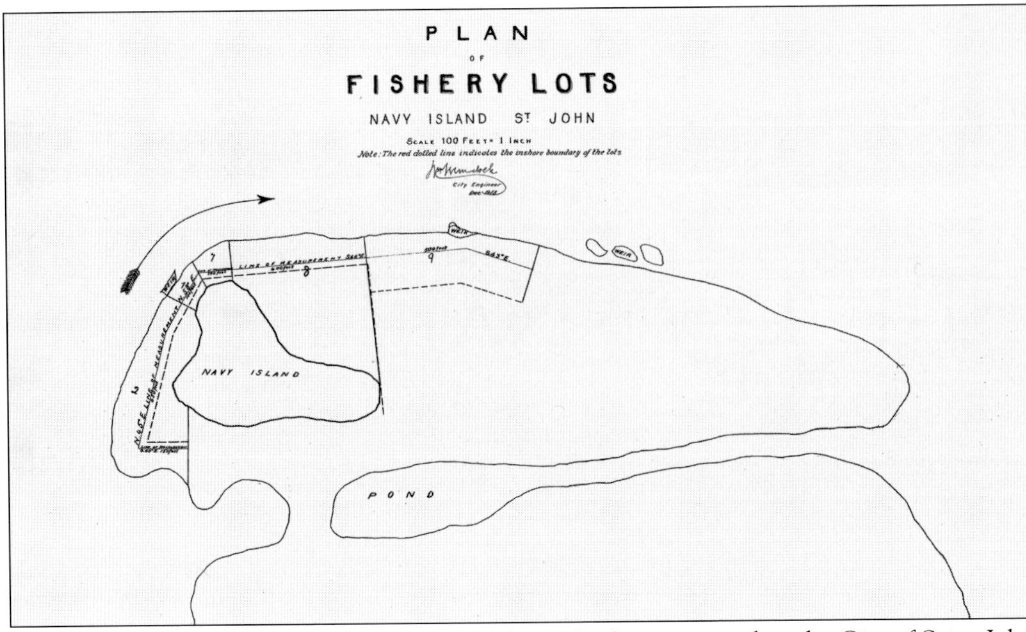

This 1913 plan shows the Navy Island fishing lots, which were vested in the City of Saint John by its 1785 charter. The island was also set aside for use by the Royal Navy during wartime. The fishing lots were licensed annually until 1930, when the island residents were removed and the island destroyed.

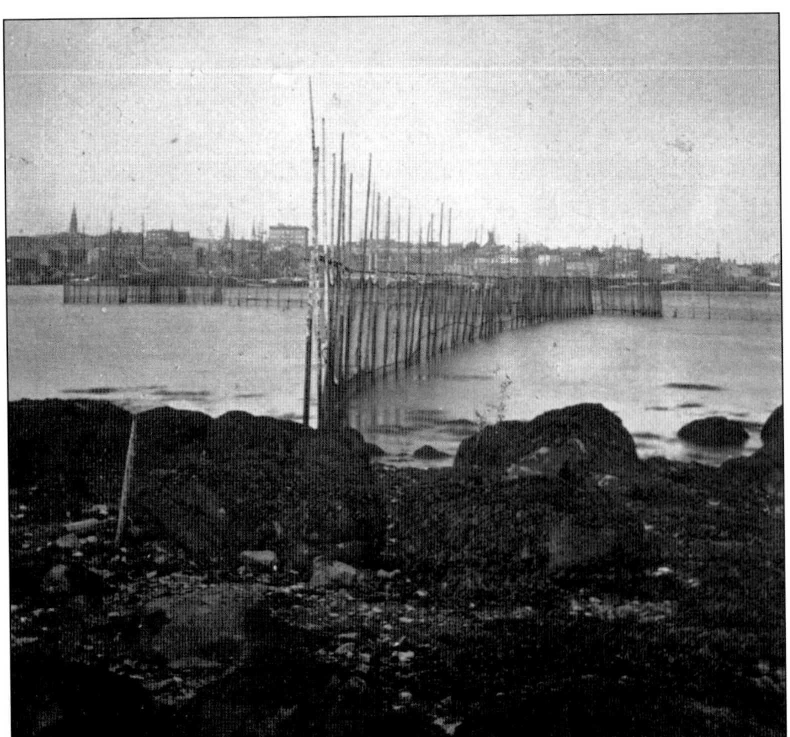

Fishing weirs were a common site around the island and in the harbour. Herring and gaspereau were caught in the nets when the tide went out. This way of life lasted until the Navy Island Terminal was completed in 1934. There had been speculation of building a pulp and paper mill on the island as well as using it as the site of Saint John's seaplane base.

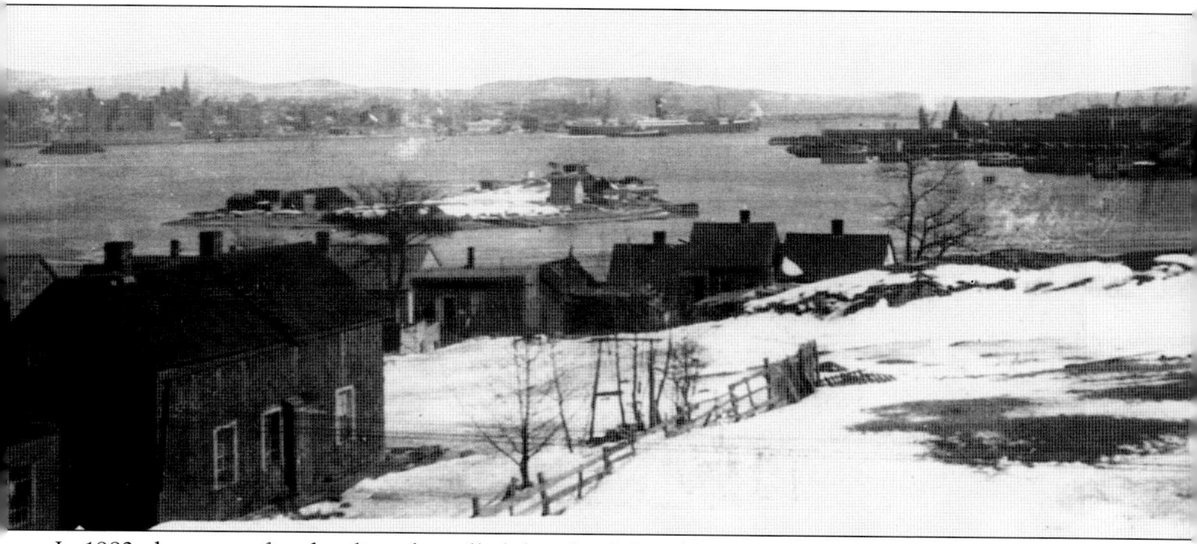

In 1883, there were five families who called the island their home. Although only a short boat ride away, the contrast between life on the two shores and the island was profound. There were tales of ghosts and buried treasures on the island. A tale of gold has existed in popular culture since the early 19th century. A sheet of lyrics was discovered in the early 1950s during the construction of postwar housing in Saint John's North End that detailed this story.

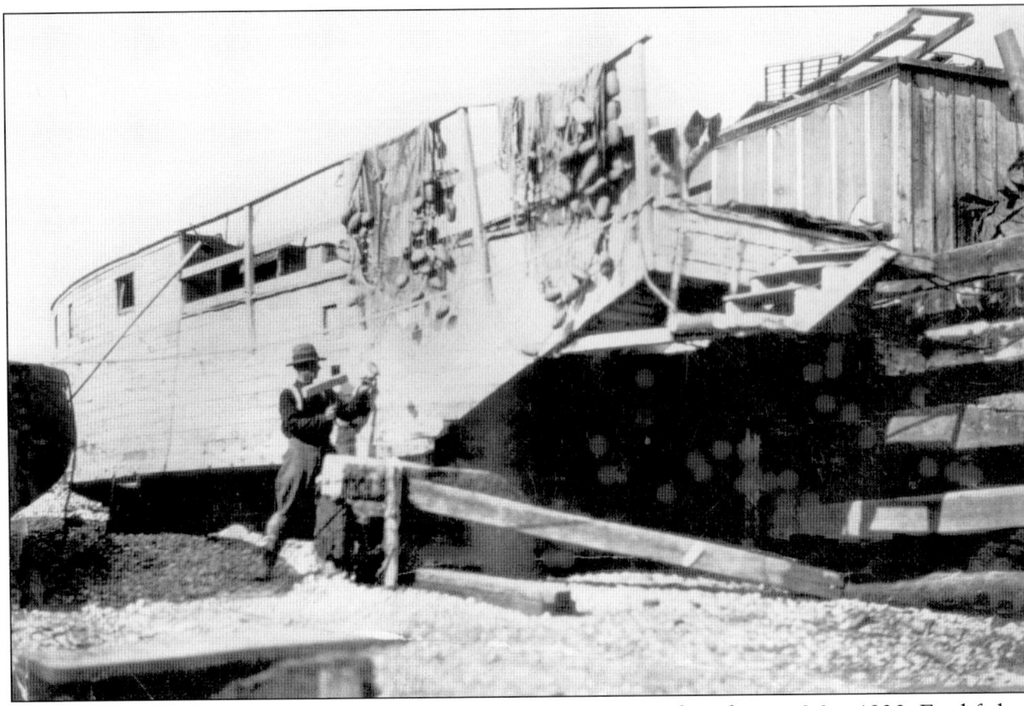

Fred Lord is shown caulking his brother Charlie's boat, the *Milwaukee*, in May 1930. Fred fished during the summer on the Saint John River to Grand Lake for eels. During the winter, he worked the winter port. Fred was killed at the port in an industrial accident shortly after moving from the island in 1930.

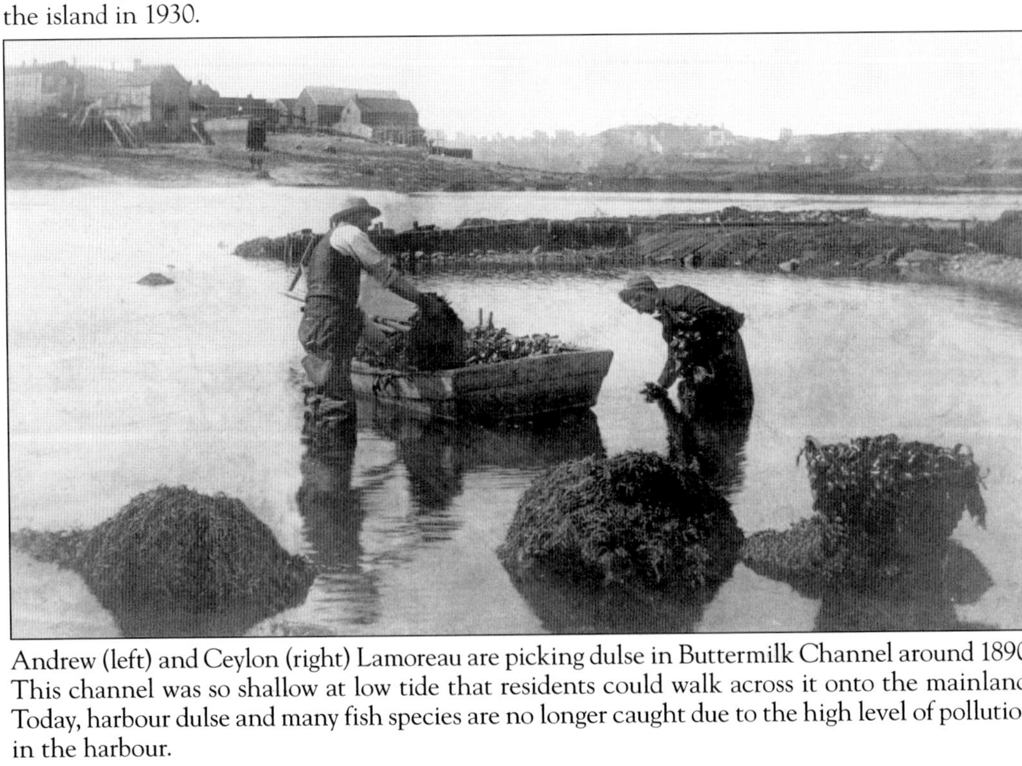

Andrew (left) and Ceylon (right) Lamoreau are picking dulse in Buttermilk Channel around 1890. This channel was so shallow at low tide that residents could walk across it onto the mainland. Today, harbour dulse and many fish species are no longer caught due to the high level of pollution in the harbour.

What was left of Navy Island is clearly shown in this 1942 photograph. The basic island shape is still visible; however, the cargo shed is approximately where Buttermilk Channel would have flowed. During the war, a small antiaircraft battery was put on the island. In the small cove at the left can be seen a sunken barge.

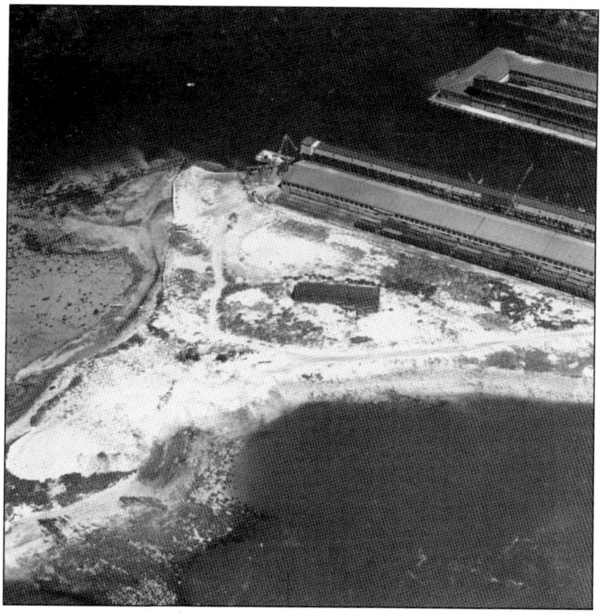

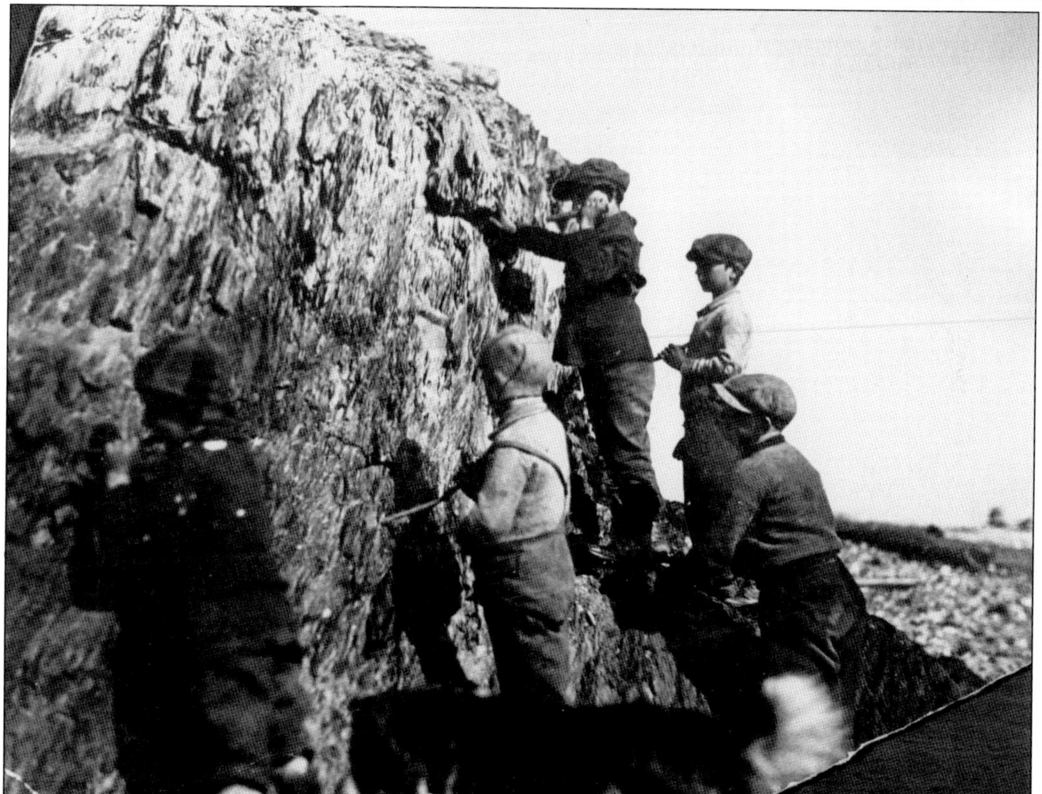

In May 1930, these island residents made one last stab at finding the gold. All they found was fool's gold. From left to right are Roy Lord, George Cogswell, Fred Lord, Leonard Lord, and Herman Donovan. There is at least one newspaper account of skeletons being found on the island, but no real gold.

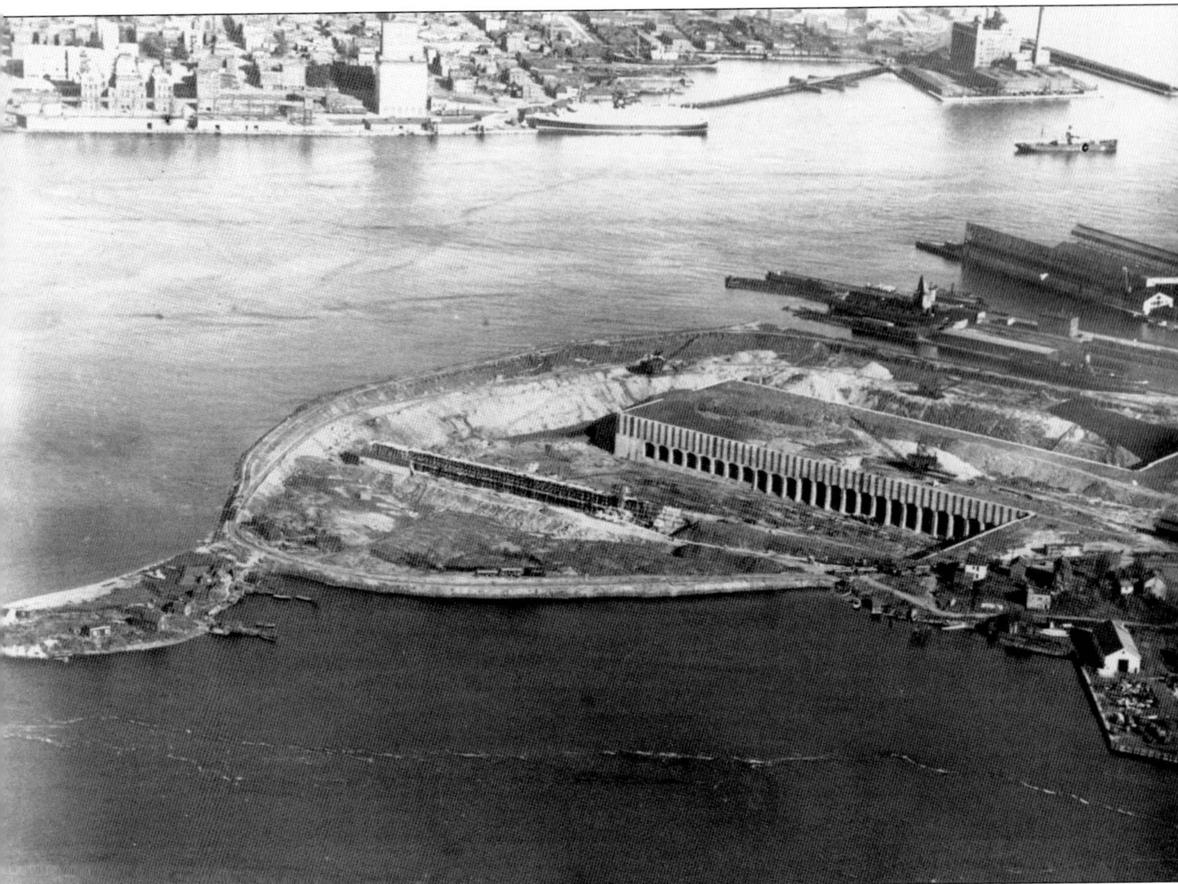

Navy Island is at the left, and the coffer dam has been pumped clear of water. This coffer dam was necessary to allow for the dredging and removal of rock for the piers of the Navy Island terminal. The following things are shown: the fishing community on Navy Island, the donkey engine and railcars and track running along the top of the coffer dam, the Dominion Government wharf at the lower right, and the SS *Saint John* ferry at Reeds Point on the other side of the harbour.

Four

NEIGHBOURHOODS DESTROYED

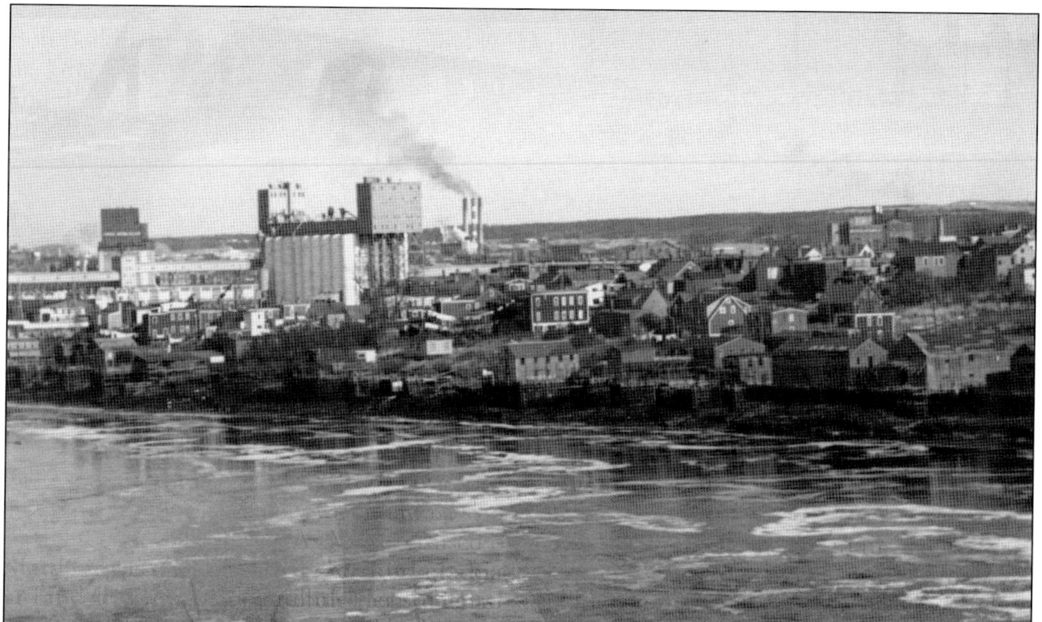

This c. 1970 image clearly shows the importance of the harbour fishing industry to west siders. Few of these fishing shacks remain, but, in 2012, the destruction of one by the tides and currents kept local residents glued to their televisions and Facebook pages as the daily changes of the shed were evident. The currents finally pulled it into the Reversing Falls Rapids for total destruction.

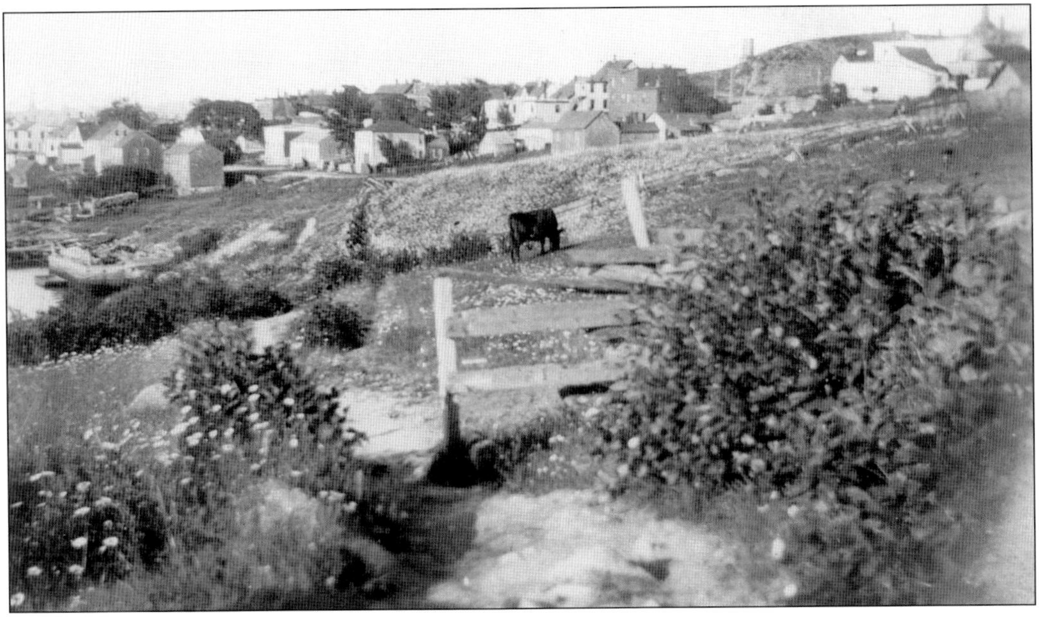

The area shown in the 1907 image above is now part of the throughway running alongside Riverview Drive. Much of the foreground was probably part of the Jewett property on Prince Street. Note the cow grazing in the area. This area is a pale shadow of itself, with few fishing sheds still along the waters' edge. The photograph below is from about 1972, which was just before all of the land along the shore was cleared for the construction of the western part of the throughway. In the centre is part of the Isolation Hospital complex of the Department of Veterans Affairs Hospital. (Above, courtesy of David Goss.)

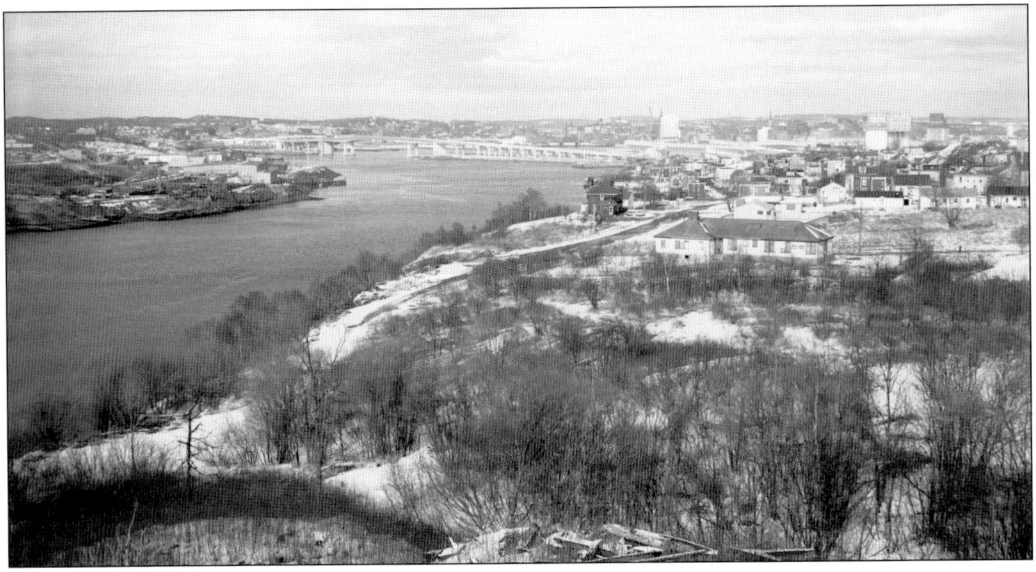

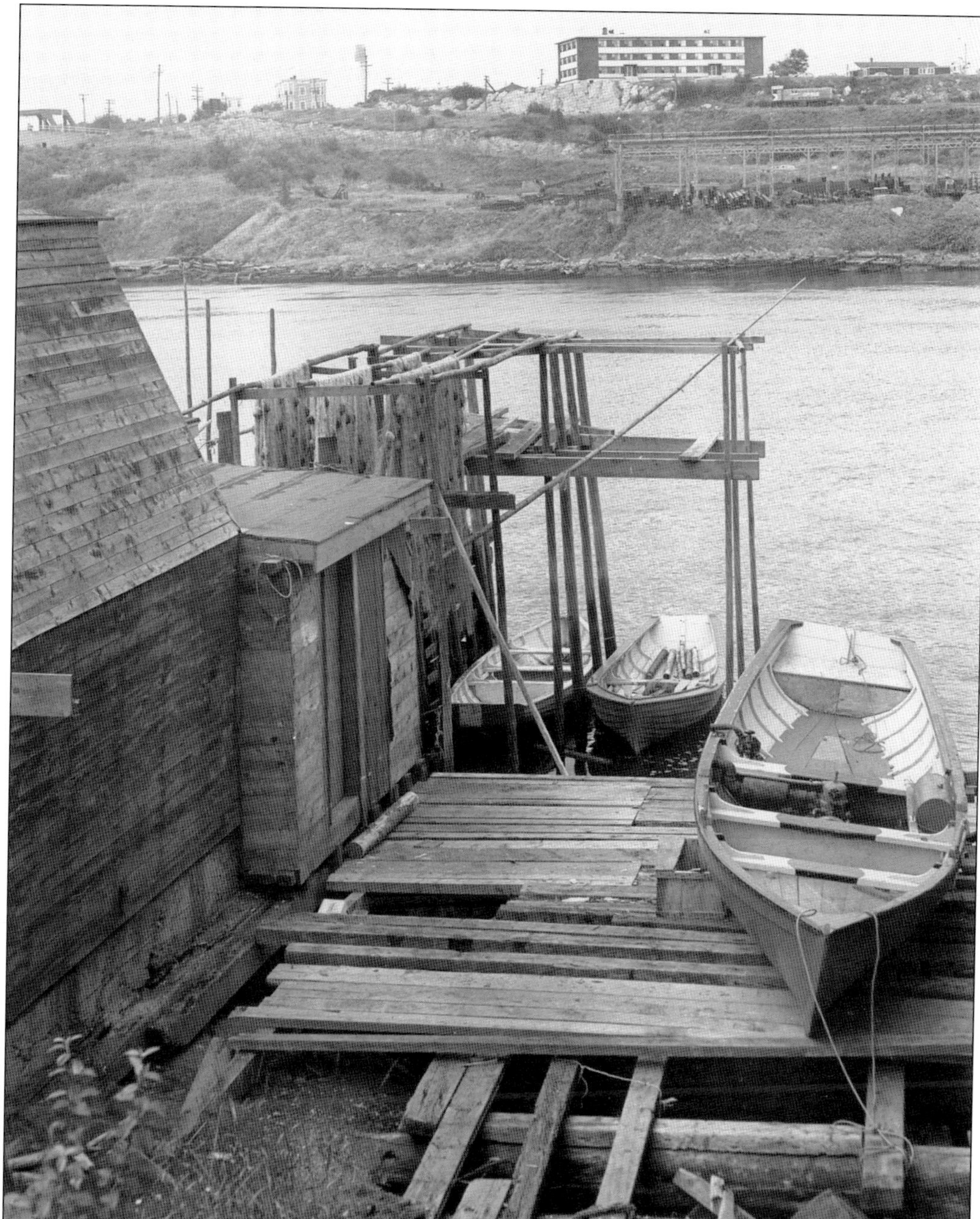

This fishing shed on Riverview Drive from the 1970s provides a stark contrast with the industrial manufacturing plant of Ocean Steel on Chesley Drive. Some ways of life were affected by industrial change, but for those who lived in this part of Saint John, the expropriation of family lands for the creation of the Saint John Harbour Bridge or throughway forced many from traditional industries.

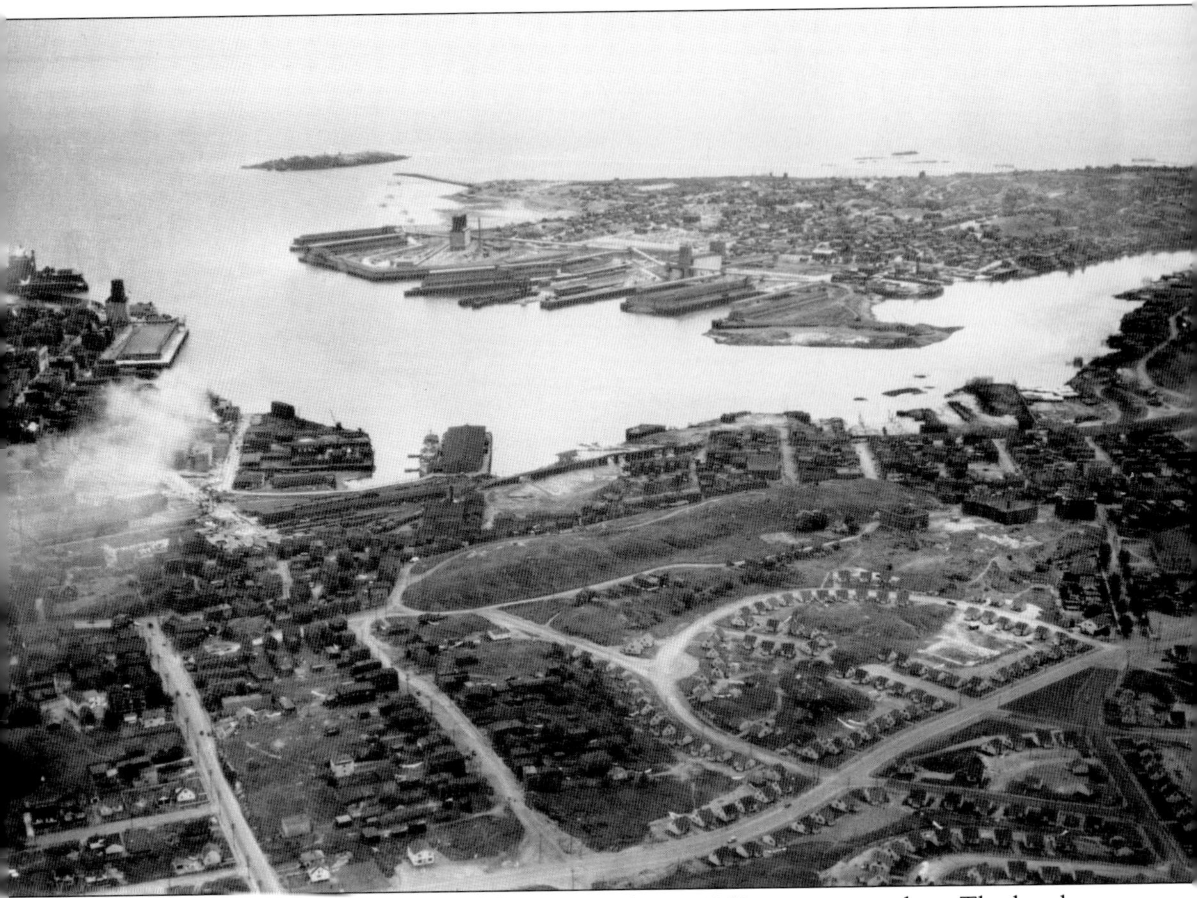

Much of the harbour has changed from when this c. 1950 image was taken. The breakwater to Partridge Island was completed in the early 1960s. The west side docks were filled in for a container terminal. At the left side of the harbour, much of the waterfront was changed for the Coast Guard base and Pugsley Terminal. In the centre is the Main Street area. This entire area was demolished for urban renewal, which included the construction of the Saint John Harbour Bridge and Throughway.

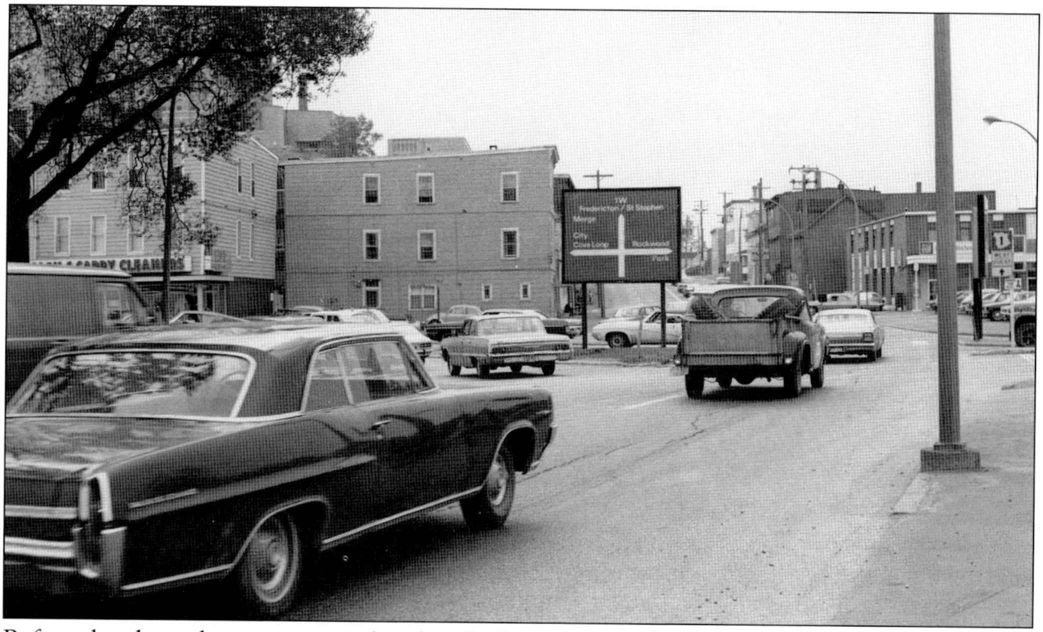

Before the throughway was completed with the on ramps for the Saint John Harbour Bridge, vehicles exiting Haymarket Square had the option to go straight along City Road to Douglas Avenue and then across the Reversing Falls Bridge. This took drivers to the highway to Fredericton or St. Stephen. Turning left went toward the City Cove Loop, while turning right went to Gilbert Street and Rockwood Park.

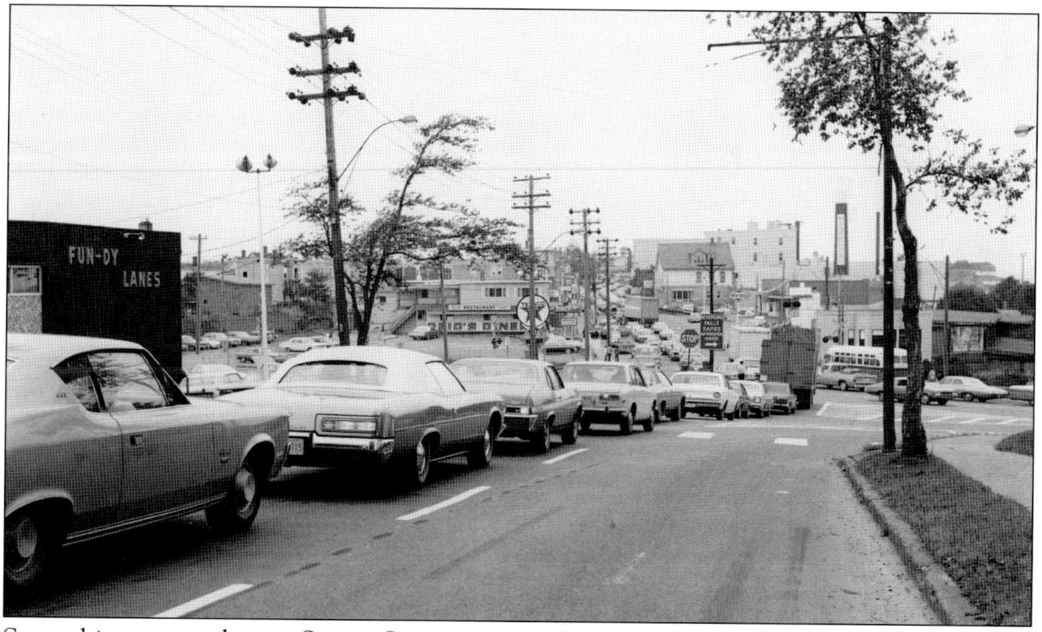

Some things never change. Simms Corner is every drivers' nightmare. The traffic that is backed up Main Street West is a long-standing tradition any time there is work done on either the Saint John Harbour Bridge or Reversing Falls Bridge. The sign in the centre shows to turn right for the Reversing Falls Rapids Information Centre. The Fun-Dy bowling lanes and Reids Diner were two west side landmarks that have been gone for almost a generation.

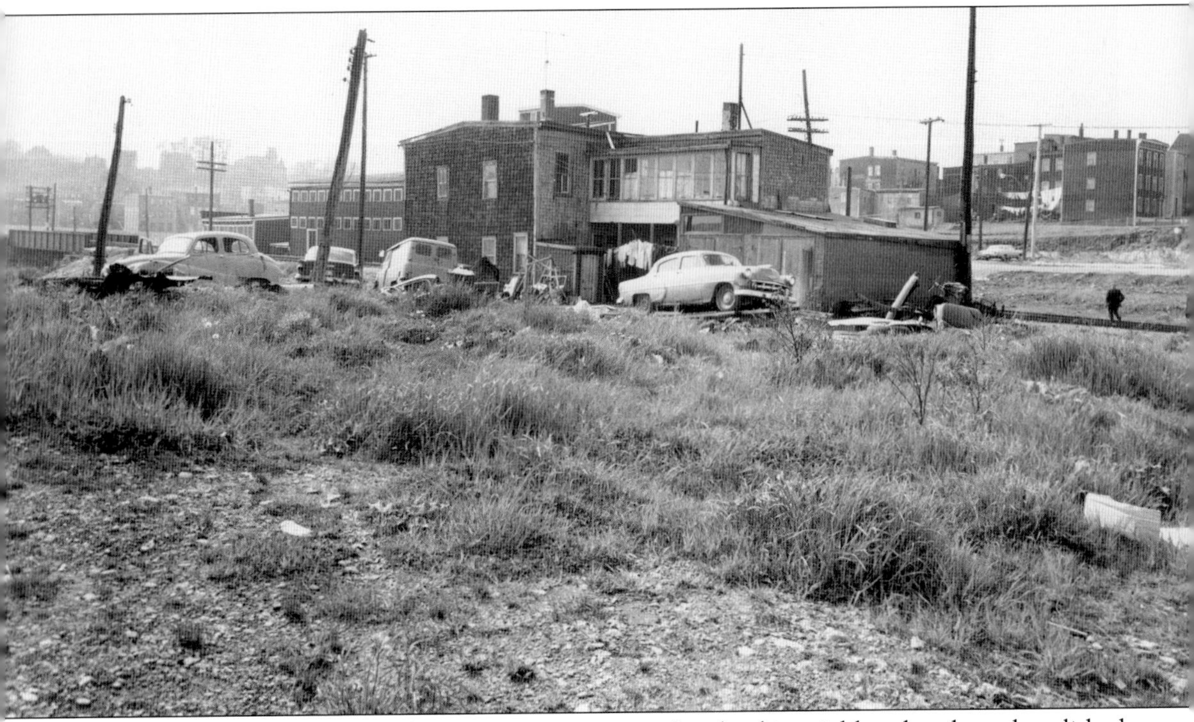

This 1966 view of 110 Portland Street suggests a reason for why this neighbourhood was demolished for the urban renewal program and the Saint John Harbour Bridge. The area was unsightly, and the buildings looked like they were ready to fall down. What the planners forgot to consider was that this was also a neighbourhood where families had lived for generations—neighbours went to the same schools or churches and played on the same sports teams.

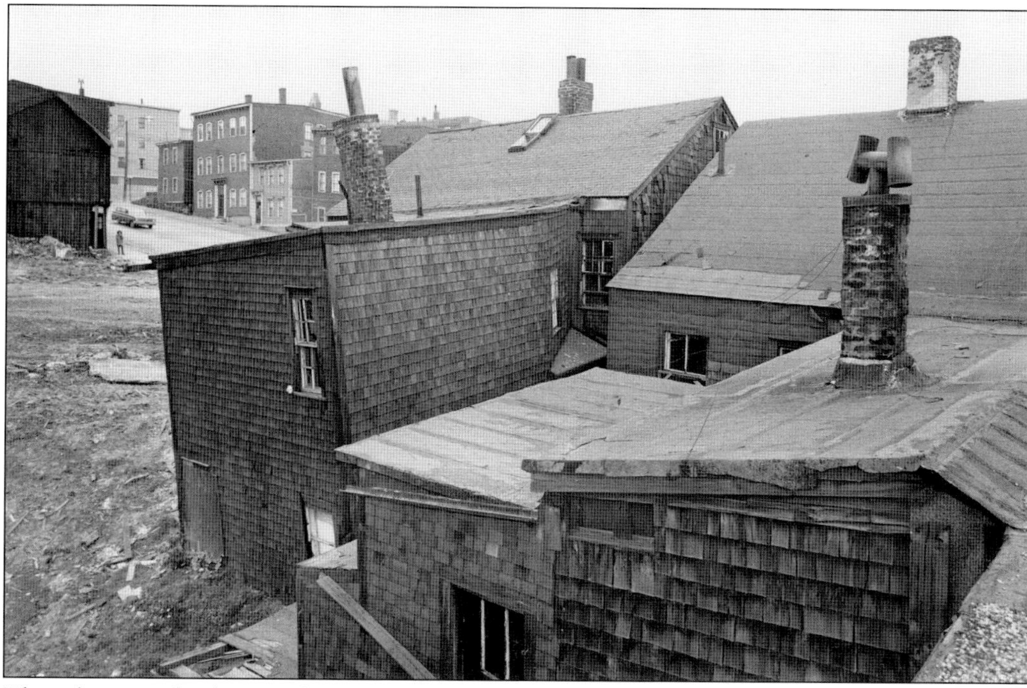

This photograph, showing houses near Portland Street, gives a distorted impression of the 11 streets that were destroyed for both the Saint John Harbour Bridge approaches, the throughway, and other commercial developments. There were many fine, outstanding buildings amongst the obvious ones that needed demolition. The chairman of the urban renewal commission, Mac Sommerville, had convinced the council that there would not be any major demolition of buildings in the area but a "comprehensive program of conservation, rehabilitation and renewal of many of the fine buildings that now exist." That did not happen.

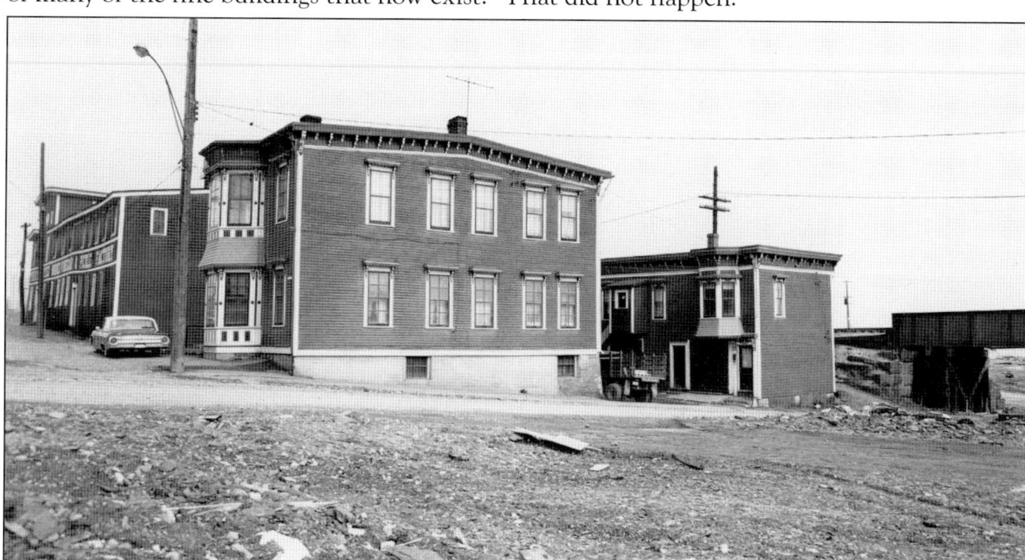

This corner of Camden and Simonds Streets shows the McCreadys Vinegar plant, one of the dozens of small and major businesses that were destroyed by the urban renewal and Saint John Harbour Bridge projects. Few of these businesses were ever reestablished.

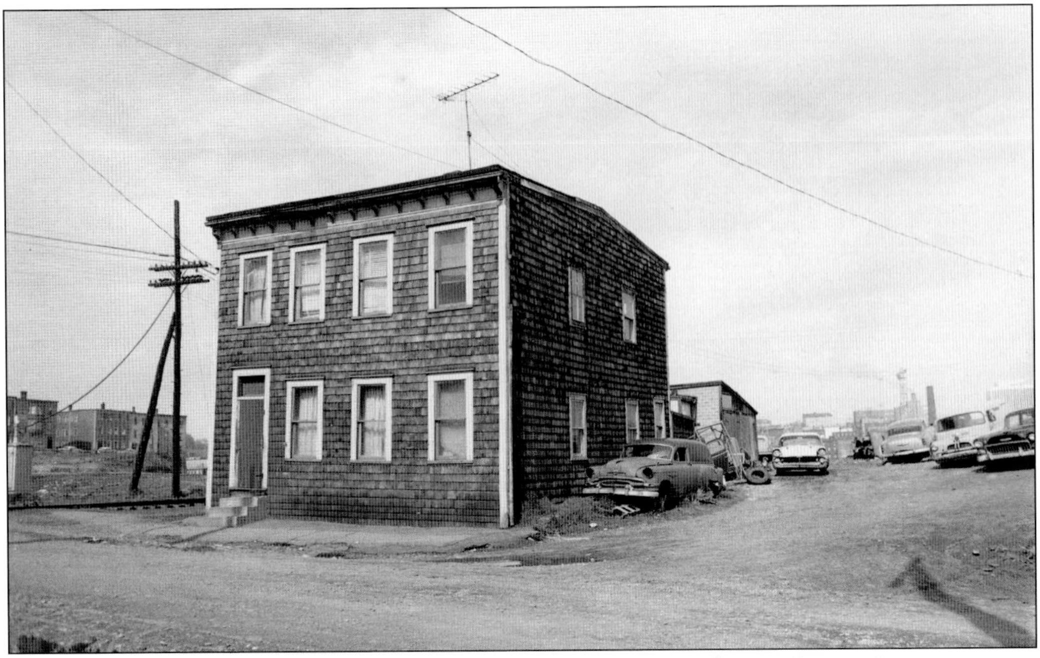

This image of Portland Street is highly suggestive of what was to replace it. Cars and more cars—in fact, these five vehicles are testament to the role the automobile had taken in the everyday life of citizens. Today, automobile collectors would probably give an "arm and a leg" for the opportunity to restore these cars.

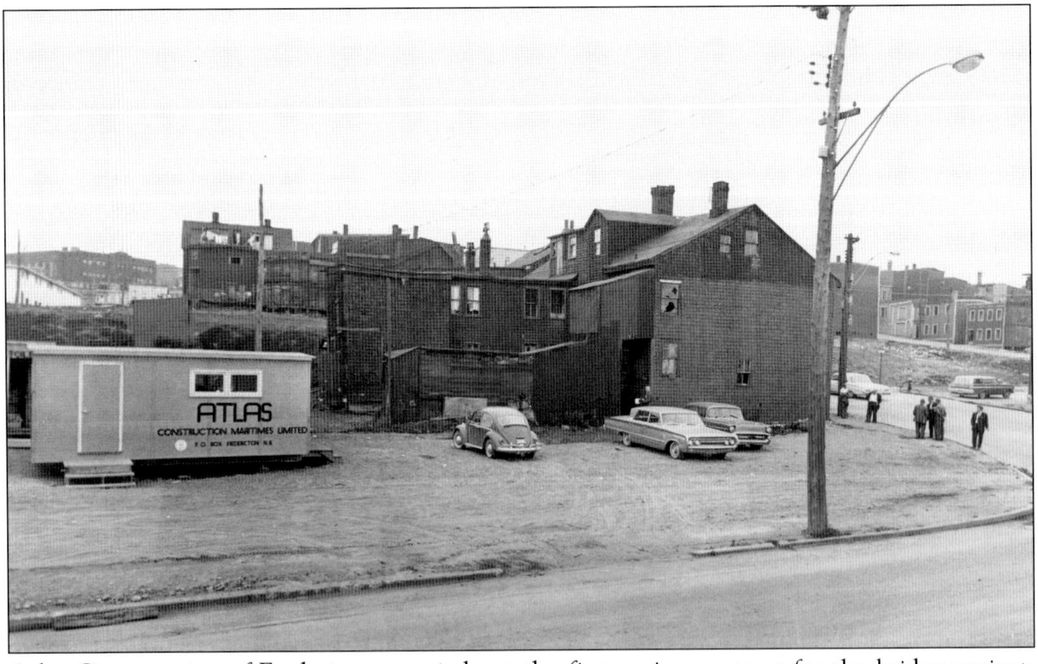

Atlas Construction of Fredericton carried out the first major contract for the bridge project. According to a newspaper article, the work "involved the installation of utilities together with the relocation of an existing city-street system, combined with the construction of temporary and permanent Canadian Pacific Railway diversions."

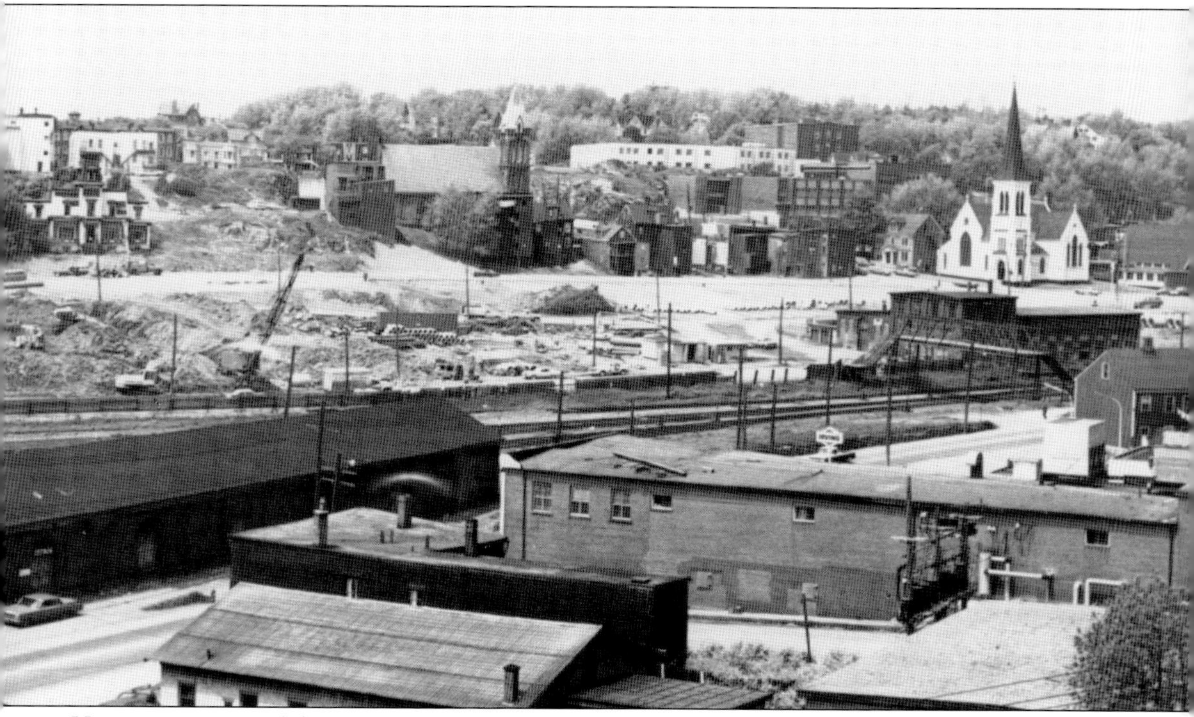

Here is an image of the construction of the throughway along Paradise Row in the early 1970s. The south side of Paradise Row, Southwark, and Lombard Streets were demolished for this section of the Saint John Harbour Bridge project. The project was complete by 1978 when the Paradise Row overpass was finished. This Lombard Street pedestrian overpass was later removed, as was the brick mill building behind it. The St. Paul's Church at the right was destroyed by fire in July 1981.

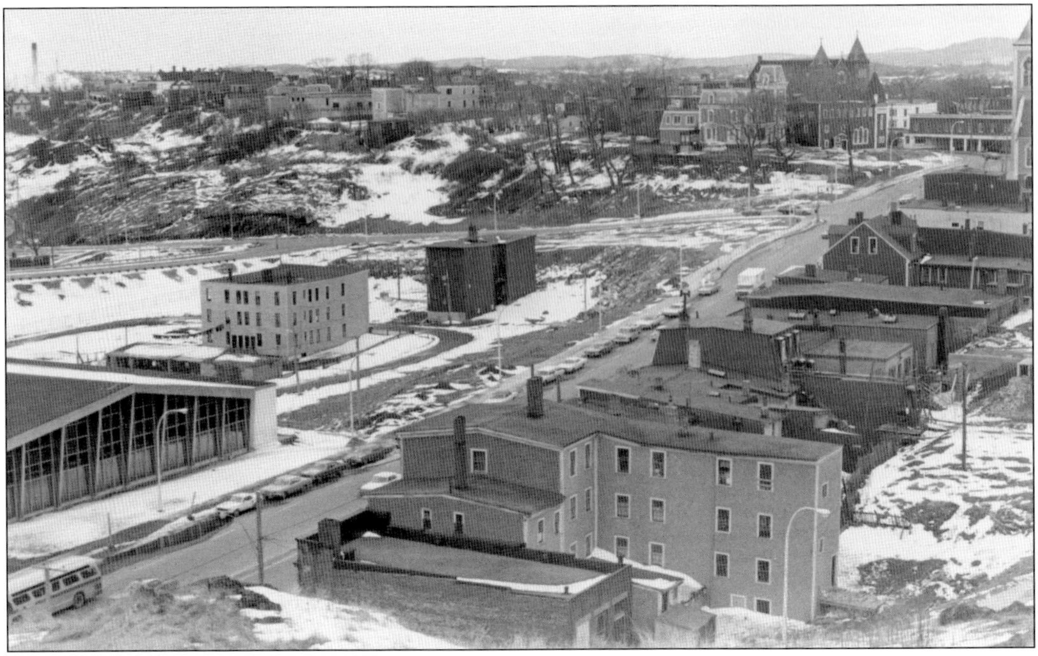

Main Street is a pale version of its former self. Only two buildings remain to be demolished for the Place 400 shopping complex. The Harrison Street ramp is clearly visible. Main Street is now beautified with the annual Marigolds on Main Street event, where students from the surrounding schools plant thousands of the hardy flowers to decorate this main vehicle artery into the uptown.

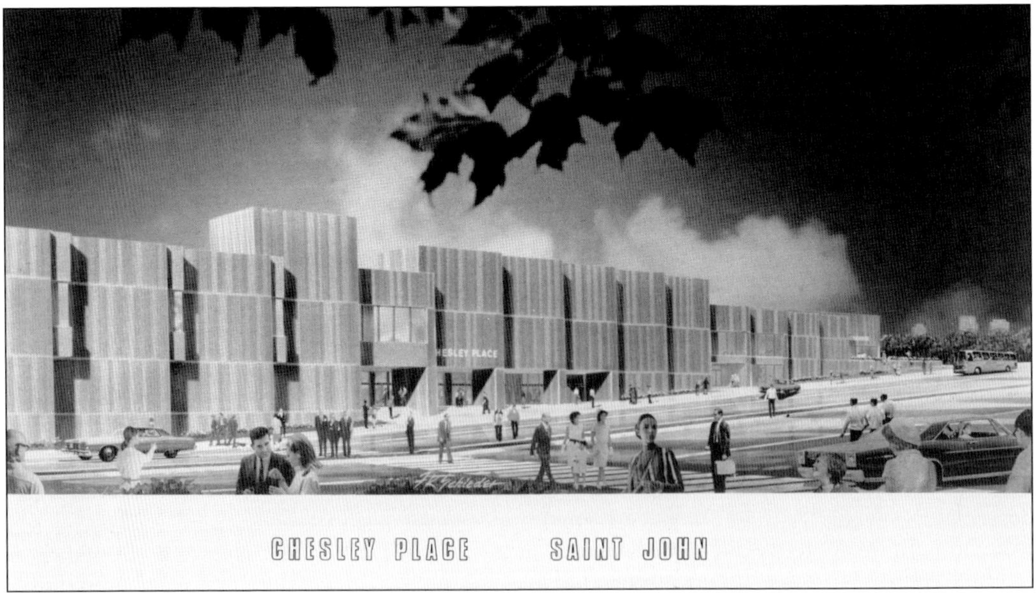

This architect's rendering of the proposed Chesley Place clearly shows how out of touch modern architecture was at the time. The few windows would have isolated the shoppers and office workers from their environment. Now renamed Place 400, this shopping complex was a dismal failure and is now an office complex of several national firms. The only part of the original concept that remains, and thrives, is the adjoining hotel, which opened as a Howard Johnson.

Five

THE SUSPENSION BRIDGE

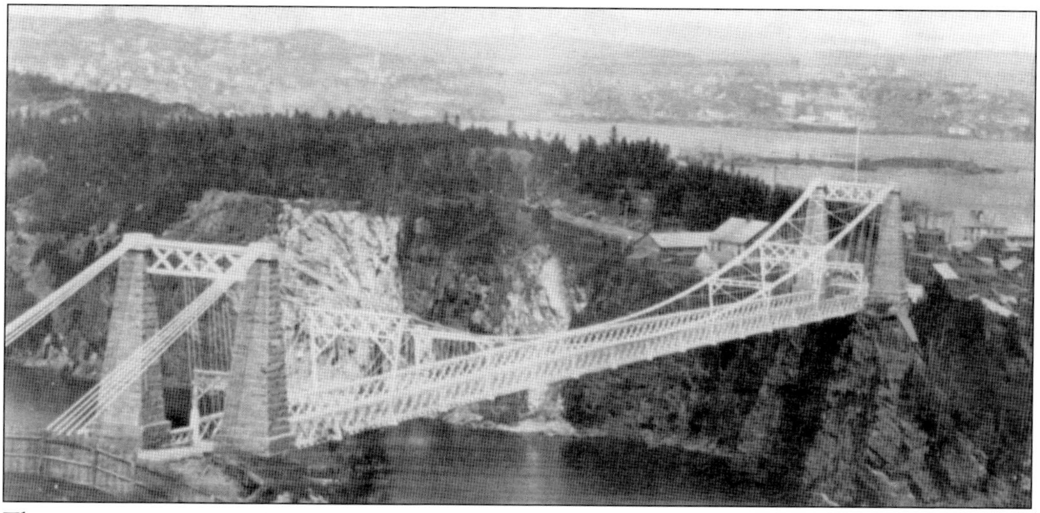

There was an attempt to build a bridge from Navy Island to the Straight Shore (now Chesley Drive) in 1837. The bridge's scaffolding collapsed, sending 14 people into the water. The following poem describes the event: "Amidst the gen'ral wreck appear'd the dead,- / Some maim'd and dying, too were brought on shore, / And some lay silent in a wat'ry bed, / While friends and kindred their sad loss deplore." Charles Simonds offered £100 sterling to anyone or company that could bridge the gap at the Reversing Falls. William K. Reynolds created the Saint John Suspension Bridge Company, and on May 6, 1848, he announced that Edward W. Serrell would design the bridge. Serrell was the designer of the Suspension Bridge across the Niagara Falls. In 1863, there were still few houses on the Douglas Road, but at the eastern end of the bridge, one clearly sees the tollhouse. In 1890, the first and only caretaker of the Suspension Bridge, J.H. Vanburen, died.

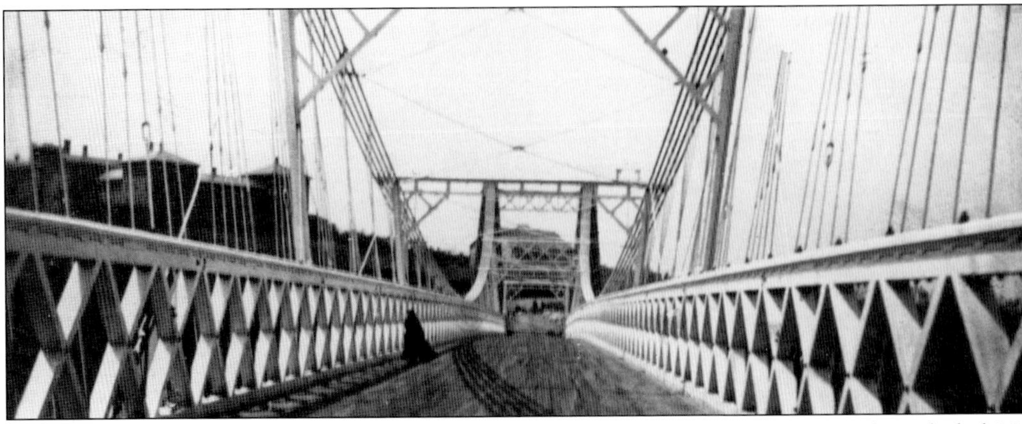

Construction began in 1850, and the bridge opened in the fall of 1853. Materials included 300 stands of No. 10 wire (3,000 in total) on four 52-foot sandstone towers. The bridge was 630 feet long, 23 feet wide, and was over 70 feet above the water. Before Reynolds received any payment for the bridge, independent engineer Alexander Light was hired to test the structure. He used 30 wagons, two tons each, which crossed over the bridge in two lines. He then used three double teams of horses with three tons, which also crossed the bridge, and it was declared safe. The tolls included fees for camels and elephants.

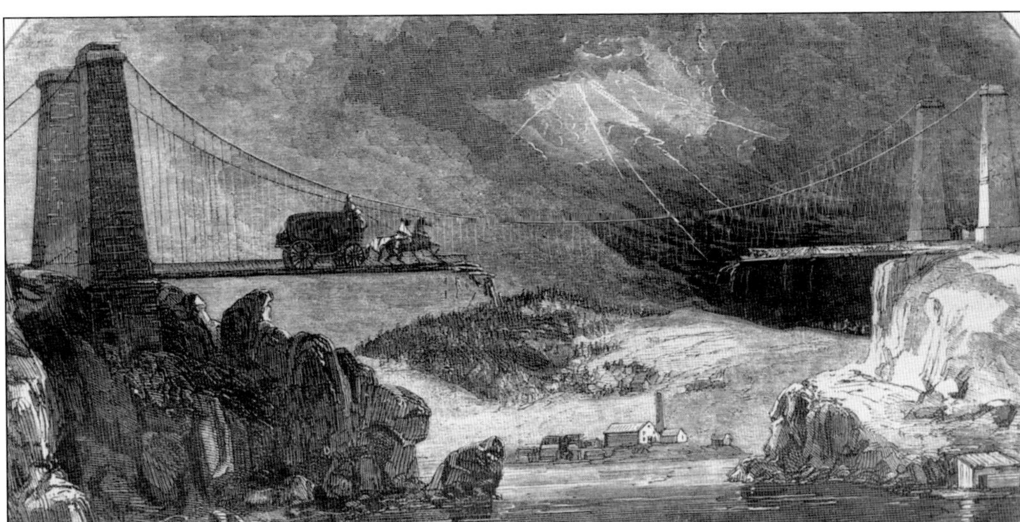

Disaster was averted when the horses of the Fredericton coach stopped dead in their tracks. On the evening on March 24, 1858, a storm raged through the province. According to *Harper's Weekly* magazine in 1858, "On Wednesday evening the wind blew a fearful hurricane at the falls from the north west, which swayed the Suspension Bridge to and fro in an alarming manner. About one third of the flooring, together with the stringers, gave way from the effects of the gale. A large number of the suspending rods, which held up the platform, are hanging loosely from the chains; and part of the wire service round the chains, passing over the pillars, seems to be chafed." The coachman whipped the horses to proceed, but they remained steadfast. He left the coach and then saw that a few hundred feet of the bridge had been destroyed; he was only inches from certain death.

The bridge quickly became part of the local tourism industry. In 1860, the Prince of Whales visited the bridge. Bass fishing became popular, both from the banks of the river and the "four or five men daily [who could] be seen on the suspension bridge from early morning until late in the evening, holding a line, . . . they [were] sometimes so fortunate to bag themselves a fish," according to a newspaper report. By 1879, there was a hotel built near the bridge to capitalize on its extensive use. It also became a local hangout for those who drank liquor, with reports of rowdy activity in 1881. A watchman was hired to crack down on speeding horses; those caught were escorted to the Portland Police Station.

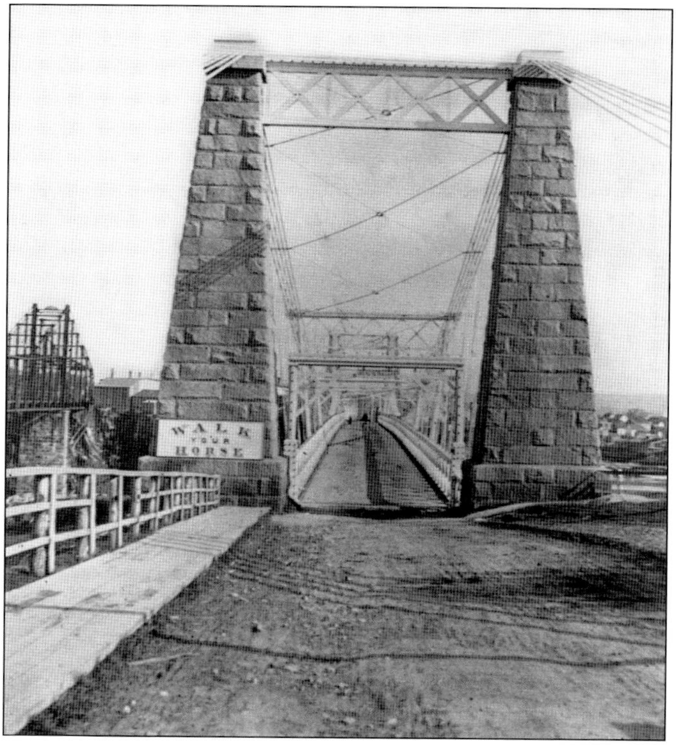

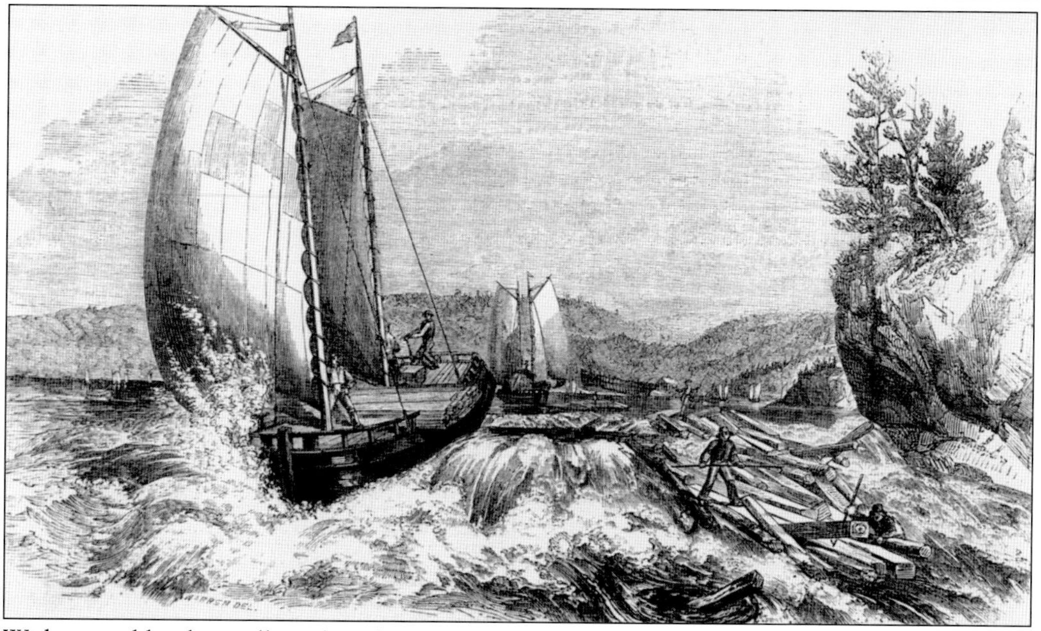

With several lumber mills within the inner harbour, timber had to be brought through the falls. While the wood boats were relatively effective in doing so, this illustration clearly shows the dangers for the men riding the timber. The dangers of such a livelihood are illustrated by the following newspaper article from the *Morning Freeman* in April 1863: "On Saturday morn., James McCREADY while passing through the Falls in a scow, fell overboard near the Suspension Bridge and but for an oar which was thrown to him, he would have drowned."

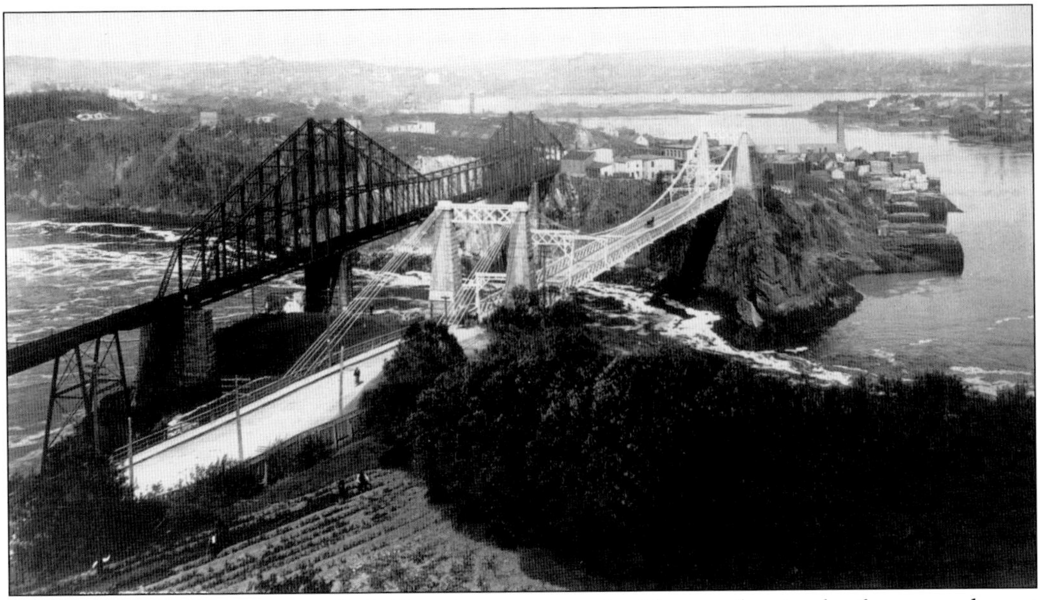

These bridges over Reversing Falls Rapids are pictured with a garden in the foreground, part of the Provincial Lunatic Asylum property, and a lumber mill at the eastern end of the bridge. Navy Island is seen in the background. Douglas Avenue at the left has been stripped of most of its tree covering.

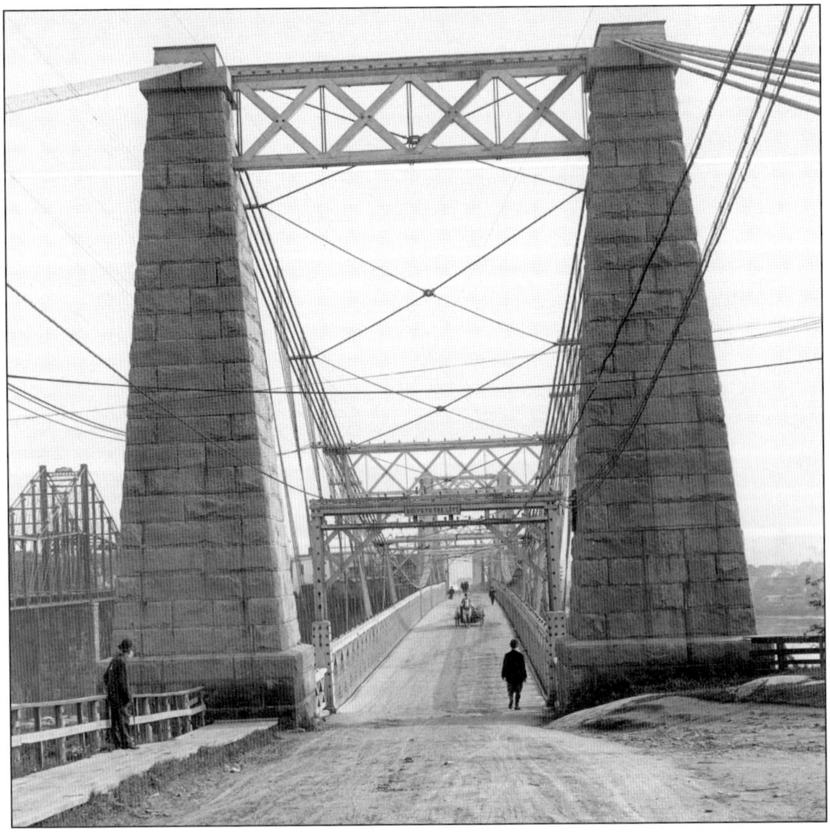

This clearly illustrates just how narrow the bridge was at 23 feet. Driving was done to the left; although, the driver pictured is in the centre of the bridge, he is playing it safe. Pedestrians shared the same space as the horses and wagons, including the mud after a rain and the droppings of the horses. The bridge deck was paved with wood paving blocks.

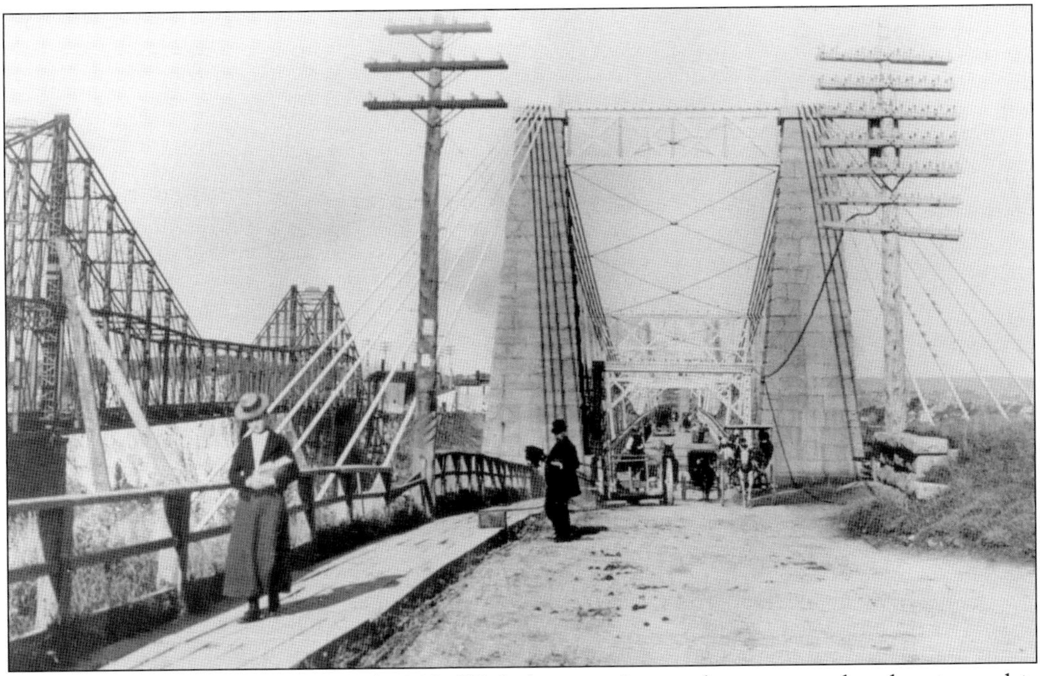

Traffic congestion is seen around 1900. With five coaches and wagons and pedestrians, this could be considered supper-hour traffic. By the turn of the 20th century, the bridge had already outlived its effectiveness as a cross-harbour link. Even when the new bridge was opened in 1916, it was still hard pressed to handle traffic at peak times.

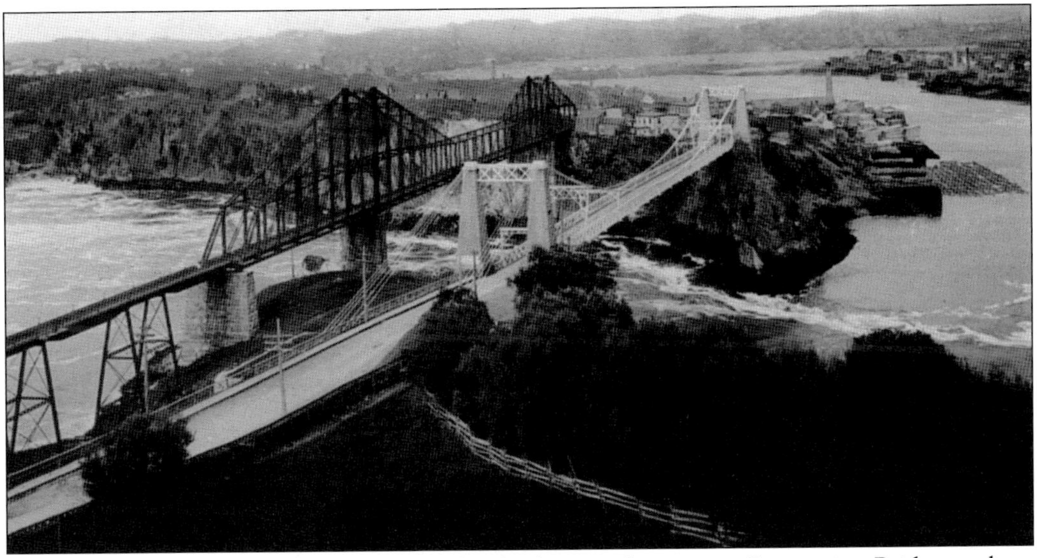

By 1911, it was evident that repairs needed to be done to the current Suspension Bridge or else a new bridge would need to be built. By the summer of 1913, in spite of speculation that government issues may cause delays, preliminary excavations had begun on work for a new bridge. Tragedy still remained part of the story of the Reversing Falls; in July 1894, a Saint John newspaper reported that "three North End fishermen drowned in the falls at 530 yesterday when the boat was caught in the falls and the whirl pools overturned the boat."

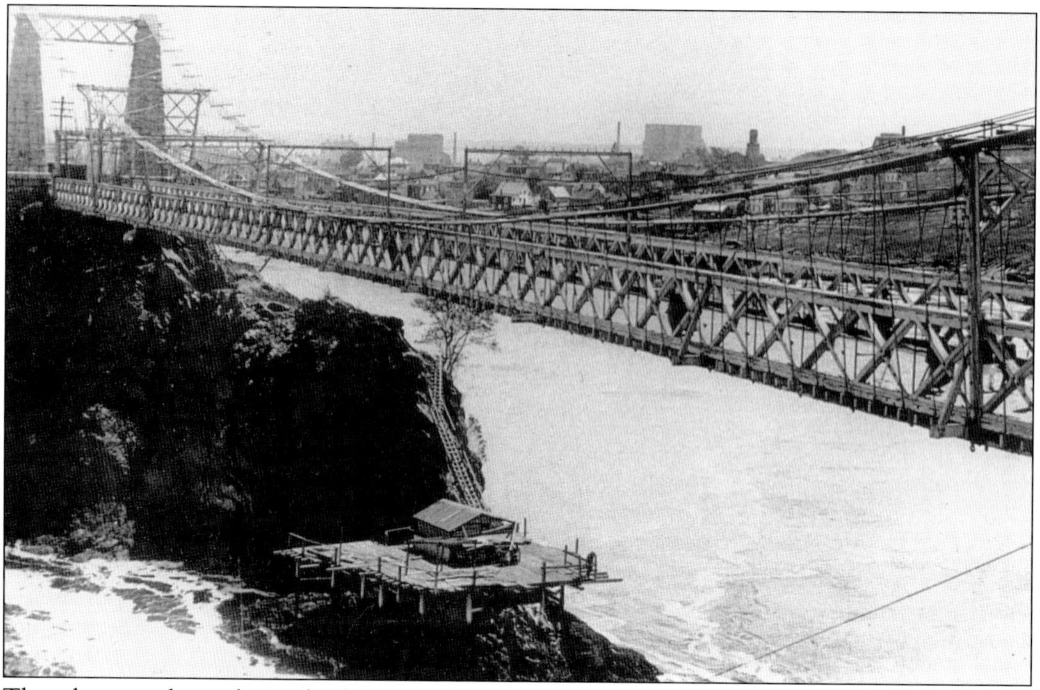

This photograph can be misleading. It shows a small wharf and shed on Split Rock about 1905. One contemporary description says it is a fishing shed. Another contemporary description says it is the wharf used to ship plumbago (graphite) from the mine at Split Rock. If one looks carefully to the left at the top of the ladder, a small round opening in the ground is visible. This was one of at least four plumbago mines at the falls.

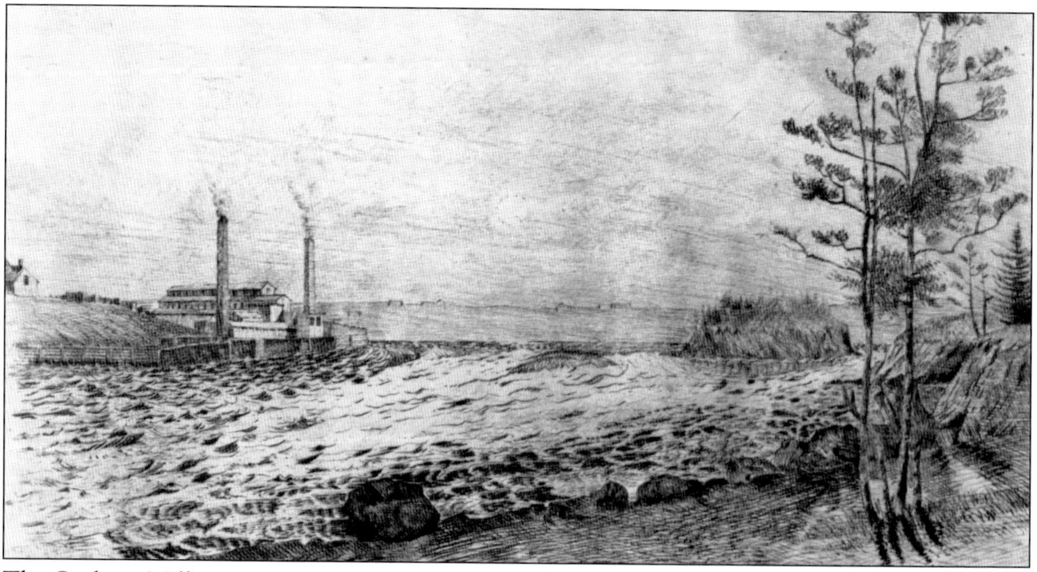

The Cushing Mill at Cunnabelle Point is depicted in 1851. The first mill at this site was erected in 1835 and was known as the Cunnabells Sawmill. In 1850, Colonel Goddard of Maine purchased the mill and, in 1851, sold it to his fellow American, Andre Cushing, also of Maine. This sawmill burned in 1851 and was rebuilt only to be again destroyed by fire in 1869. The island at the right would be False Island.

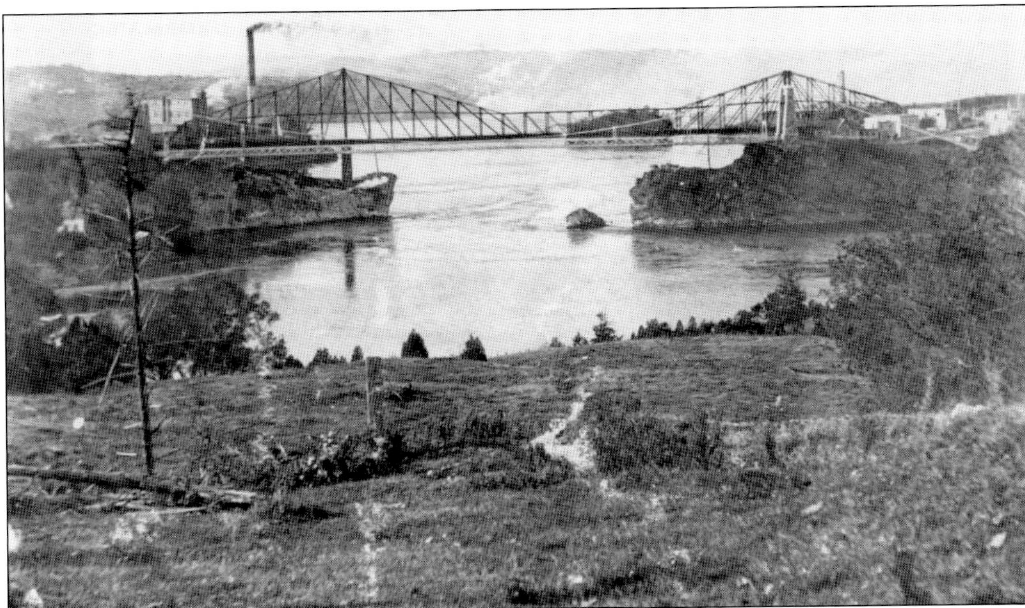

This view of the Reversing Falls and bridges is from the Jewett property on Prince Street, which later became the site of the DVA Hospital. If the bridge could speak, it might tell of the 1872 escape from prison of James McGarbon, who shot and robbed Mr. Welch, the former toll keeper of the Suspension Bridge, in 1858.

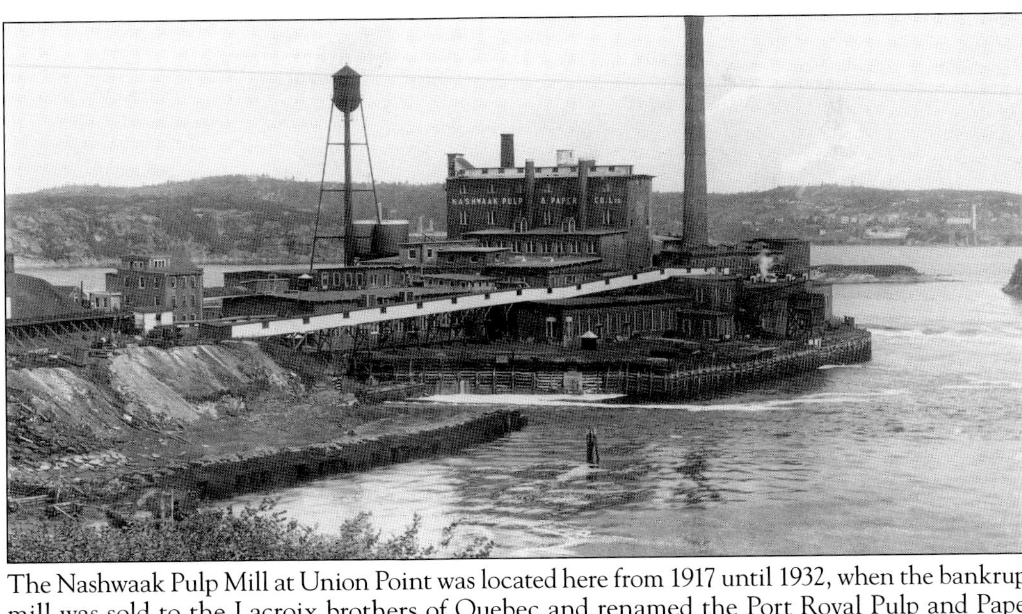

The Nashwaak Pulp Mill at Union Point was located here from 1917 until 1932, when the bankrupt mill was sold to the Lacroix brothers of Quebec and renamed the Port Royal Pulp and Paper Company. The Nashwaak Pulp Mill produced up to 45 tons of bleached sulphite for high-grade book paper. The mill went bankrupt when the owners could not finance upgrades.

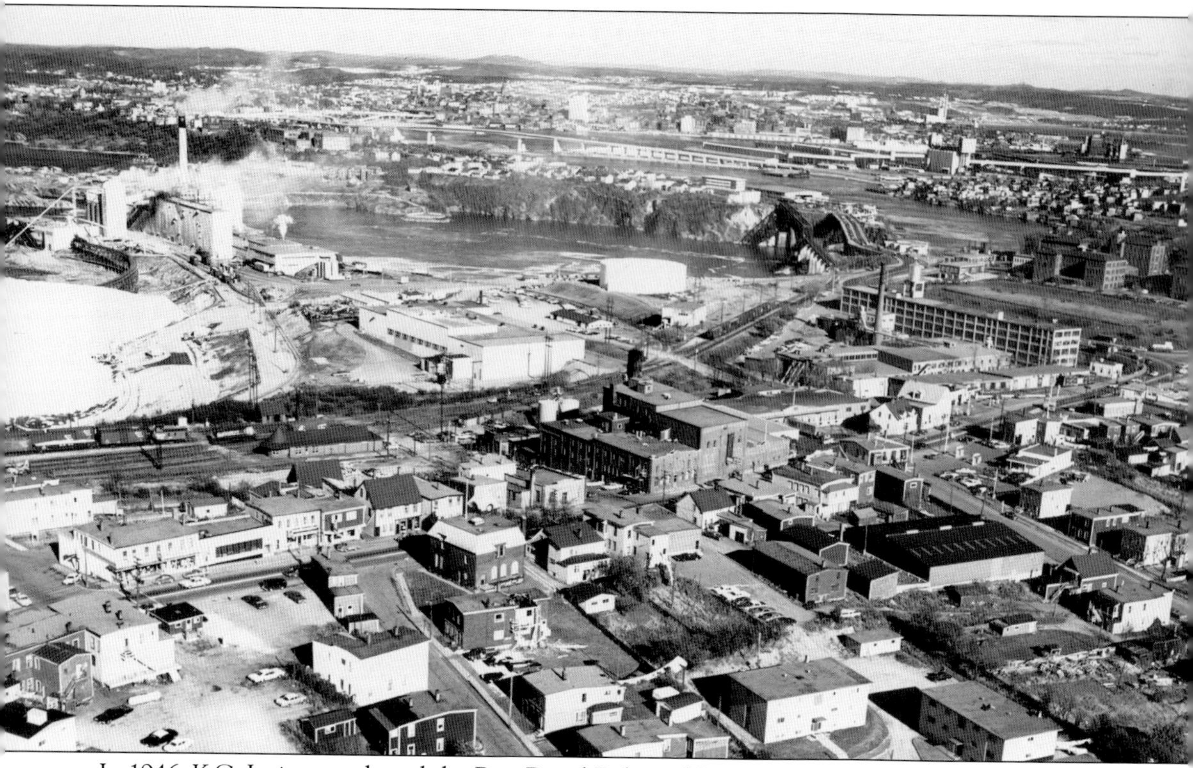

In 1946, K.C. Irving purchased the Port Royal Pulp and Paper Company's mill and its associated woodlands in Maine from the Lacroix brothers. In 1952, the name was changed to Irving Pulp & Paper, Limited, and since that time, the mill has been one of the major employers in the city. The company has made great strides over the decades to reduce its effluent and emissions. It produces in excess of 1.036 tons of kraft pulp daily. Other major employers seen in this image include Moosehead Brewery on Main Street and TS Simms on Bridge Road. Across from Simms is the former Centracare hospital, now Wolastoq Park, maintained by J.D. Irving, Limited.

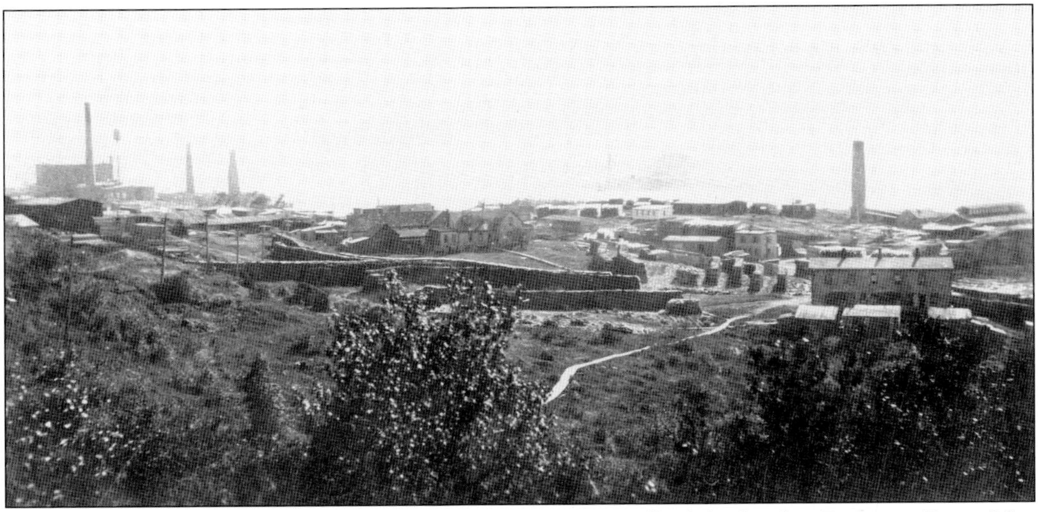

In 1921, the Murray & Gregory Mill encompassed almost all of the land at Prospect Point. Not only were there mill operations and storage areas, but there were also residences built for some of the staff. A few of those residences remain today; the main mill buildings were destroyed by fire several decades ago. The firm milled lumber in various forms, did custom mill work for doors and windows, and even produced stained glass. William H. Murray and Fraser Gregory were the proprietors, and both lived on Douglas Avenue.

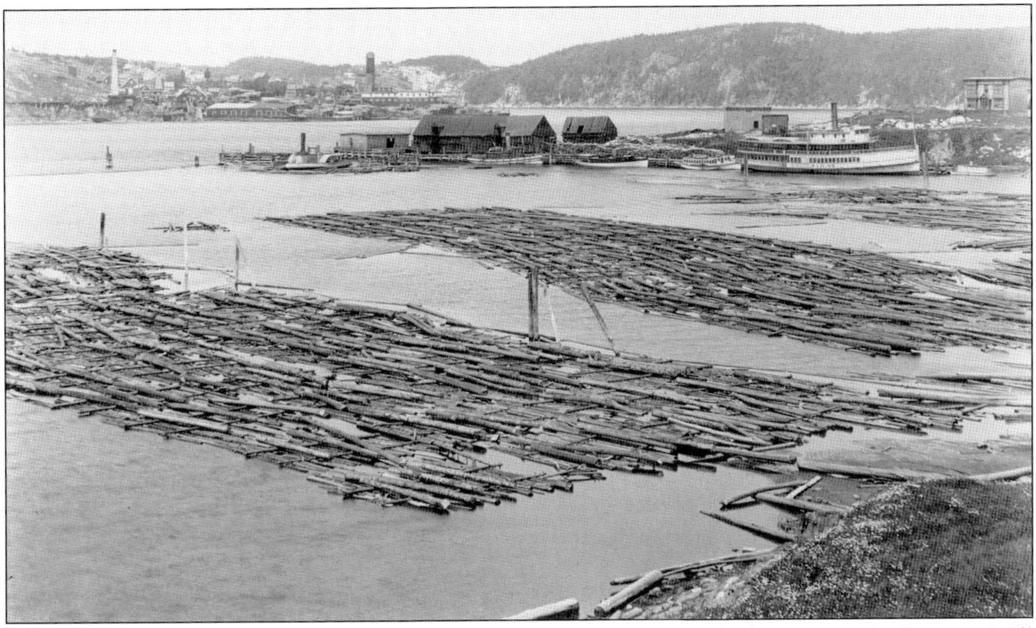

This 1913 view of Marble Cove shows its use as a millpond for both the Murray & Gregory Mill and the Goddard Mill, shown at the centre. At this time, the cove was also home to the Saint John Powerboat Club as well as storage for the riverboat *Elaine*. Across the river at Pleasant Point can be seen the Lewis & Rivers Sawmill.

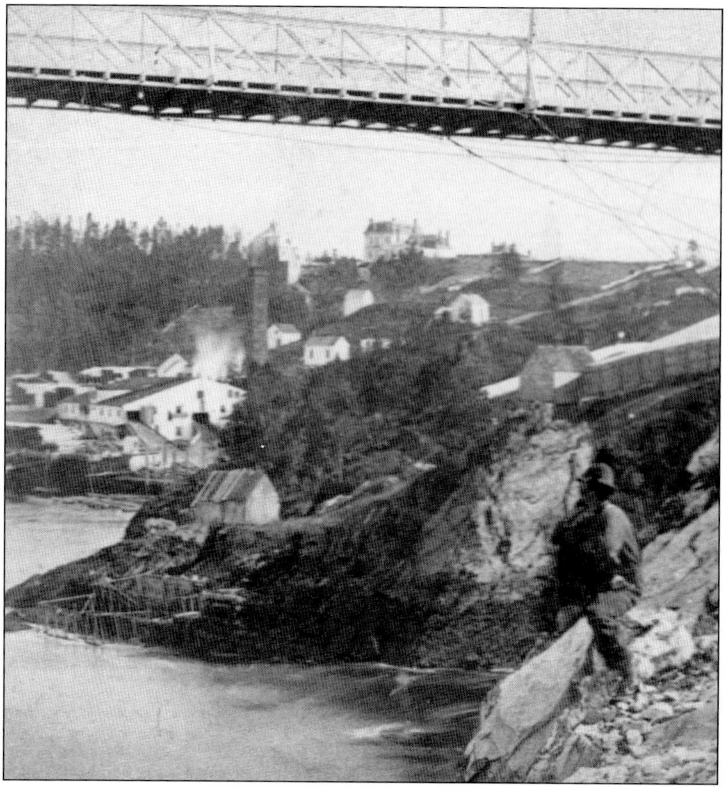

Edward D. Jewett's sawmill is seen at Deadmans Cove. Remnants of the mill are still visible at low tide today. In 1855, the mill published a notice of the dozen marks they placed on their timber, cautioning and forbidding all persons "not duly authorized by us, from buying, receiving or taking charge of, or into their possession for any purpose whatsoever, any of the above Timber and Logs, and will be liable to prosecution for so doing."

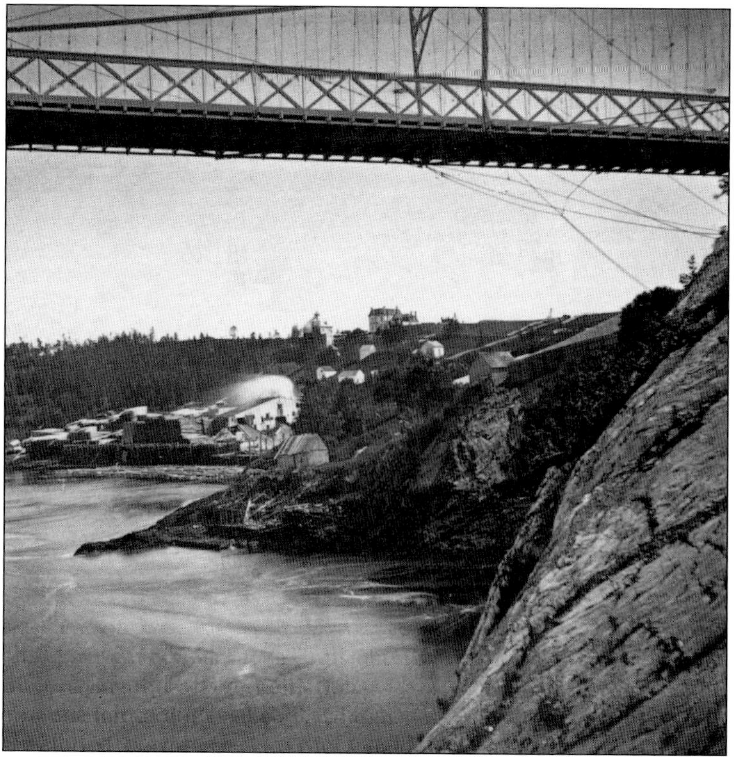

Here is another view of Deadmans Cove, which got its name from the bodies that surfaced from both the boating accidents and those who jumped from the bridge. At the top centre of the image is the home of Andre Cushing, which as named Keystone. In 1872, he and E.D. Jewett had their homes painted in the fresco technique. In the 1970s, the former location of Jewett's mill became the short-term location of a marine museum started by Harry Bagley.

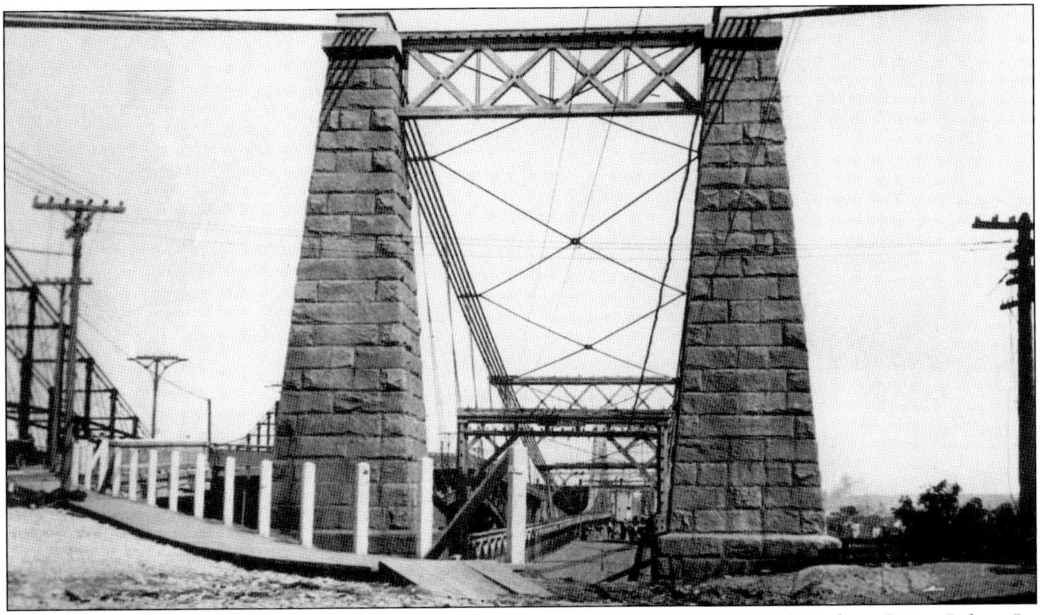

In August 1895, Mary Babin of Moncton received a letter from her husband in Saint John. In part, it read as follows: "Dear Mary, I am writing this on the Suspension bridge and by the time you receive it, I will be floating down the river. I have not been a success in life and am no good to anyone. Good-bye." This is one of the dozens of sad tales that the Suspension Bridge could tell. This 1915 view of the bridge shows the beginning of its dismantling. The new cantilever bridge is seen through the cables.

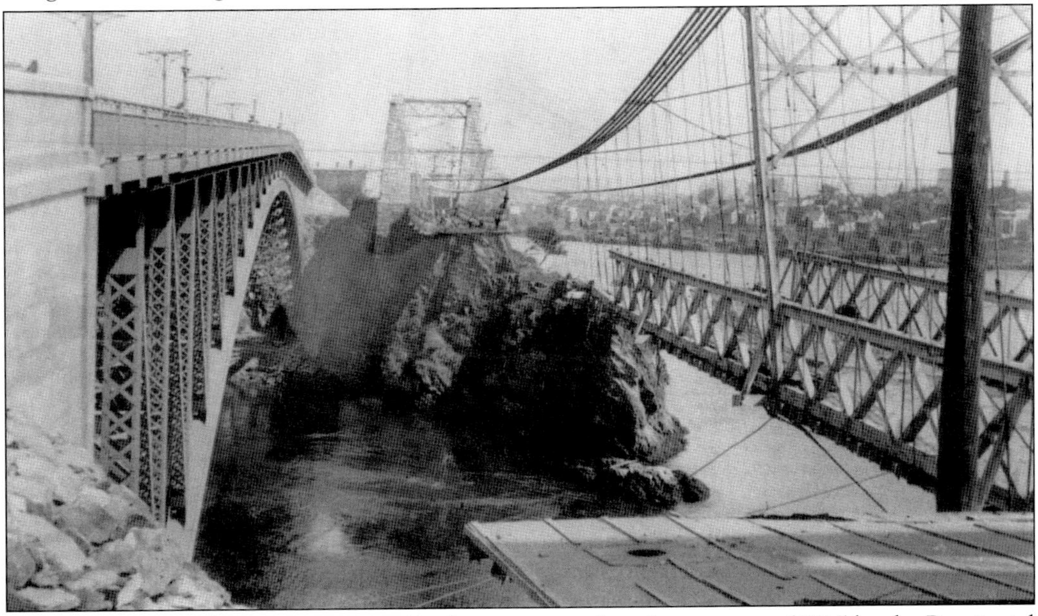

Tenders to dismantle the Suspension Bridge were issued in the summer of 1915 by the Provincial Public Works Department. The removal included all wood, wires, and the granite tower supports. By that fall, only a bit of wood was left as well as some cables and two stone towers. In September, the New Brunswick Historical Society began a campaign to have two of the stone towers remain as a monument to the bridge.

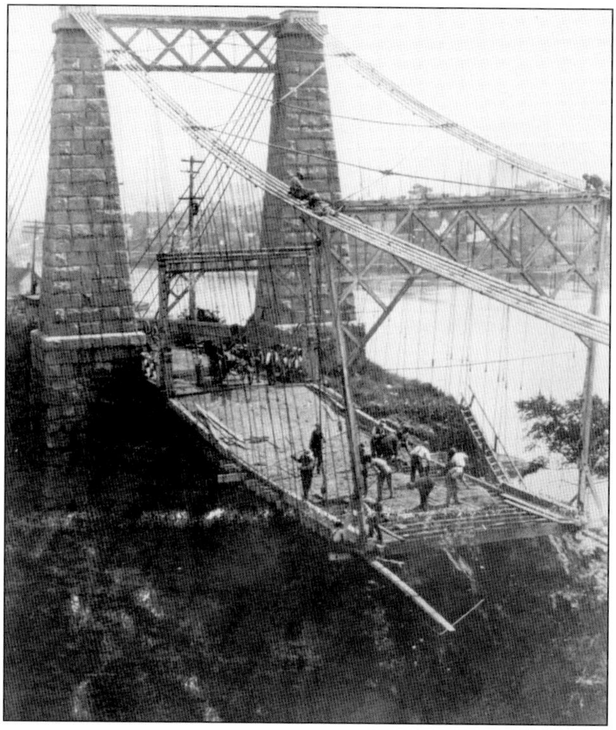

The contractor for the demolition was Joseph McVey. He expected it would take three weeks to remove the woodwork. McVey was also responsible for cutting off a corner of the southern anchorage at the western approach so that the street railway company could proceed with the laying of rails for the new bridge.

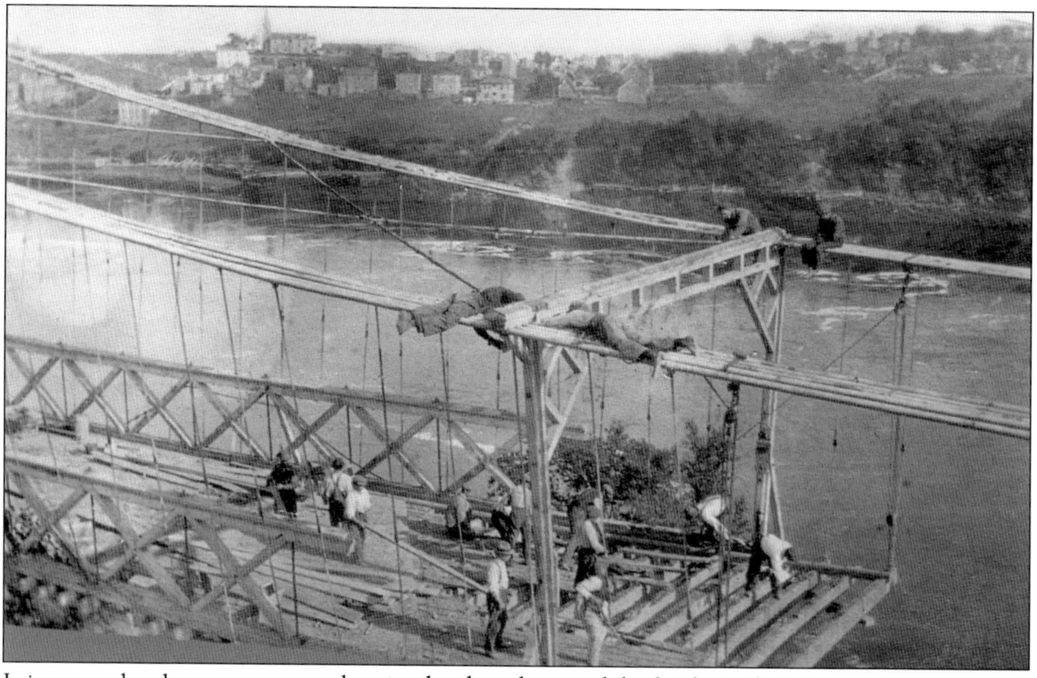

It is a wonder that no man was lost in the demolition of the bridge. There appears to be a total lack of safety devices. Eighty feet of flooring was removed on September 13, 1915, the last day for the wood removal. Then the cables were removed, which was a far more difficult job. When the cables were originally installed, the wires had been boiled in linseed oil and franklinite to prevent corrosion. (Courtesy of David Goss.)

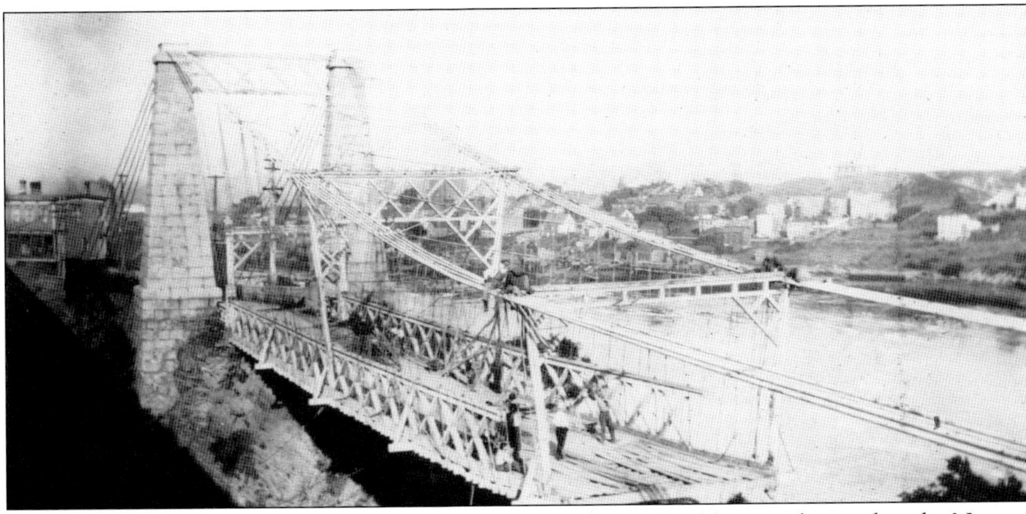

When the bridge was dismantled, pieces of the wood deck and cable were donated to the Natural History Society Museum. It is believed these pieces are still part of the New Brunswick Museum's collection. The stone from the pillars was recycled into a new bridge foundation in Moncton.

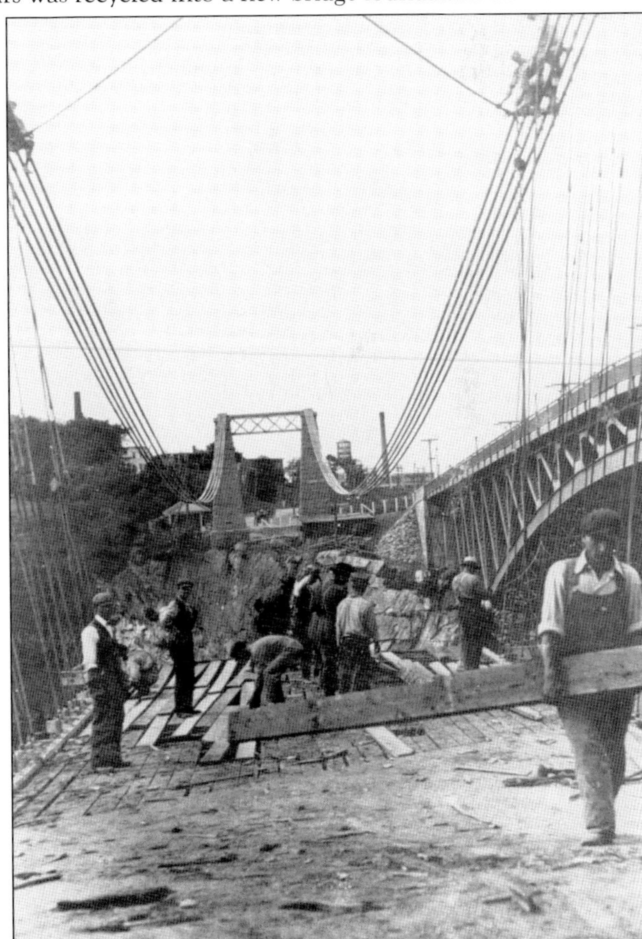

When the tenders closed for demolition of the bridge on August 18, 1915, the contract specified that the job had to be completed by October. That it was done in such a timely manner, as well as without accidents involving the workers, is testament to the work ethic of the men. This image clearly shows the dimension of the deck flooring.

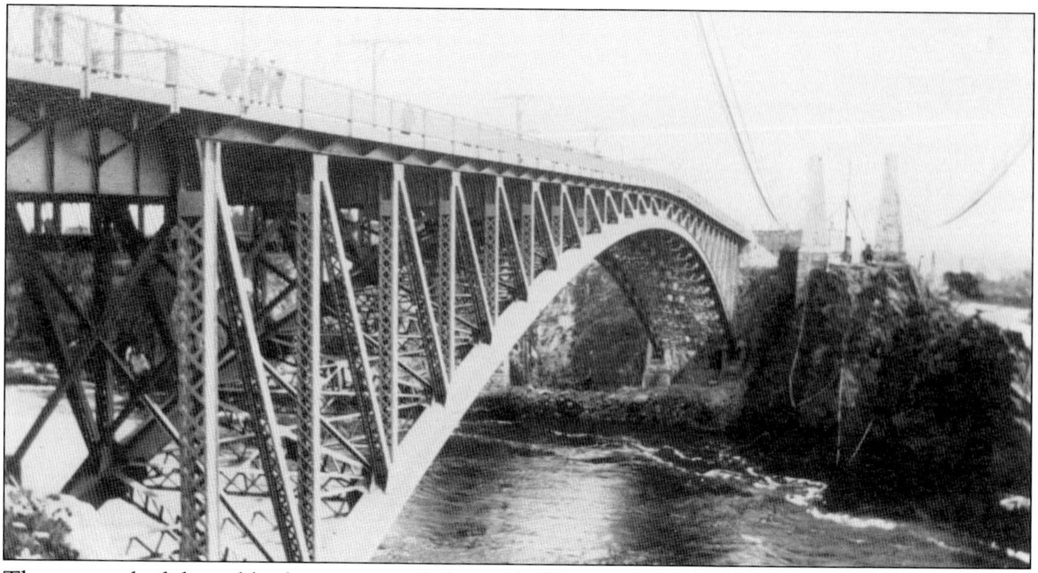

The removal of the cables began toward the end of September 1915. The first cable was tied to a large rope, with the intent of lowering it when cut and then pulling it up from the other side. The first cable was not co-operative. It broke from the tackle and crashed against the opposite cliff face. Each cable was about seven inches in diameter and weighed several hundred pounds apiece.

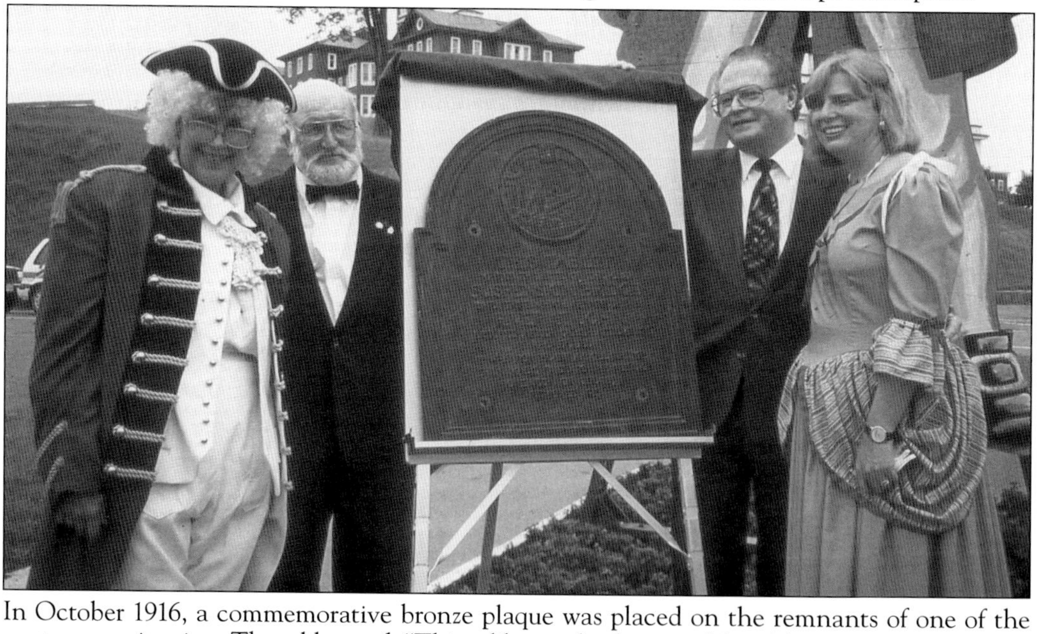

In October 1916, a commemorative bronze plaque was placed on the remnants of one of the western granite piers. The tablet read, "This tablet marks the site of the old suspension bridge, the first which spanned the Saint John River. Erected after other attempts had failed, it was for years a toll bridge then made free to the public open for use 1853 removed 1915." The tablet stayed at the site until it was removed in 1961. In 1995, Harry Marr found the plaque in the Spruce Lake dump. Co-author Harold E. Wright arranged for its donation to the New Brunswick Museum in 1996, and the rededication ceremony during the Festival by the Falls. Shown are, from left to right, Jane Barry, member of the Legislative Assembly for Saint John West; Harry Marr; the Honorable Sheldon Lee, Minister of Transportation; and Her Worship Mayor Shirley McAlary.

Six

THE CANTILEVER BRIDGE

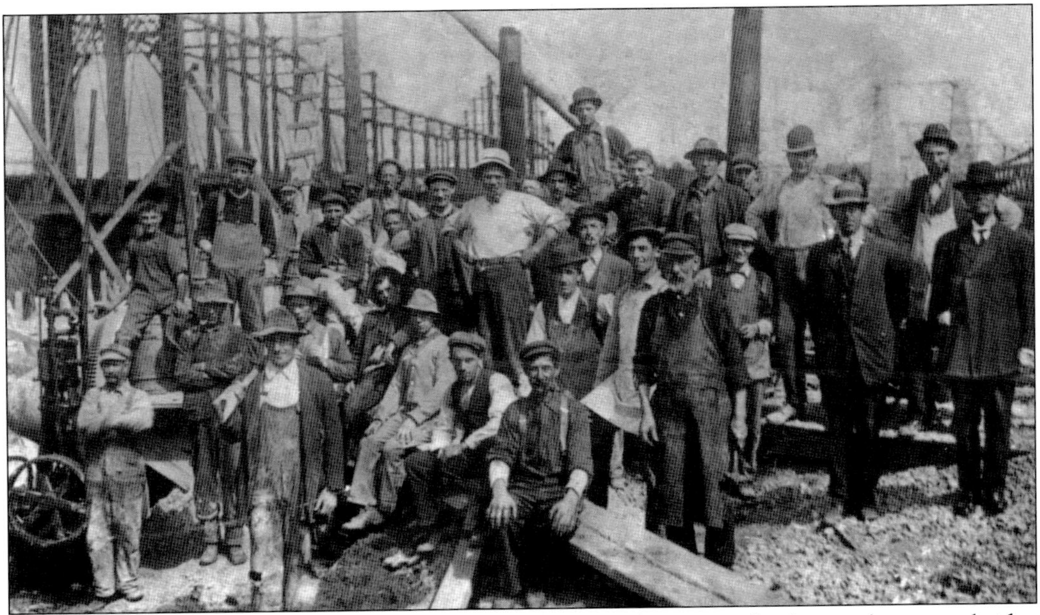

By 1911, it was evident that repairs needed to be done to the current bridge or else a new bridge would need to be built. With the growing automobile traffic and the expansion of the street railway system, the government decided on a new bridge. In the summer of 1913, excavations began for a new bridge. It was designed by C.C. Schneider of Philadelphia and was to be built by the Dominion Bridge Company.

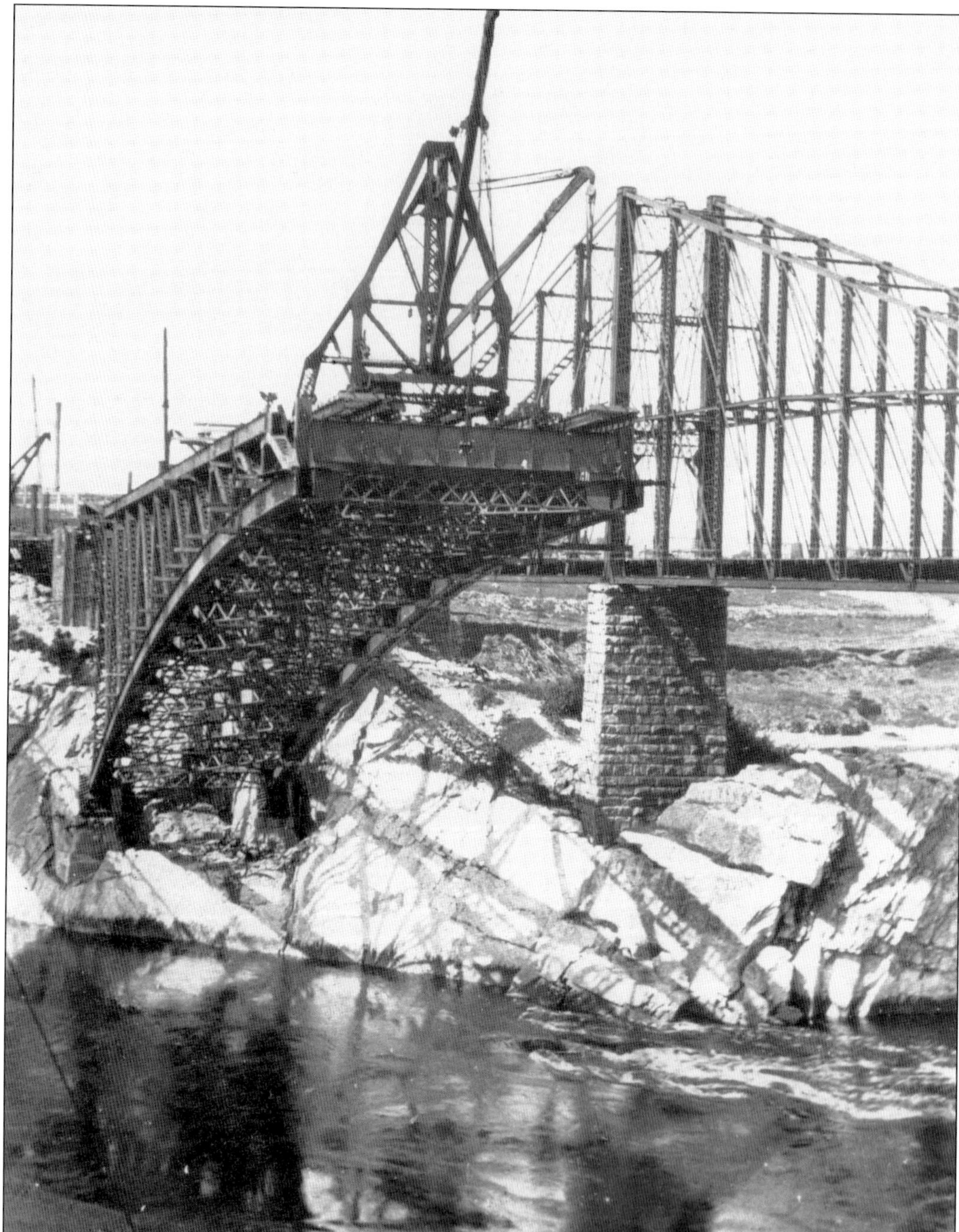

As work progressed on the steel superstructure, the first accident happened. Foreman John Johnson fell from a scow while attempting to get onto Split Rock. The first woman to cross the bridge was Lena Gibson. It was still under construction when on the morning of November 29, 1914, she walked the central girder with a friend—no bridge deck, only hoses, rivets, and bolts—with no rope or safety devices. She froze but was helped by her friend who was one of the bridge workers. The police took her to jail, but after a public outcry, the charges were dropped.

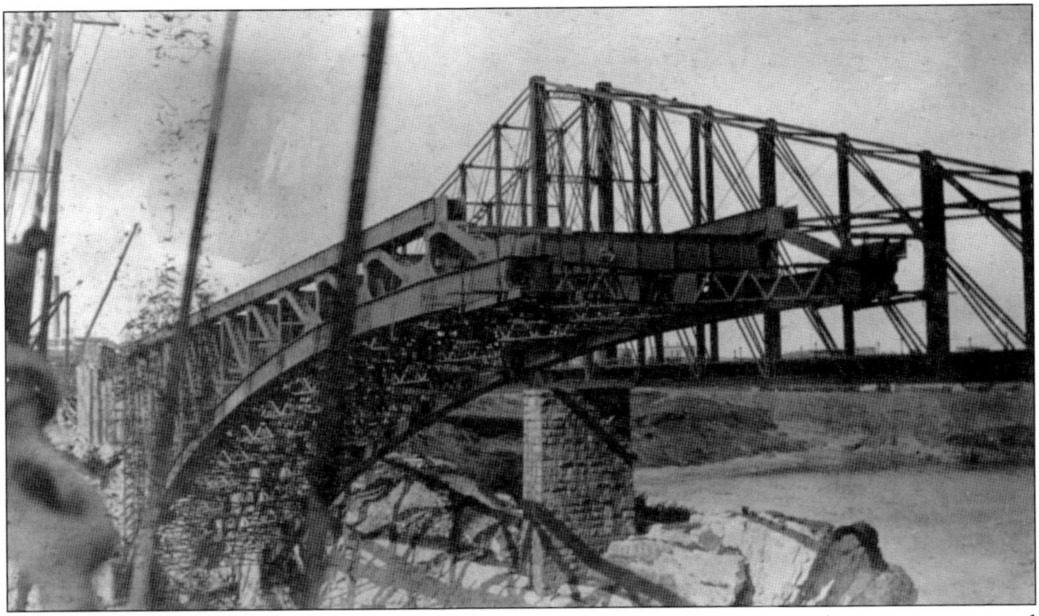

A Dominion bridge report of 1915 described the construction as follows: "The span was erected as a cantilever from both ends, and upon the junction being made at the center, the condition for a three-hinged arch was secured. By the insertion of the center portion of the top chord, accurately fitted and under no stress, all further dead load such as flooring and minor steel work as well as live load, was carried by the truss as a two-hinged arch."

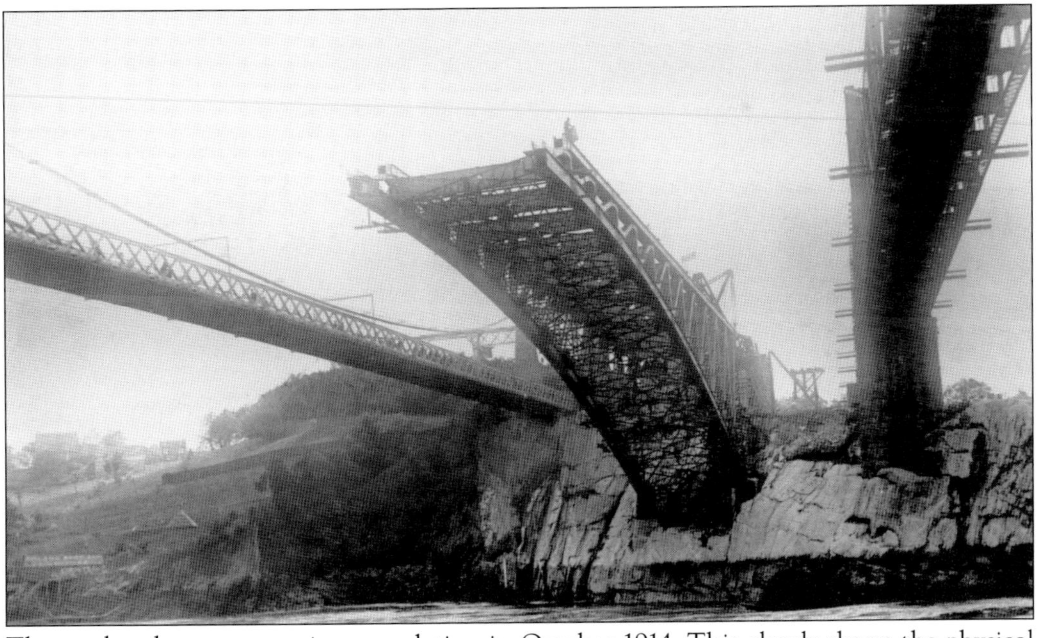

The steel arches were nearing completion in October 1914. This clearly shows the physical difference between the suspension and cantilever means of construction. The Provincial Lunatic Asylum grounds are in the background.

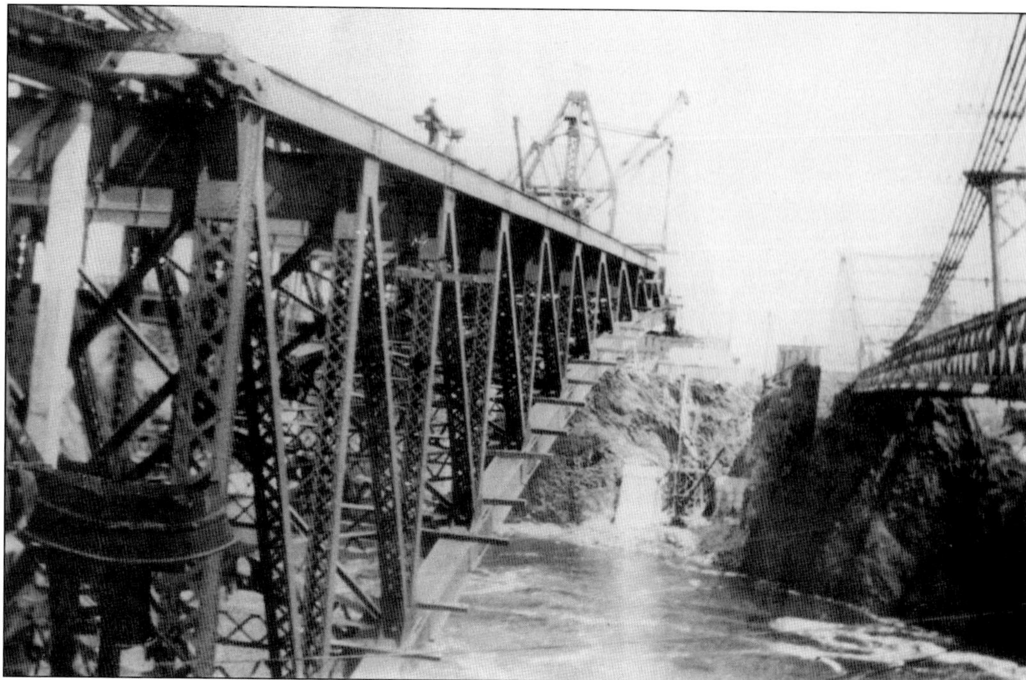

This shows the method of construction clearly. Spans from both sides of the falls were cantilevered over the water, where they met in the centre and were literally pinned together. The original bridge remained in constant use until the summer of 1915, when the new bridge was opened.

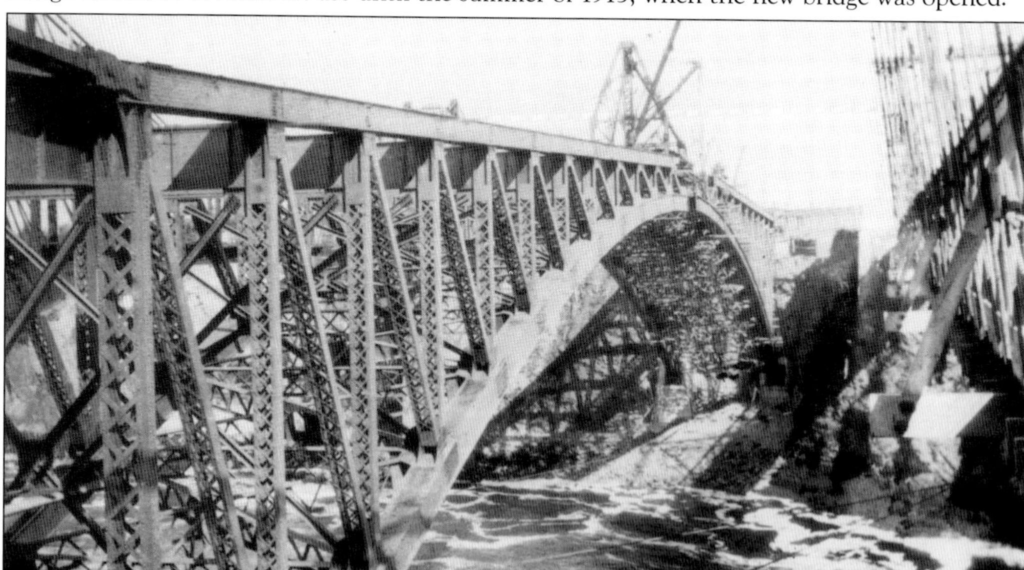

With the final section in place, it was not long before the bridge was opened to vehicle and pedestrian traffic. One of the first new bridge casualties was Pte. J.R.W. Scott. He was a returned soldier suffering from nervous shock but was on the road to recovery. Crossing the bridge on December 23, 1915, he was partway across when a gust of wind blew his hat from his head and over the bridge. He reached out to grab his hat but fell over. Private Scott is commemorated in the *Canadian Book of Remembrance* in the Peace Tower of Canadian Parliament.

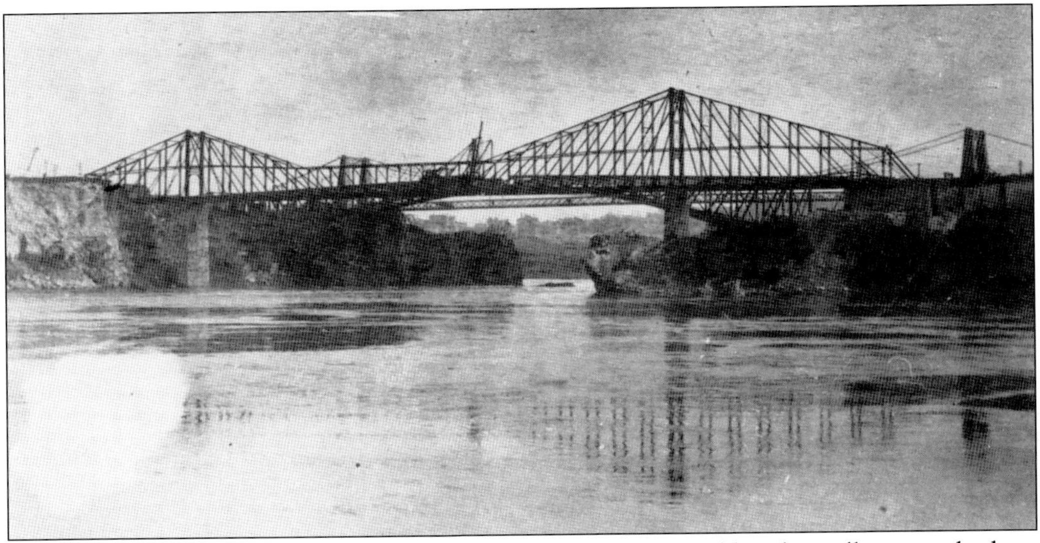

Crossing the Reversing Falls Bridge by foot on a windy day would make walkers wonder how difficult and dangerous it was to work on this structure. By October 8, 1914, the eastern section of the bridge had been extended halfway across the falls. The company was averaging three sections of bridge a week.

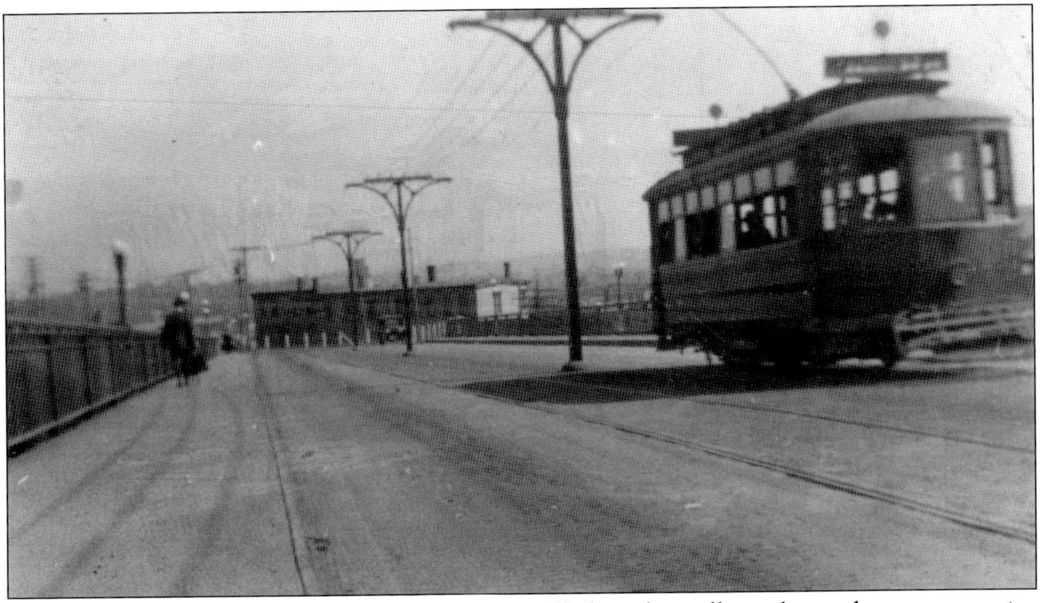

By the end of September 1915, the wires were installed on the trolley poles, and streetcar service was almost ready to begin service across the Reversing Falls for the first time. By the third week of October, the streetcar finally crossed the bridge. There were two sets of tracks across the bridge on a 36-foot-wide roadbed and two 7-foot-wide sidewalks. (Courtesy of Carol Harris.)

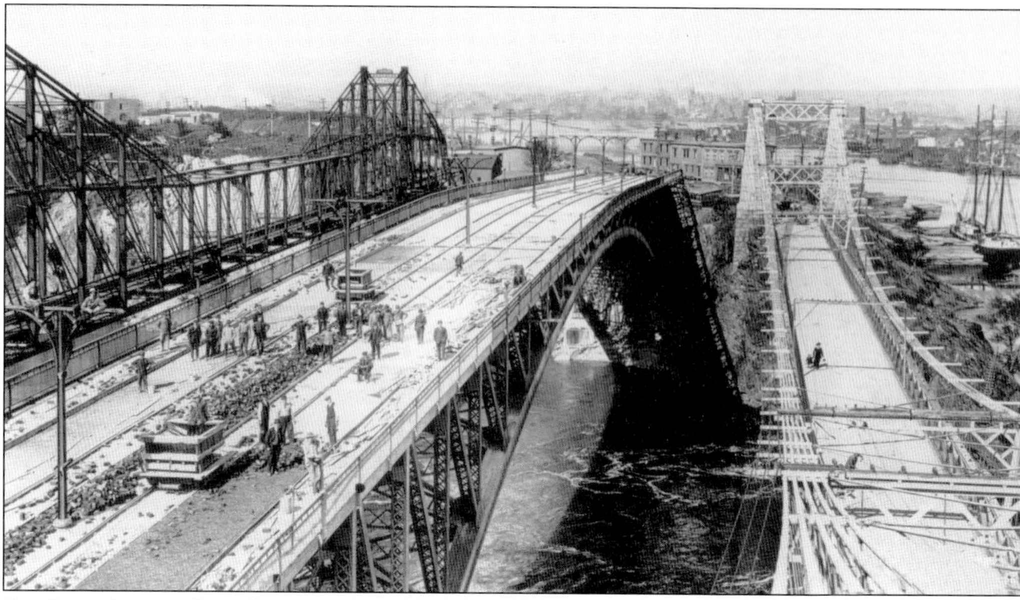

Final touches, such as the wires for the electric streetcars and granite paving blocks, were being installed between the streetcar track. This was the only time that three separate spans crossed the Reversing Falls at one time: suspension, cantilever, and the arched rail bridge. After 62 years of service, the Suspension Bridge closed in October 1915.

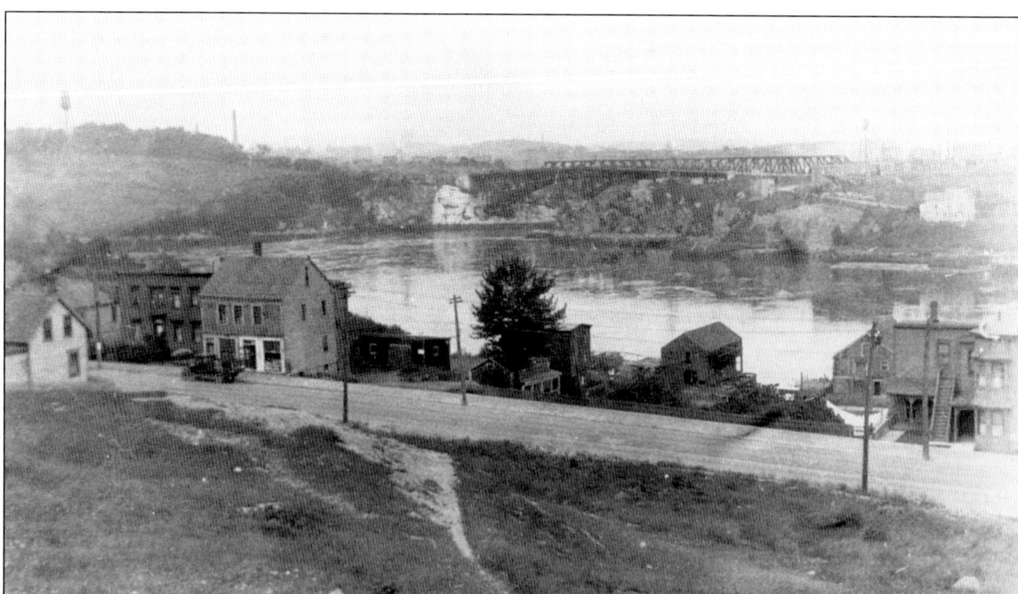

The falls are seen from Prince Street west. One of the more interesting stories of the falls involves a "moving picture" shot here in 1915. The actress, possibly Betty Bouton, refused to jump into the falls, and the scene had to rewritten where a Mr. Law was tethered to a stunt rope and lowered from the bridge into a whirlpool. Men on the bridge held him above water with ropes.

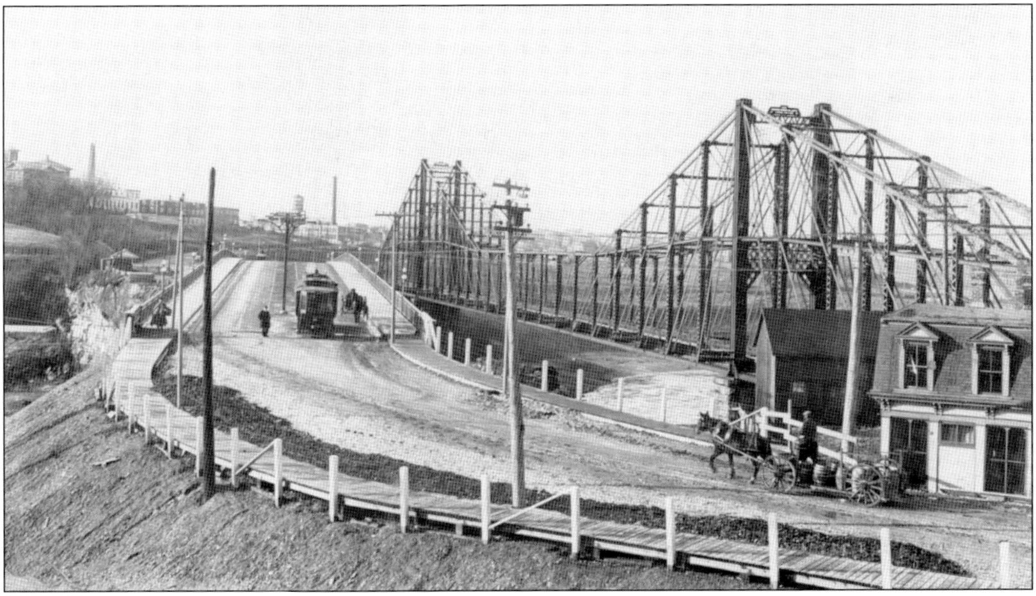

October 21 was the first day that streetcars could officially cross the new bridge. On the reverse of this photograph was the following caption: "The toll house on Douglas Avenue 'Where H.H. Gallant of 17 Main St., Fairville works, Engineer.'" The sidewalks are made of wood, and like the previous bridge, driving was still to the left.

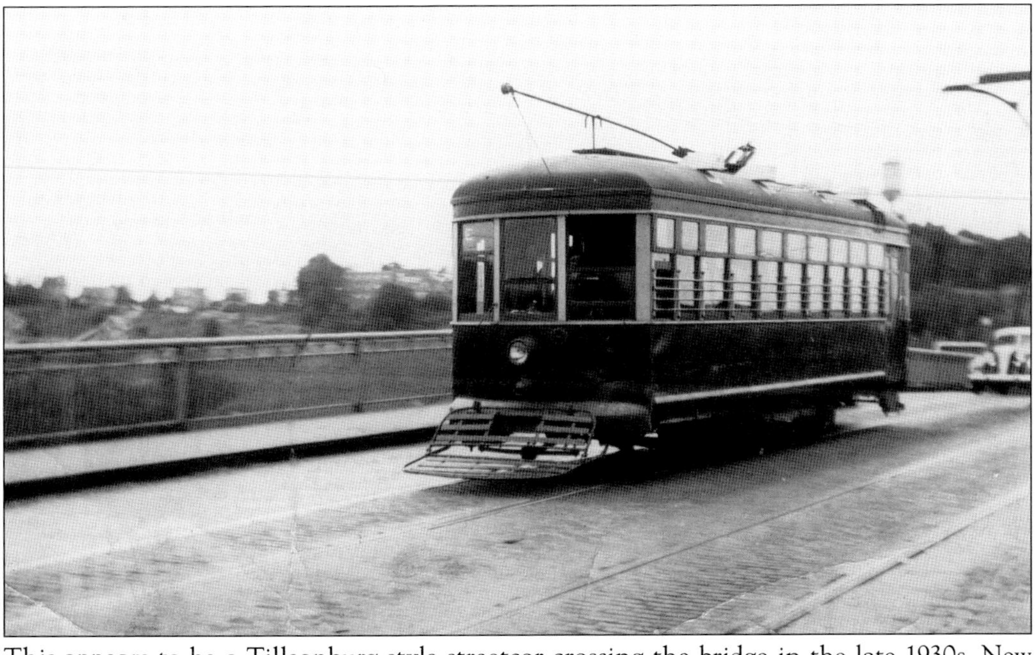

This appears to be a Tillsonburg-style streetcar crossing the bridge in the late 1930s. New Brunswick Power, which operated the streetcar system at the time, purchased 20 of these cars from the Tillsonburg Electric Car Co. in 1914, and they remained in operation until 1948. Note the granite rectangular paving blocks on the ground. These are not cobblestone, as many believe. Cobblestones are naturally occurring round stones. (Courtesy of Lois Ellis.)

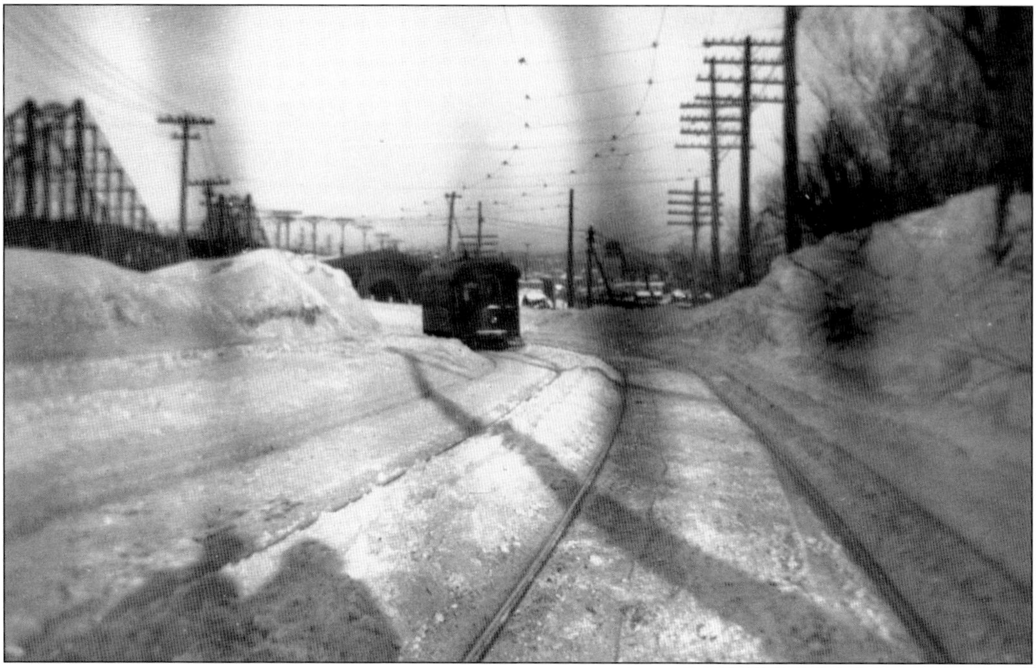

The wicked S curve leading onto the new bridge has posed a problem for motorists and streetcar drivers. The original curve was deemed dangerous for streetcar service. The options were to build a new retaining wall or straighten out the current approach before the cars went into service, which was eventually done.

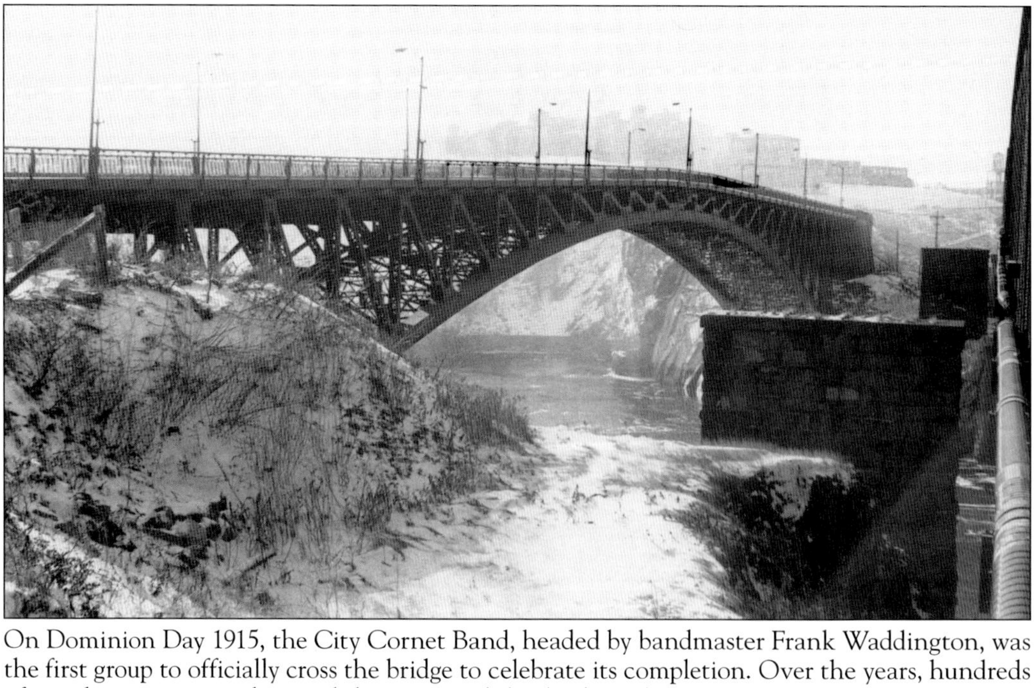

On Dominion Day 1915, the City Cornet Band, headed by bandmaster Frank Waddington, was the first group to officially cross the bridge to celebrate its completion. Over the years, hundreds of parades, runners, and animals have crossed this bridge. The stone foundations of the original train bridge are shown at the right. (Courtesy of David Goss.)

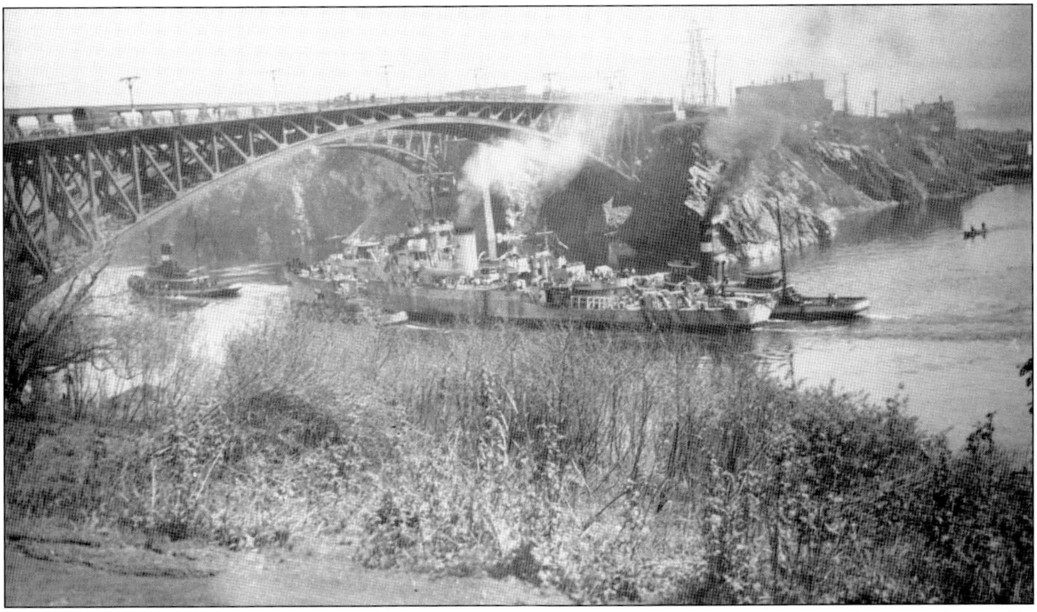

Navigation under the bridge is a dicey affair, regardless of the type of ship. There are basically two windows of safe sailing time, which are both about 20 minutes long. After undergoing engine repairs at the Saint John Drydock in 1944, HMCS *La Hulloise* went upstream to the Long Reach for speed trials. This ship was paid off in December 1945.

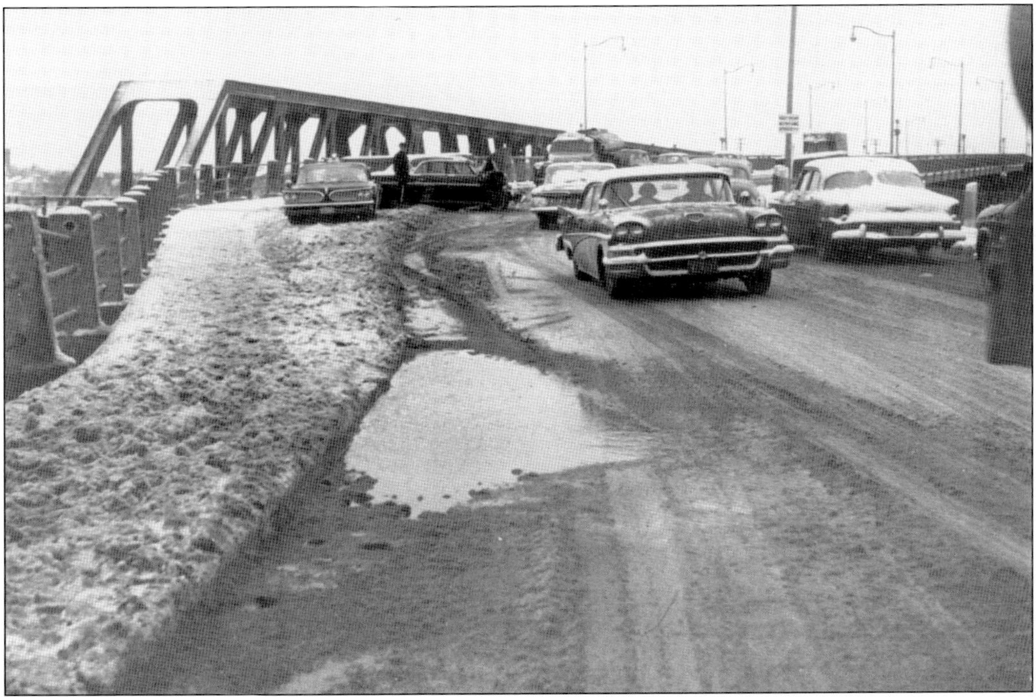

The Reversing Falls was the only road link across the harbour for 50 years. With upwards of 32,000 vehicles a day, accidents were bound to happen. In January 1960, it was probably a combination of speed and weather that caused this car to crash into a city transit bus. Lancaster police officer Harold Mayes investigated.

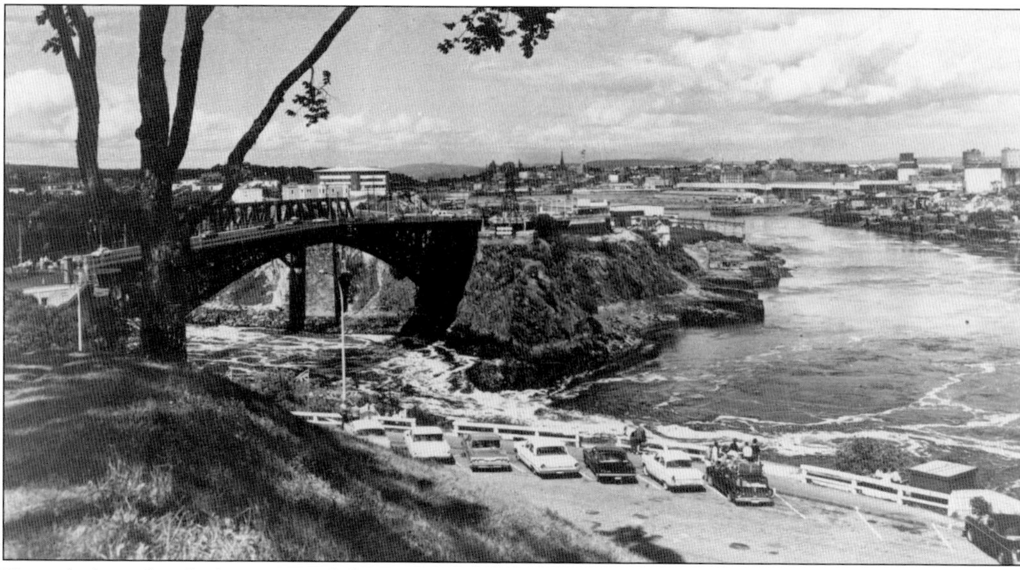

Deep below the dark waters of the Reversing Falls lies untold horrors, or at least according to some of the stories. There is the local lore of a diver with jet black hair who went into the falls and surfaced pale as a ghost, unable to speak, and with hair as white as snow. There is also the story of the Victorian woman who threw herself from the bridge only to be saved by her hoop skirt acting as a parachute.

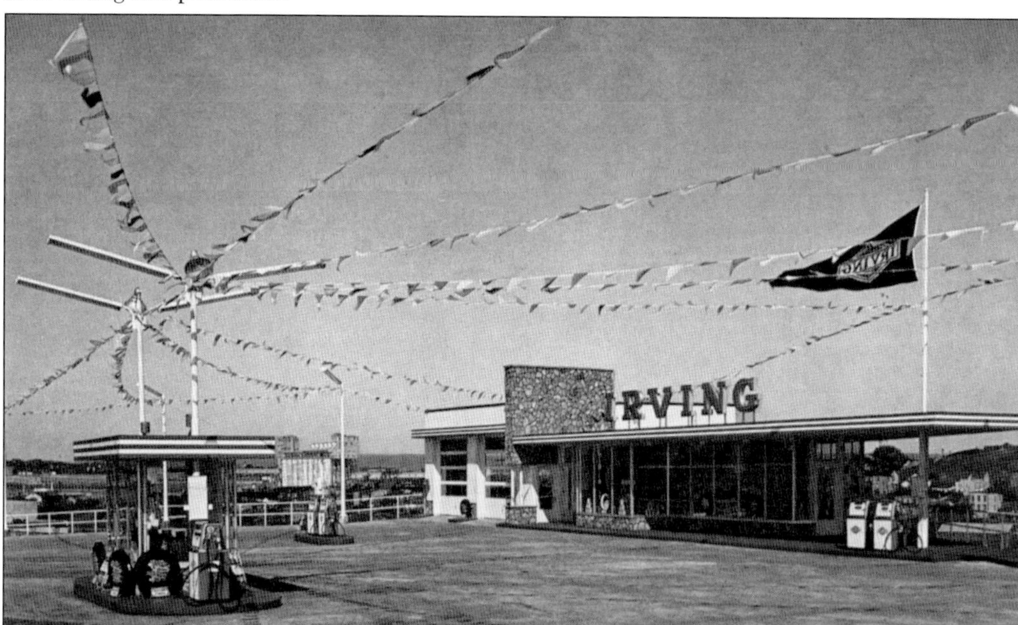

By 1960, this gas station had serviced thousands of cars and trucks and would do many tens of thousands more until January 4, 1974. That evening, an accident at this station caused one of the largest explosions seen in the city. Five people were killed. In 2012, a memorial park was installed on site with a plaque listing these names. The bridge was closed for several days while engineers determined if it had suffered any damage. They declared the bridge was safe, but within three years, the bridge was almost entirely rebuilt.

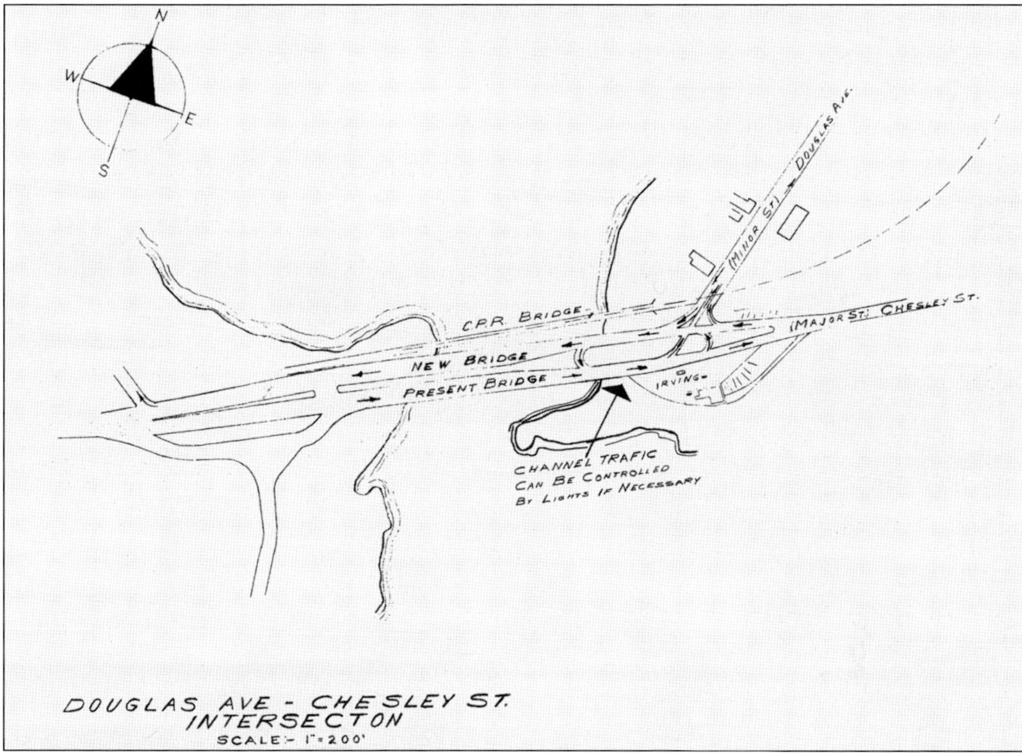

In the 1950s, there was a proposal to build a new bridge at the falls, between the existing road bridge and the rail bridge. Each bridge would carry two-lane traffic in one direction, and Douglas Avenue would be relegated to a minor role. This plan was shelved and replaced with the Saint John Harbour Bridge proposal.

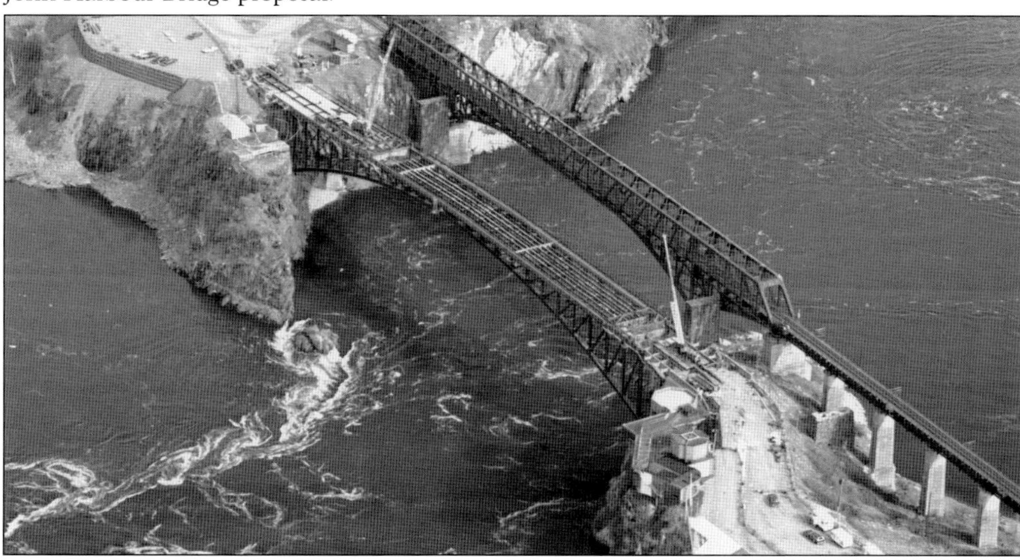

Almost a year before this work began, Saint John Common Council asked the province to ensure that the Saint John Harbour Bridge tolls would be removed. This was the first major repair to the bridge since it opened in 1915, and council wanted to reduce the headaches for motorists. (Courtesy of Bob Boudreau.)

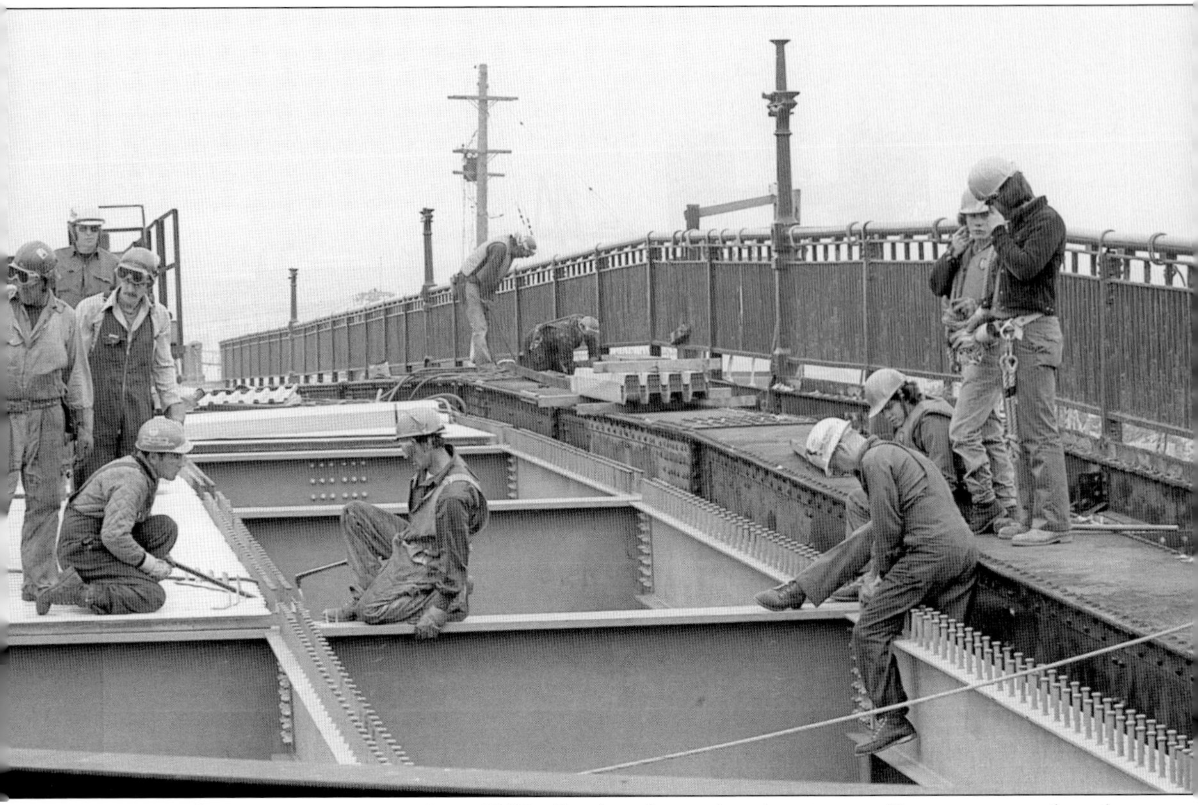

During these major repairs in June 1977, all vehicular and pedestrian traffic was rerouted to the Saint John Harbour Bridge. All of the steel framework was replaced. Once these were in place, new concrete was poured and then covered in asphalt. Notice the original light standard minus the round globe, located on the railing. Also note that most of the workers are not wearing any safety harnesses. (Courtesy of Bob Boudreau.)

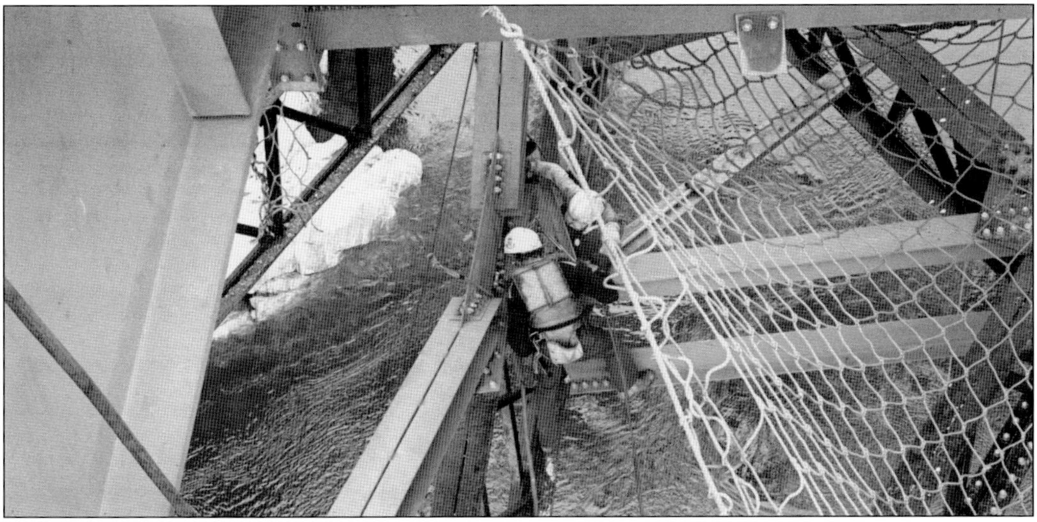

It has been 35 years since the bridge had this level of repair work. The Provincial Department of Transportation seems to have been quite diligent over the years in ensuring regular maintenance has been carried out. However, whenever repairs are done, the driving public are inconvenienced with long line ups, delayed completion dates, and until recently, the tolls at the Saint John Harbour Bridge. (Courtesy of Bob Boudreau.)

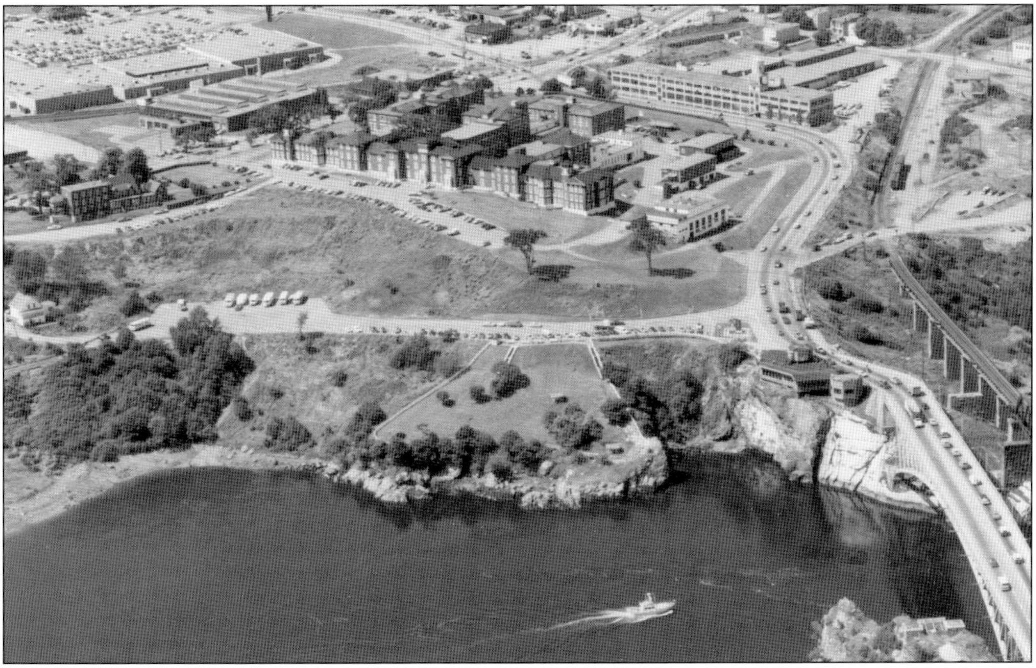

With the Centracare hospital overlooking the falls, one can clearly see the area of the 1949 landslide in front of the hospital. An attempt by the city to build a shortcut road to the left of the falls caused a massive landslide. The S curve from the bridge to Bridge Street in front of the Simms brush factory is clear. Also shown are the former Ford plant on Lancaster Avenue, the Lancaster Mall just behind it, the Golden Mile, and then at the right Main Street West and Moosehead Breweries. In 1967, this part of the city, then known as Lancaster, amalgamated with Saint John and became known as West Saint John.

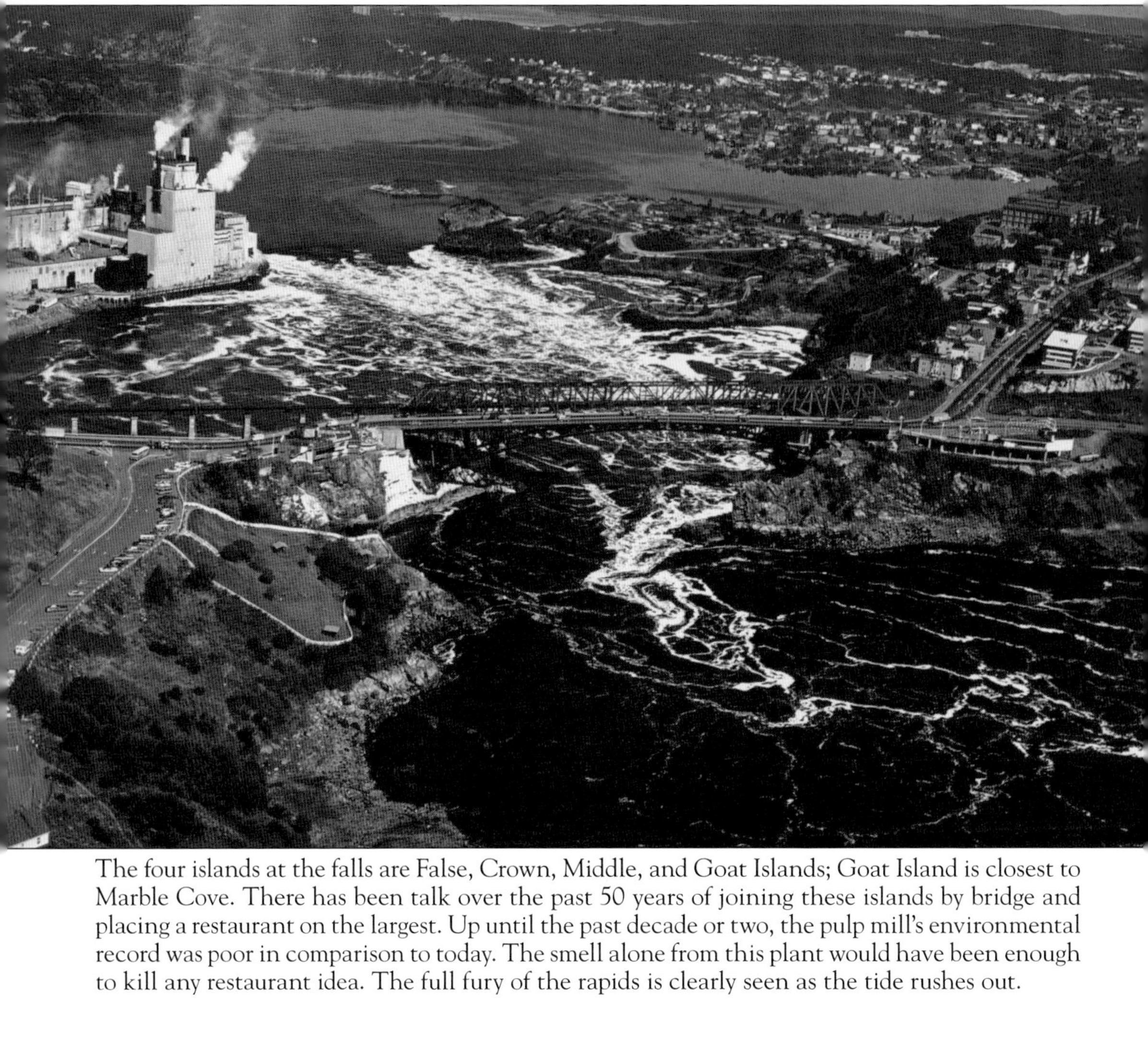

The four islands at the falls are False, Crown, Middle, and Goat Islands; Goat Island is closest to Marble Cove. There has been talk over the past 50 years of joining these islands by bridge and placing a restaurant on the largest. Up until the past decade or two, the pulp mill's environmental record was poor in comparison to today. The smell alone from this plant would have been enough to kill any restaurant idea. The full fury of the rapids is clearly seen as the tide rushes out.

Seven

The Rail Bridges

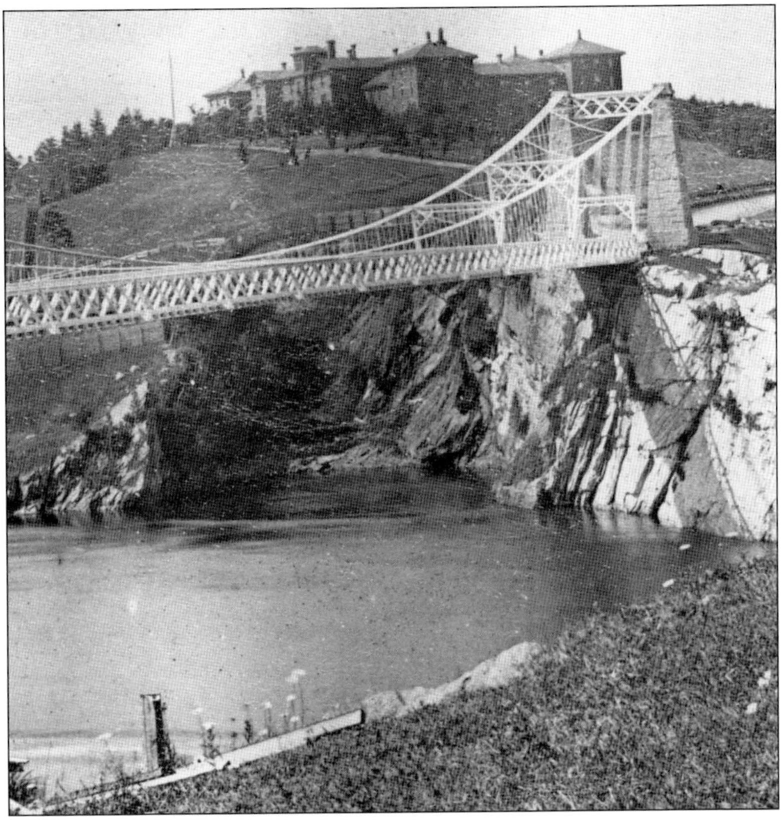

There were two rail lines serving the city, but they had no means to connect. The Reversing Falls separated them. To solve this issue, the Saint John Bridge and Railway Extension Company was formed. The best location was next to the Suspension Bridge.

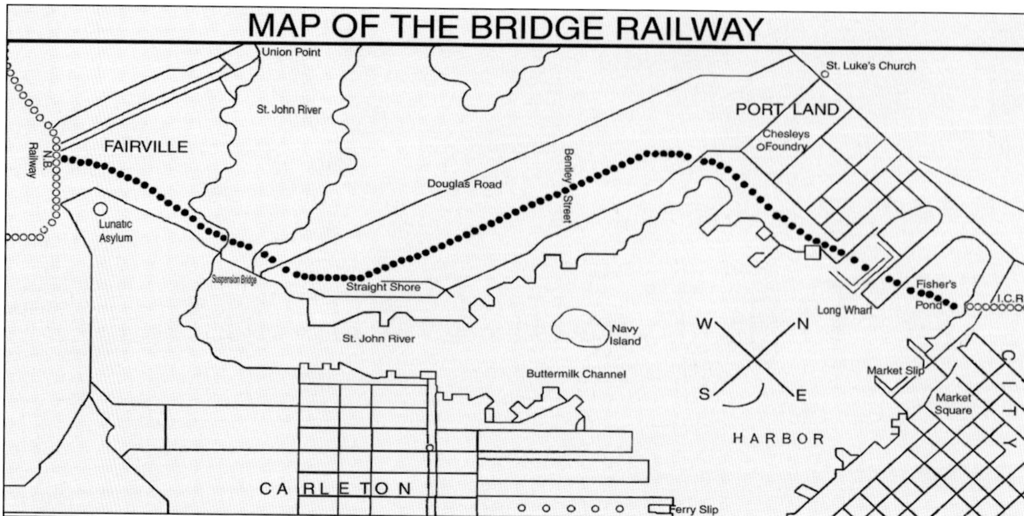

The Dominion Bridge Company won the right to construct the rail bridge, and Sir Samuel Leonard Tilly backed the project with public funds. This bridge would connect the New Brunswick Railway down the Straight Shore, over Fisher's Pond at Long Wharf, to the Inter Colonial Railway line on Paradise Row.

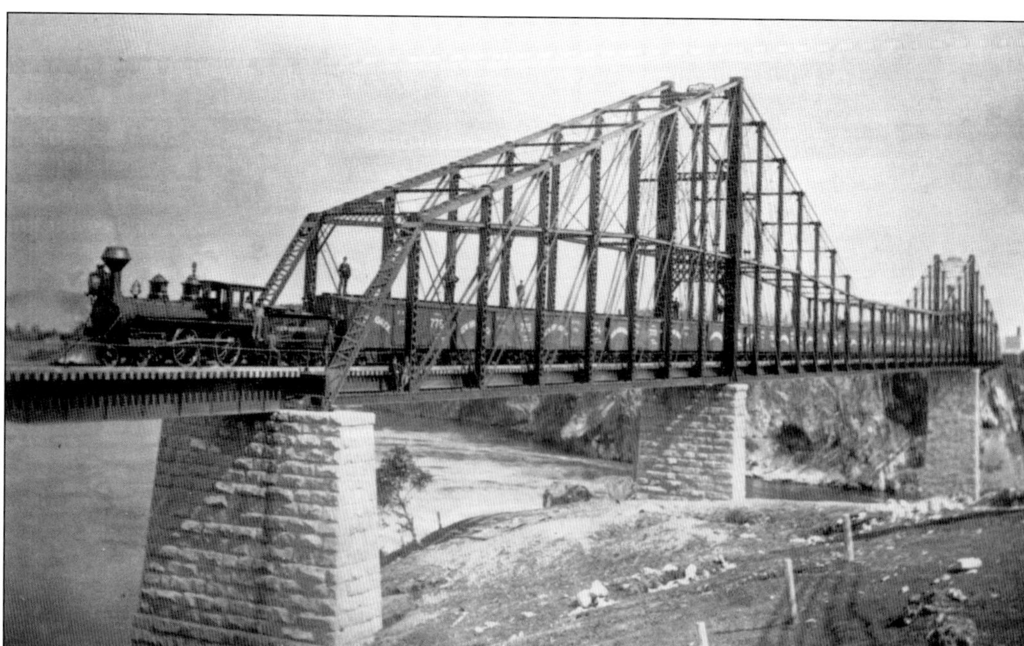

The first cars of the New Brunswick Railway passed across the new bridge on July 20, 1885. The steel was placed between April and July 1885, and the last spike was put in place on July 9, 1885.

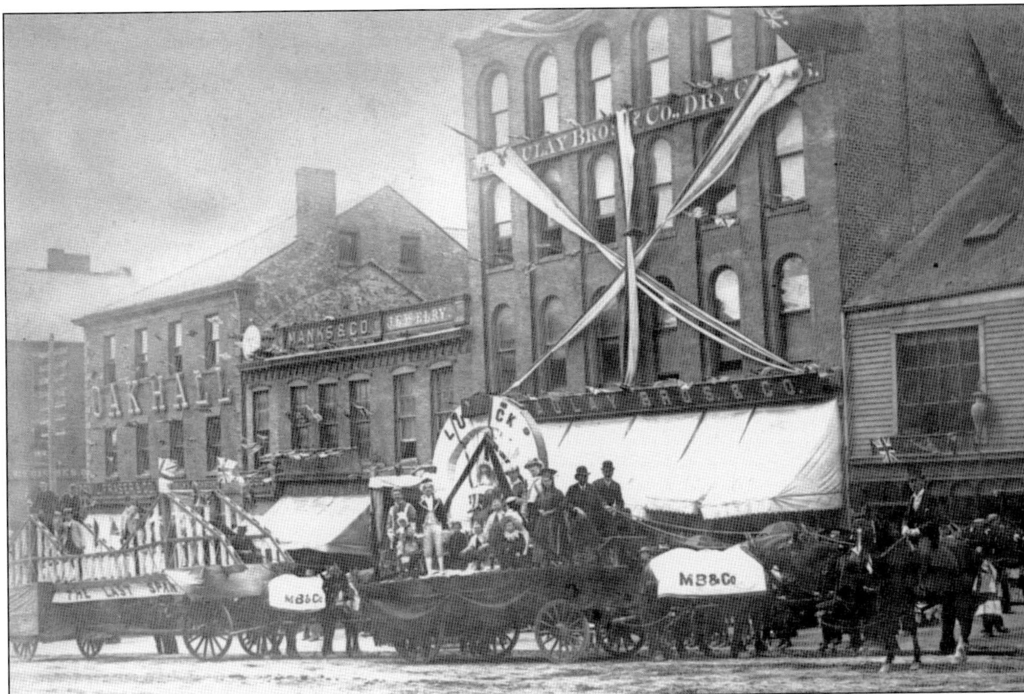

The bridge opened on September 30, 1885. The ceremony started at 10:30 a.m., and shortly after, the train stopped on the bridge to allow passengers to get off and look around. Citizens from around the city waved handkerchiefs in excitement, and inmates from the Provincial Lunatic Asylum watched from their windows and hospital grounds. This McCaulay Brothers parade float on King Street includes a "Last Spike" float.

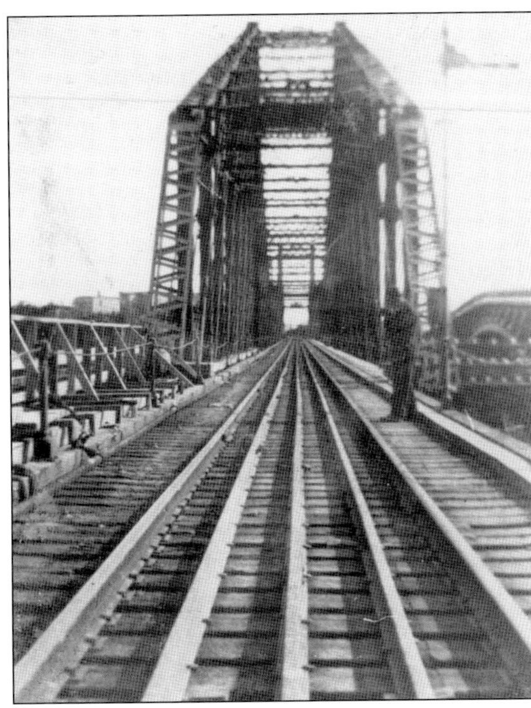

Like a brand new baby, the *Saint John Globe* announced the bridge's weight and size. The bridge spanned 1,431 feet, with 477 feet between the piers. This bridge shortened the route from Carleton to Portland by a significant margin.

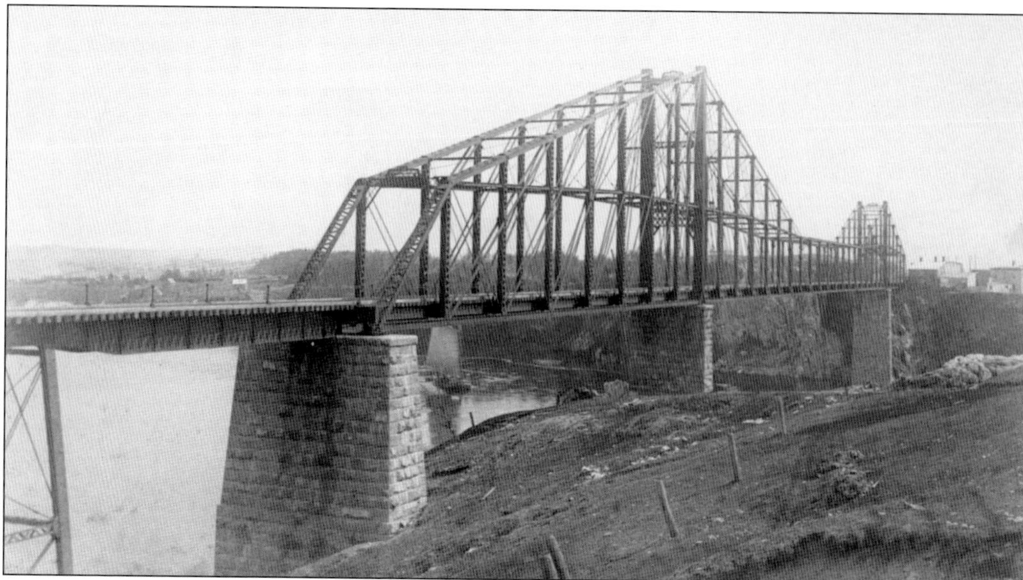

The piers of this giant structure are still visible today. They are worse for wear due to the constant harbour weather and lack of maintenance. What once held up thousands of pounds of steel is now the base for moss, grass, and the odd bird that calls this post its home.

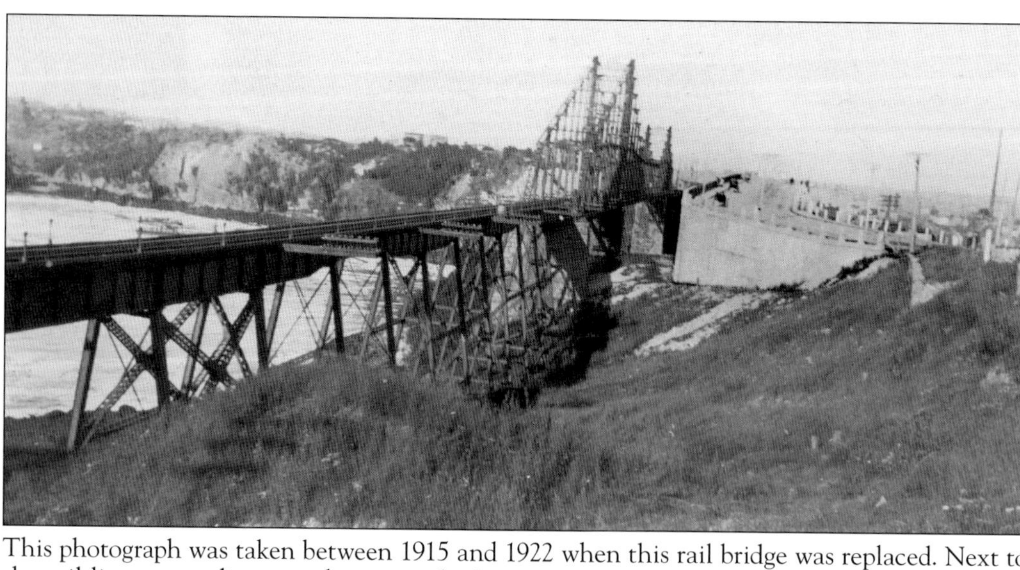

This photograph was taken between 1915 and 1922 when this rail bridge was replaced. Next to the rail line, power lines can be seen, which were carried alongside the bridge. In later years, water pipes were added to the bridge's infrastructure. The retaining wall built for the S-curve access road to the new cantilever bridge is clearly at the right.

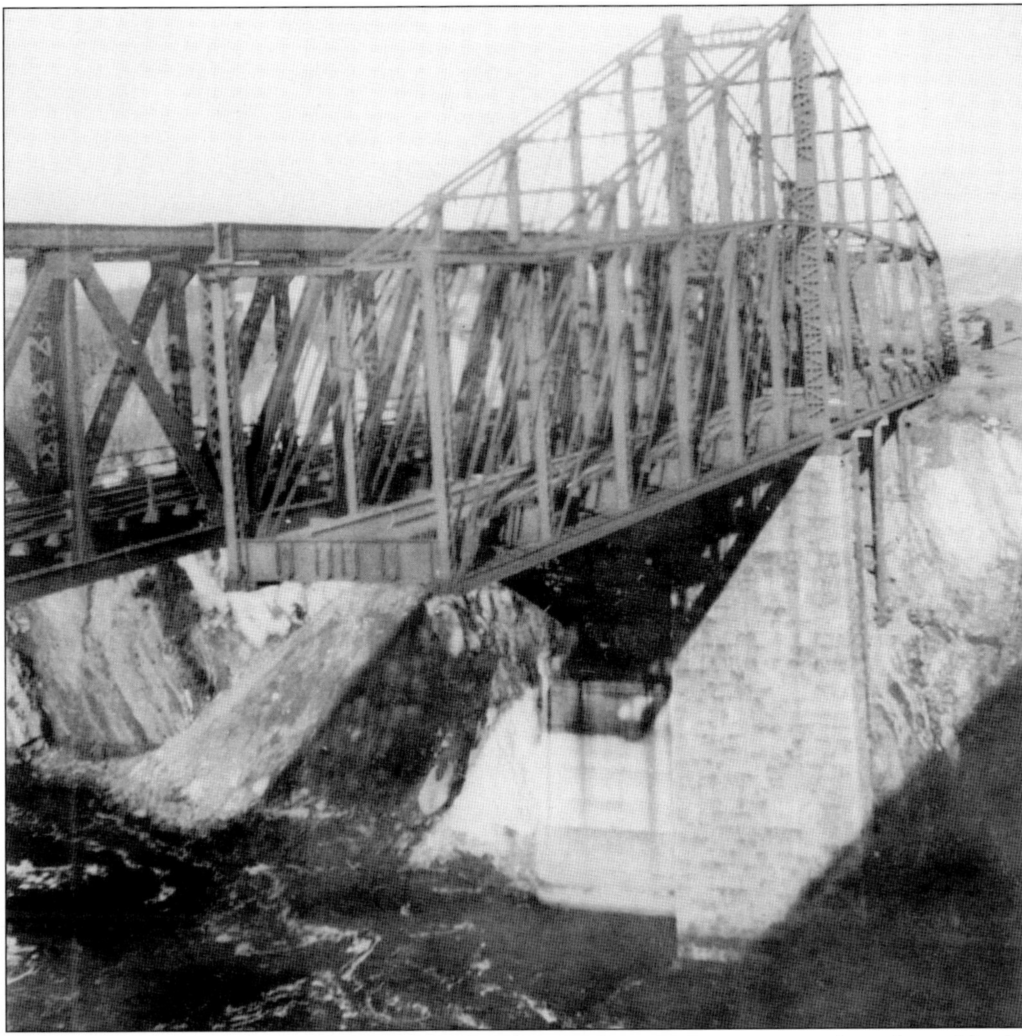

In 1920, the Canadian Pacific Railway made it known that it was going to replace the rail bridge at the falls. Another cantilever bridge would be built; however, this time rivets, instead of pins, would be used, and it would look more symmetrical. The bridge opened on November 24, 1921.

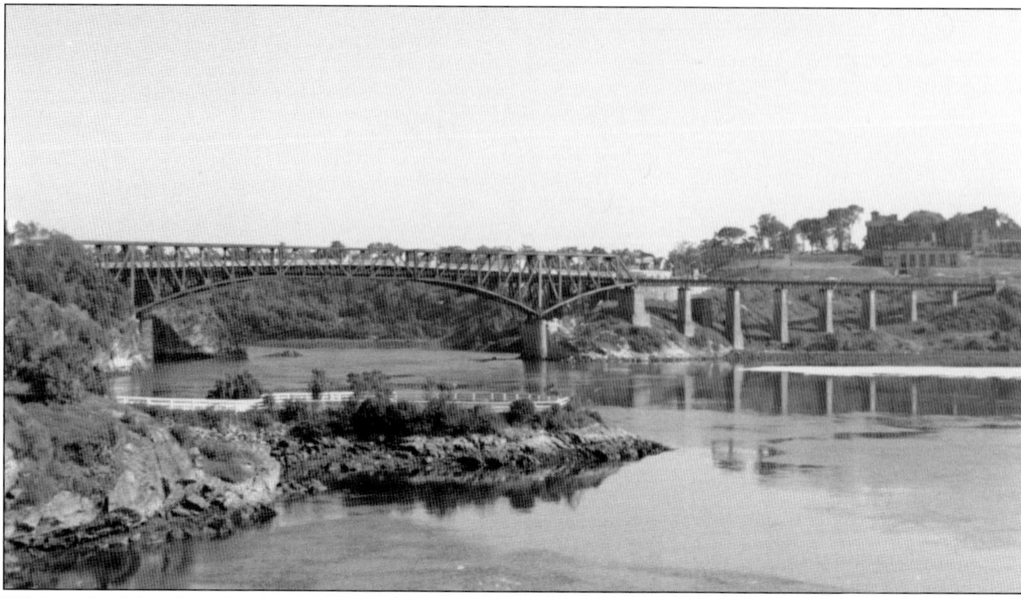

With False Island in the foreground, the new 1921 rail bridge is quite a bit lower than the cantilever bridge. This has impacted larger sailing vessels wanting to go upstream to the Saint John and Kennebecasis Rivers.

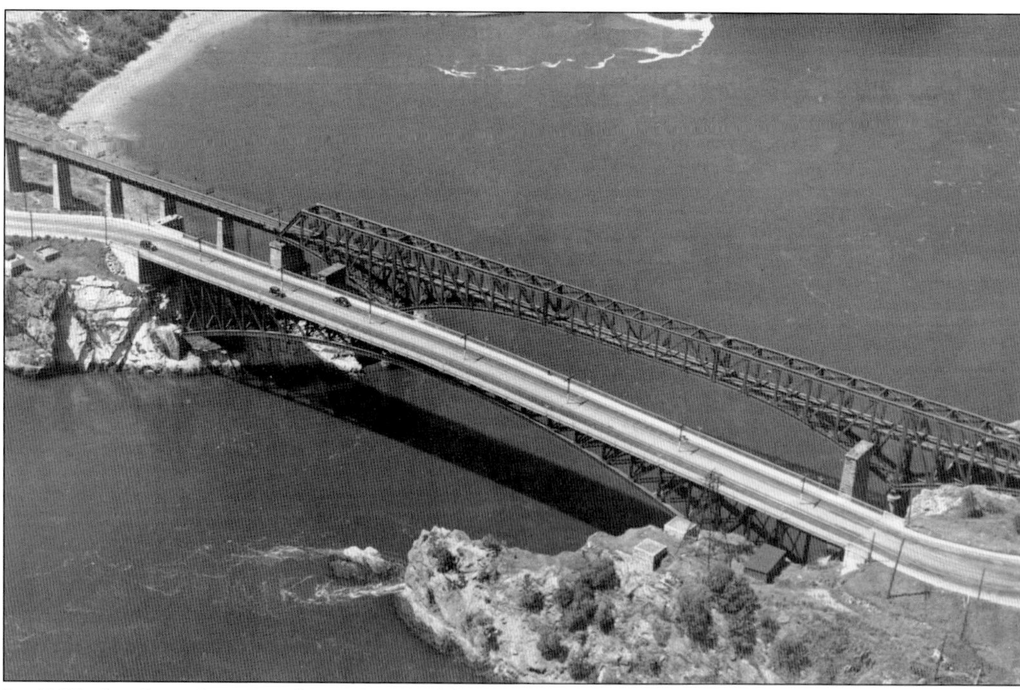

In 1995, the Canadian Pacific Railway sold its Canadian Atlantic Railway subsidiary to the New Brunswick Southern Railway, owned by J.D. Irving, Limited. The City of Saint John uses the bridge to carry water supply pipes. In 1976, New Brunswick Power constructed the Lorneville pipeline from Irving Oil's Canaport, and this pipeline crosses the river using this bridge.

Eight

Tourism at the Reversing Falls Rapids

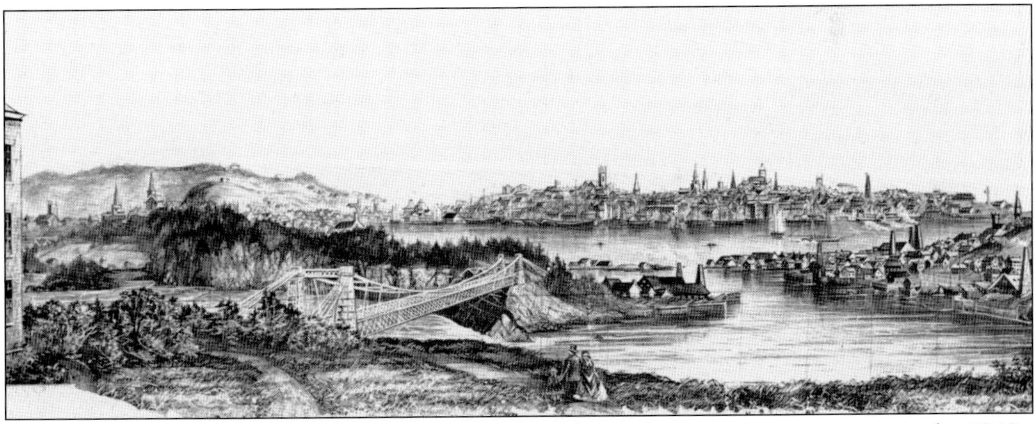

The Reversing Falls and its rapids have been part of the city's tourism attraction since the 1840s. In 1865, John March, an amateur photographer, took a photograph from the balcony of the Provincial Lunatic Asylum. It showed part of the walkway around the falls, called the Rocky Road to Dublin. This illustration was made from the March photograph. (Courtesy of Saint John Regional Library.)

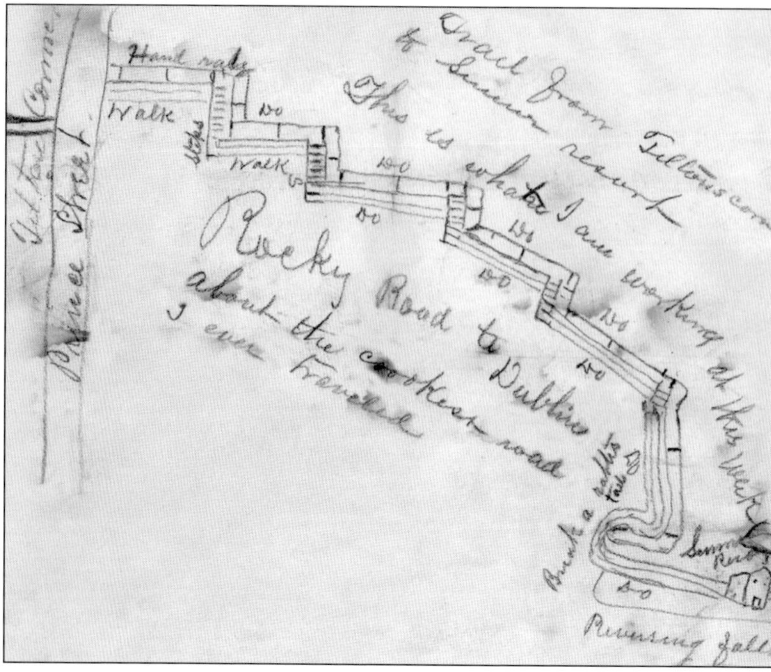

The Rocky Road to Dublin was "about the crookest road . . . ever traveled" and was a tourist path from Prince Street at Tiltons Corner to the summer resort at the Reversing Falls. The contractor's name is not known, but this was what he was "working at this week." (Courtesy of David Goss.)

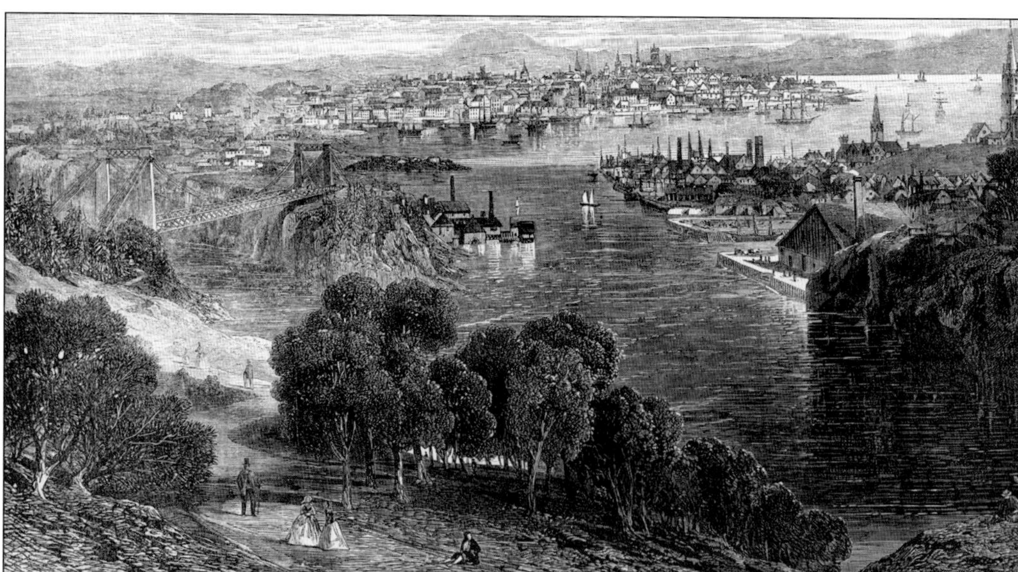

The *Illustrated London News* printed this image of the Rocky Road to Dublin at the Reversing Falls in 1866. It shows the quaint country scene, which Saint John was promoting at the time. It certainly does not show the Provincial Lunatic Asylum. Although the specific buildings and industries have changed, visitors to this area today get the same basic view. (Courtesy of David Goss.)

There is a distinction between the location of the bridge and the name of the tourist attraction. The bridge is at the Reversing Falls. The tourist attraction is the Reversing Falls Rapids. These ladies and child are visiting the rapids. For most of the 19th and part of the 20th centuries, the tourist amenities here were a small shelter and picnic table.

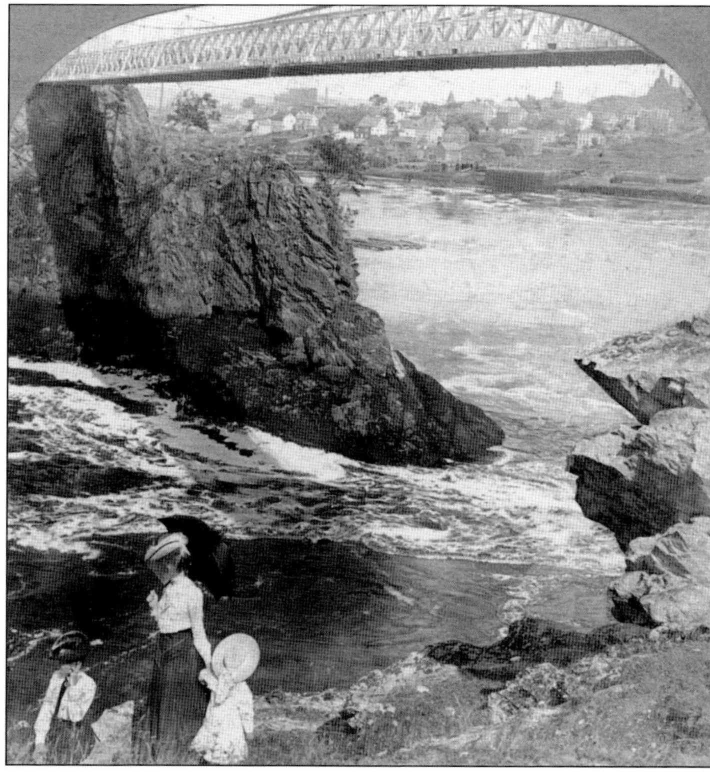

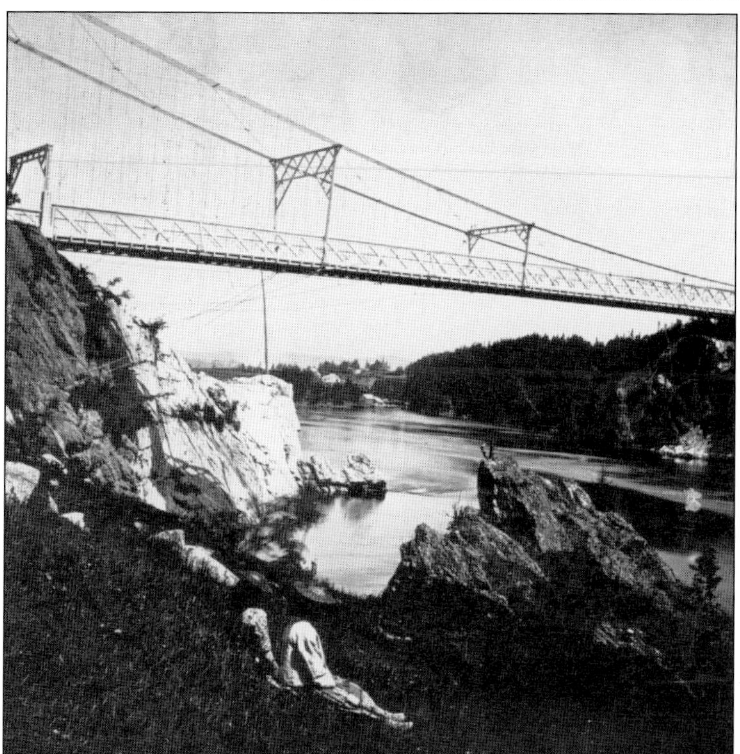

This part of the falls overlooks Deadmans Cove and was certainly not high on most tourists' lists of places to see. The attractions here were the rapids and the currents.

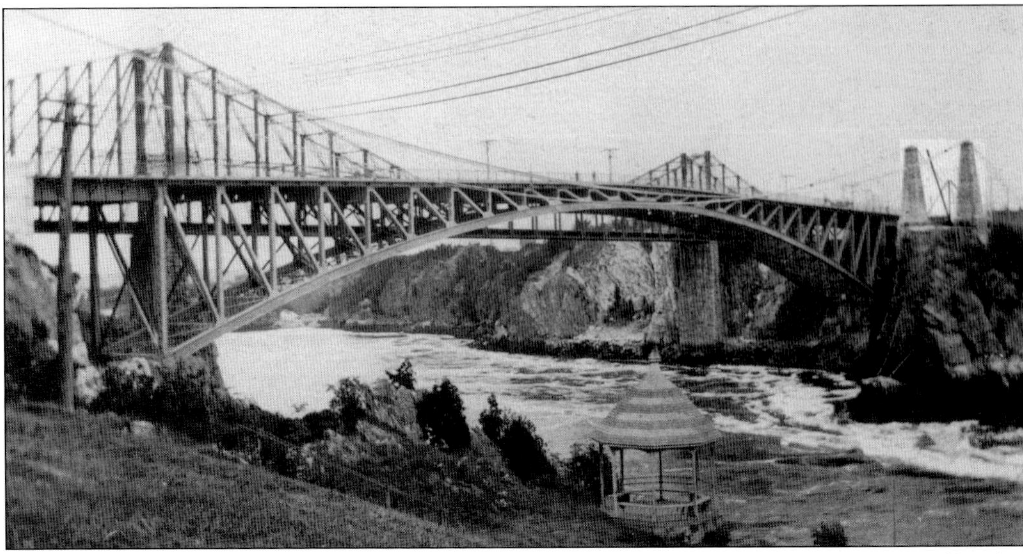

The tourist rest house at the Reversing Falls Rapids was about the only amenity offered to visitors for the first half of the 20th century. Postcards of this scene are plentiful, but the local tourist association seemed to have been only concerned with having visitors view the falls going backwards.

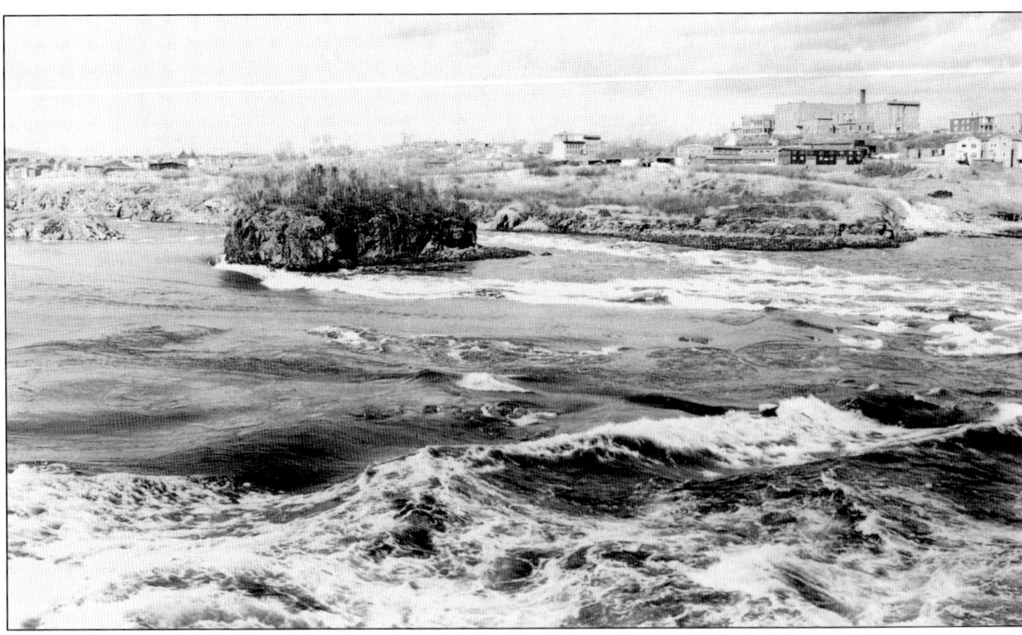

With Crow Island at the centre and the rapids in full fury, it is easy to see why first-time visitors would find this view attractive. In the 1920s and 1930s, the Reversing Falls Rapids were popular with travelogues and tourist writers. In the background are the Murray & Gregory Mill and Vocational School (now Harbour View) on the hill.

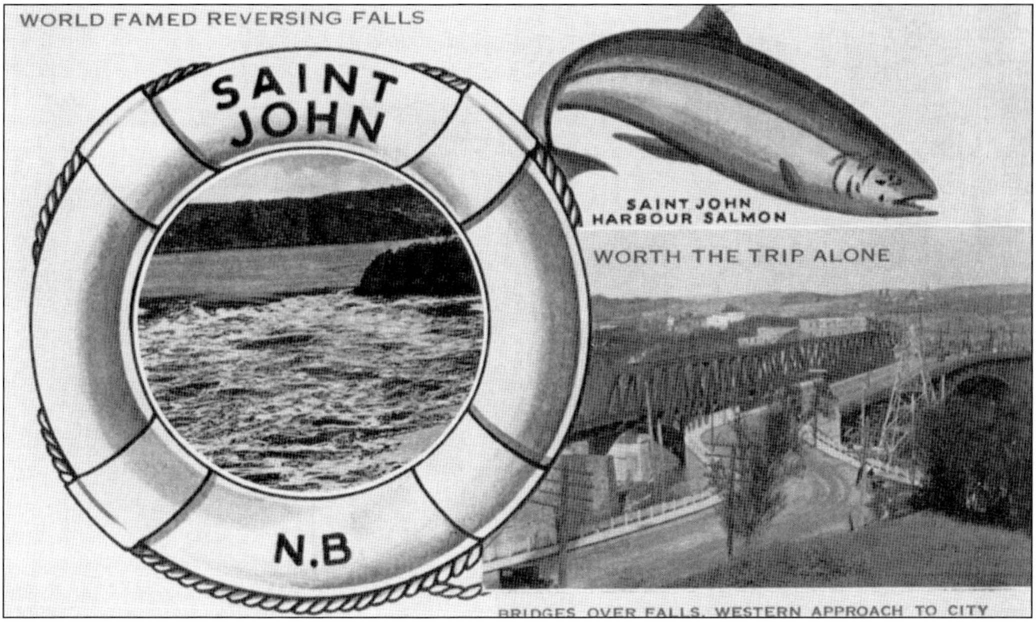

While the postcards offered to visitors presented the falls as world famous and the harbour salmon as plentiful, visitors were often disappointed that the falls did not look anything like Niagara Falls going backward and that they could not catch salmon at the falls.

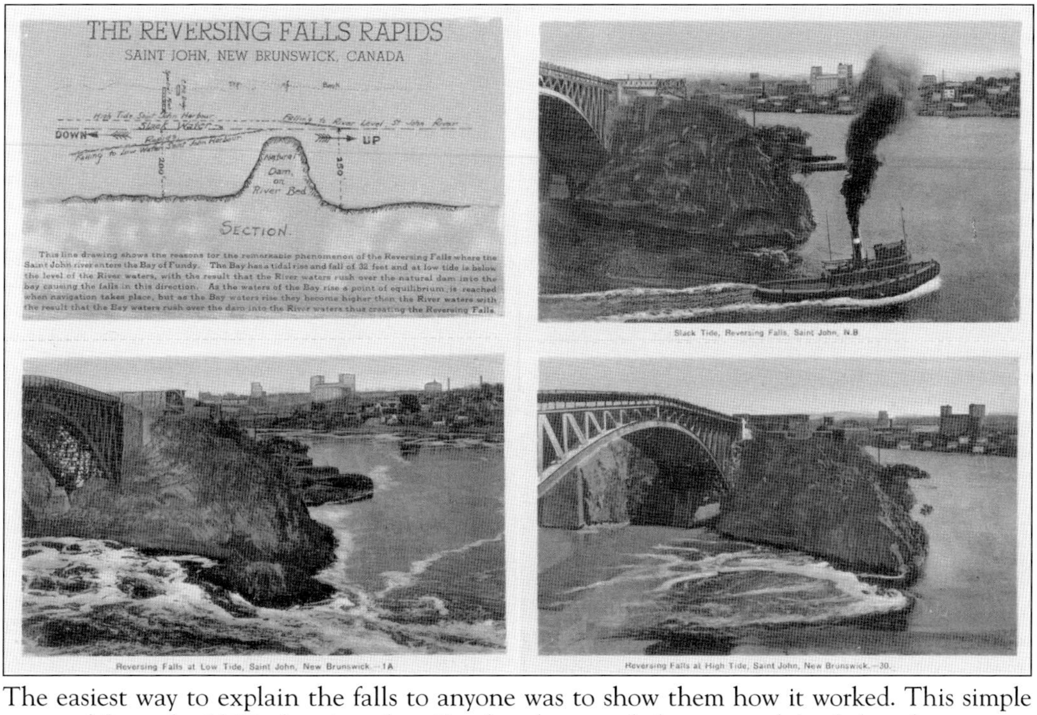

The easiest way to explain the falls to anyone was to show them how it worked. This simple postcard from the 1940s does just that. For decades, people have complained that they cannot see the falls reverse to their convenience. The entire tidal cycle is 12 hours.

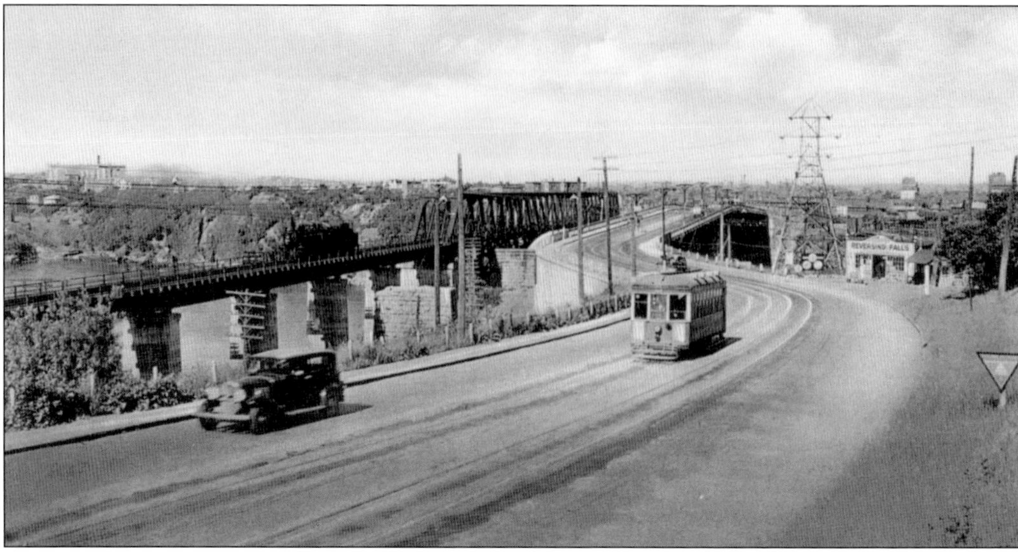

In the 1930s, the bridge was lit up at night by a series of large spotlights. These were eventually removed to the Millidgeville Airport for nighttime landing. The first attraction at the falls turned out to be the Trading Post, where one could buy postcards and souvenir china and look at the tide clock next to the post.

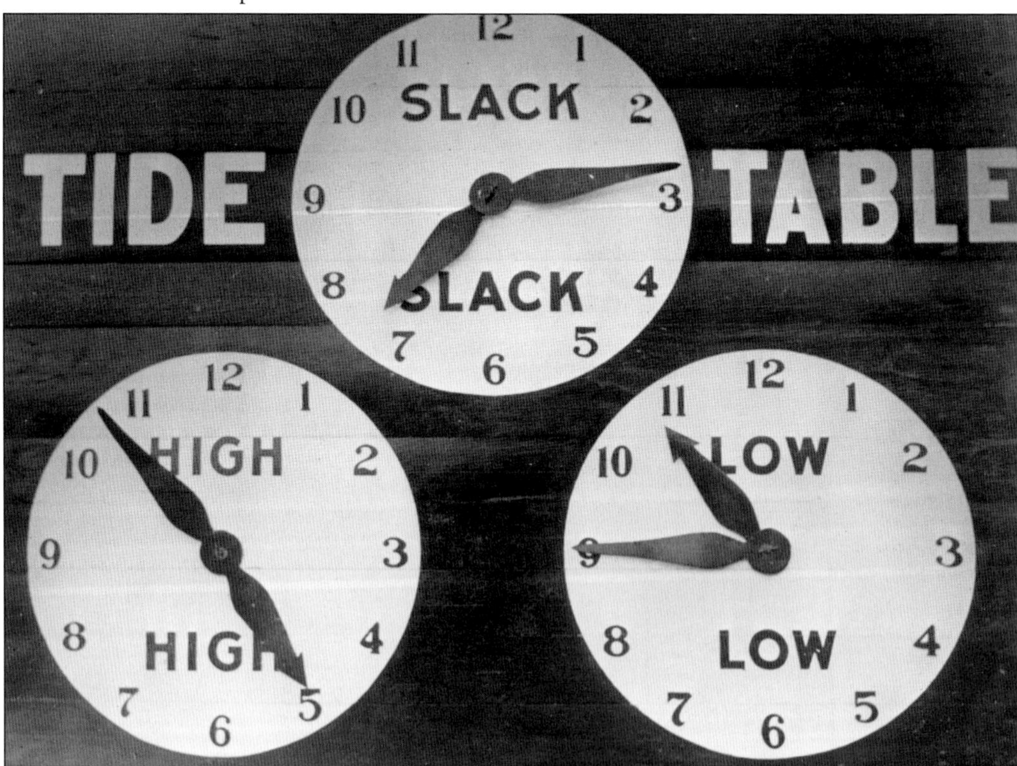

This tide table clock was placed outside of the Trading Post so that visitors had an idea when the tides would change. For many years, the tourism literature included a fully printed tide schedule for the entire year. Today, these tide clocks have been replaced by chalk on a blackboard.

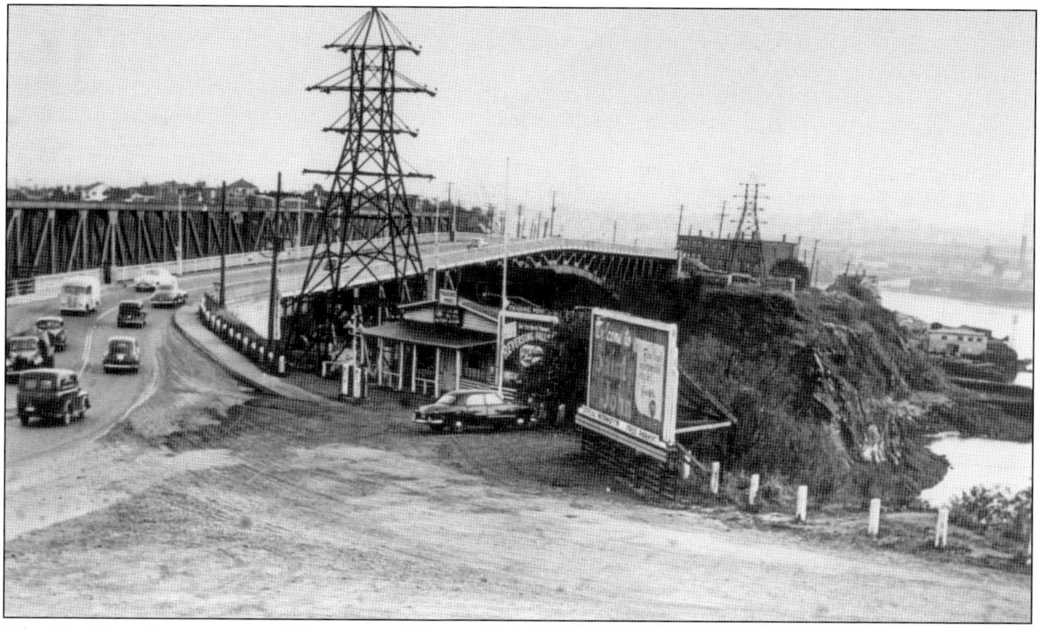

The Trading Post remained here until the early 1950s. There had been a plan in 1947 to relocate the tourist bureau to one of the islands in the falls. Over the years, the tourism literature alternated between calling the attraction the Reversing Falls or the Reversing Falls Rapids. This confusion came to a head in the 1970s with comical results. (Courtesy of David Goss.)

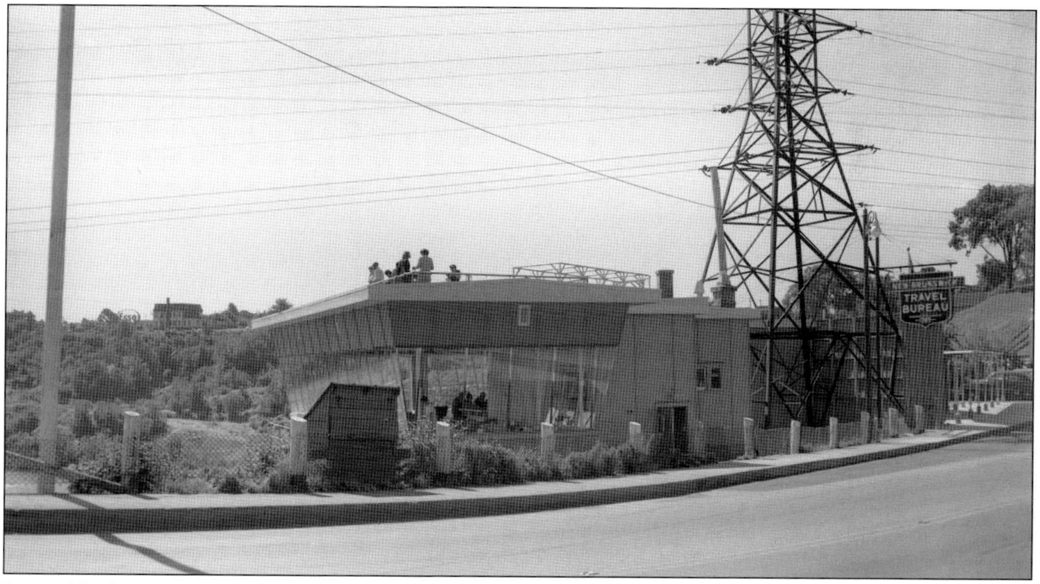

In 1955, the new tourist bureau opened with all the modern amenities, including the power tower. At this time, the New Brunswick Travel Bureau operated the information booth. At times in the 1950s and 1960s, there were tens of thousands of visitors registering at the bureau. Of course, this was also at the same time that the Reversing Falls Bridge was the only means of crossing the river.

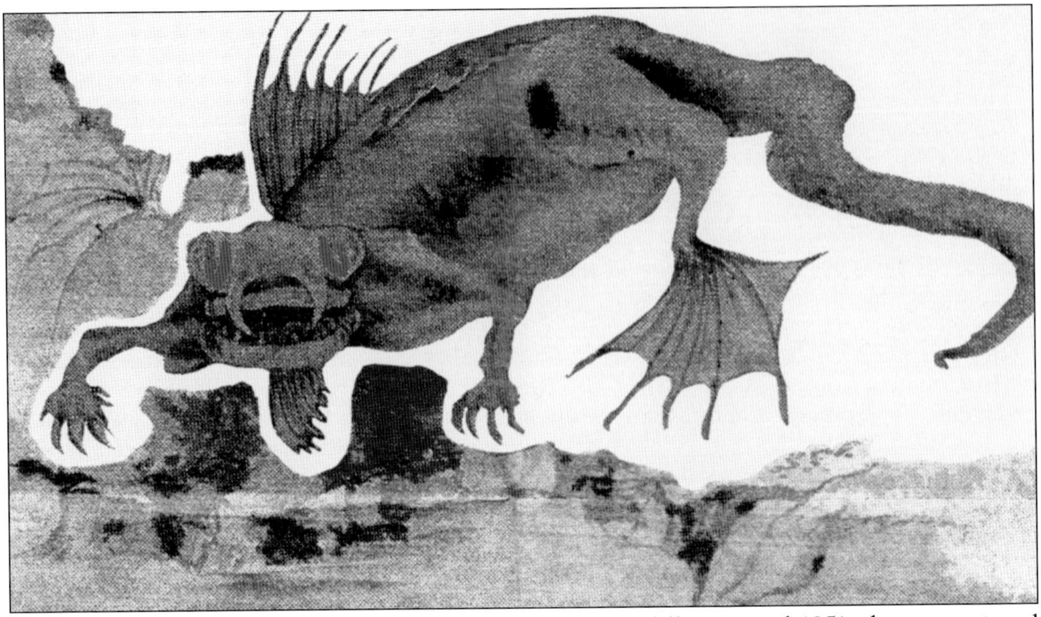

The Ug Wug is a mythical creature that lives beneath the falls. Around 1951, this was painted on a wall in the tourist bureau. After enough visitors complained, the Ug Wug was covered over and eventually destroyed. Apparently, the best time to see an Ug Wug is when one has had a few too many to drink.

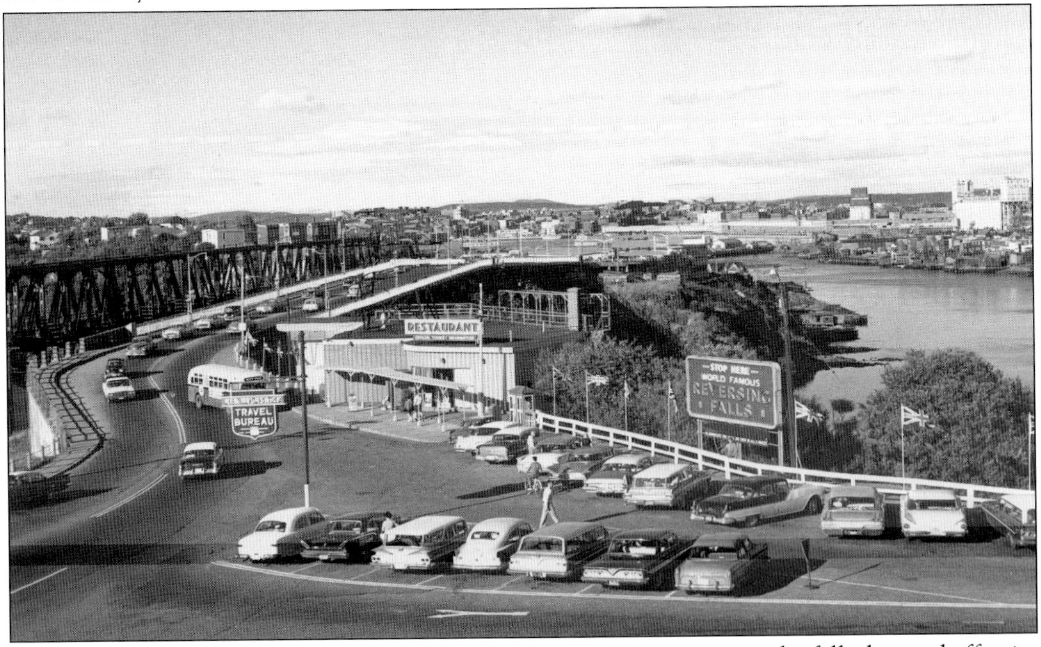

After the Saint John Harbour Bridge opened in 1968, tourist visitation at the falls dropped off quite dramatically. To try and recover some of those lost visitors, the city tourism department changed the promotion of the falls. All reference to the "rapids" was eliminated, and the impression to be created for the visitor was to see Niagara Falls going backwards. This backfired as tourists felt cheated and robbed at not seeing the falls going backwards. This was told to co-author Harold E. Wright by two directors of Saint John Tourism, Seward McDonald and Ray Butler.

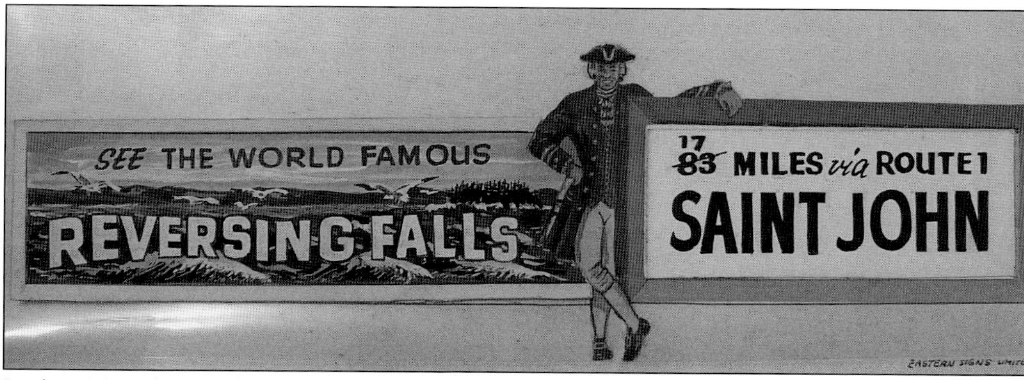

In the 1950s, the Loyalist Man became the tourism icon for the city. Conceived by Jim Stackhouse and painted by Ron Howard, this man was the stereotypical Loyalist—white, male, well dressed, and well off. This large billboard kicked off the new promotion by dropping off the word "rapids" to create the Niagara Falls syndrome.

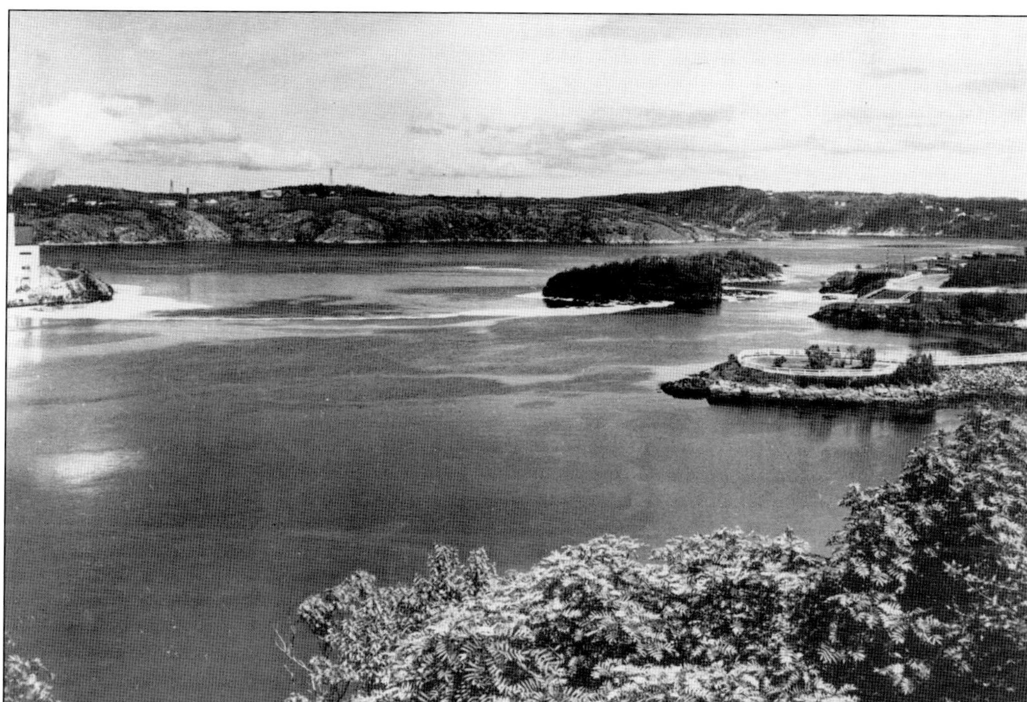

At low tide, there was little water between False Island and the mainland. In the 1950s, the small water opening was filled in, a visitor's lookout was set up on the island, a few trees were planted, and that was the extent of tourism development. Recently, tourists were blindsided again. While the area has been known as the Reversing Falls for hundreds of years and the tourist site was called the Reversing Falls Rapids, the Waterfront Development Corp. decided to rebrand the site without any understanding behind the tourism history. They renamed it the "Reversing Rapids." And now, tourists and locals alike are confused trying to find three places—the falls, the rapids, and this new creature, the Reversing Rapids.

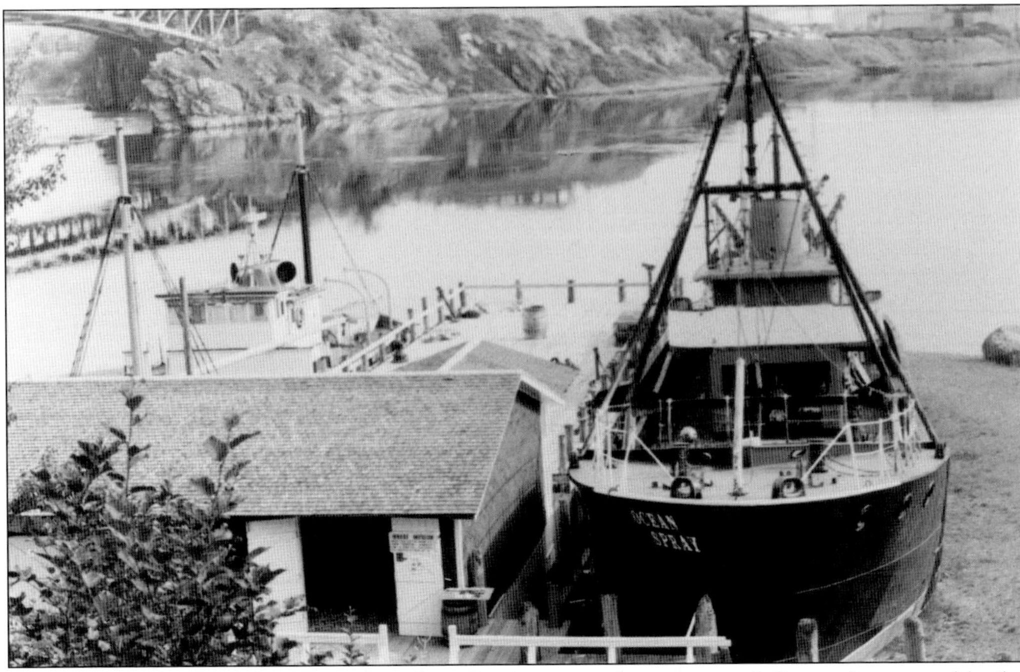

In the mid-1970s, Ralph Bungay bought a few boats, with one named *Ocean Spray*, and built a small wharf museum at the former Jewett Mill site. He filled the building and boats with nautical and local history items. That is as far as he went, as city tourism officials would not support his operation and, in fact, worked against him by not promoting his museum and by steering tourists away from the place. (Courtesy of David Goss.)

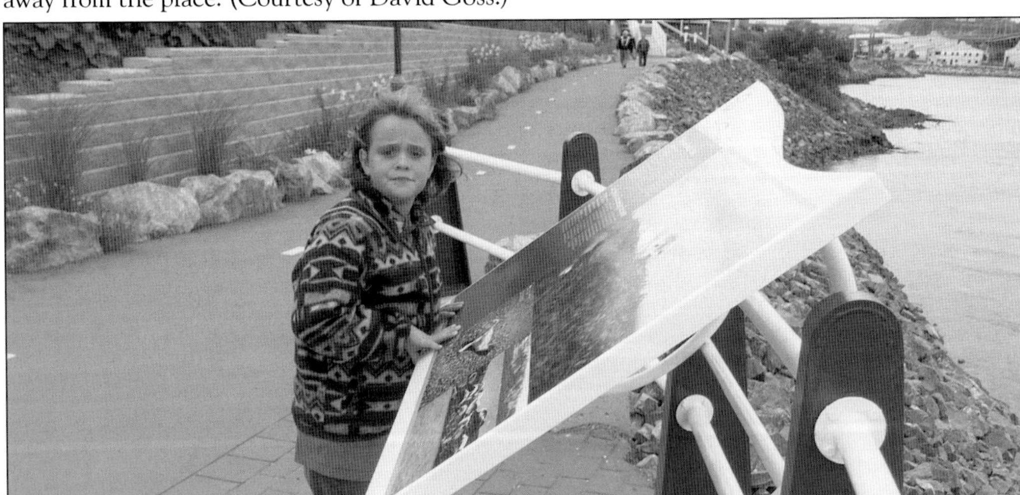

Harbour Passage is a cranberry-coloured waterfront trail that begins in St. Patrick's Square at Reeds Point in the South End and travels up Water Street, around Market Slip, along Portland Point, and then down Chesley Drive, up Bentley Street, and also to the Reversing Falls. The plan is to eventually have this pathway snake its way along the harbour front. While beautiful when it opened, it has suffered considerably from lack of maintenance and poor-quality craftsmanship. Here, Jessalyn Wright exams one of the many information panels along the path. (Courtesy of Harold E. Wright.)

Nine

THE 100-YEAR DREAM GETS BUILT

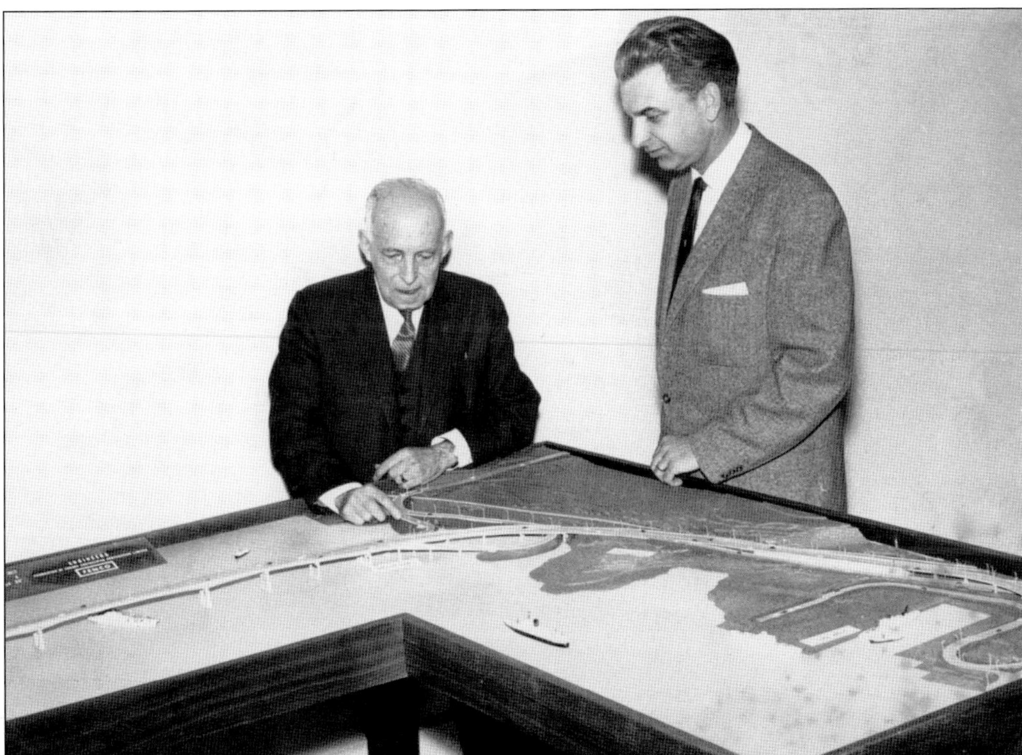

Lancaster City councillor George Cameron was once quoted as saying, "We've been waiting for the bridge for a hundred years." That dream was years in the making, dating from the 1857 attempt to cross at Navy Island, the 1889 Portland amalgamation with a bridge proposal, and the 1909 attempt to have a bridge built. Harry F. Hopkins (left), honorary chairman of the Saint John Harbour Bridge Authority, examines a model of the Saint John Harbour Bridge with H.W. Shaven, the general manager of the Saint John Harbour Bridge Authority.

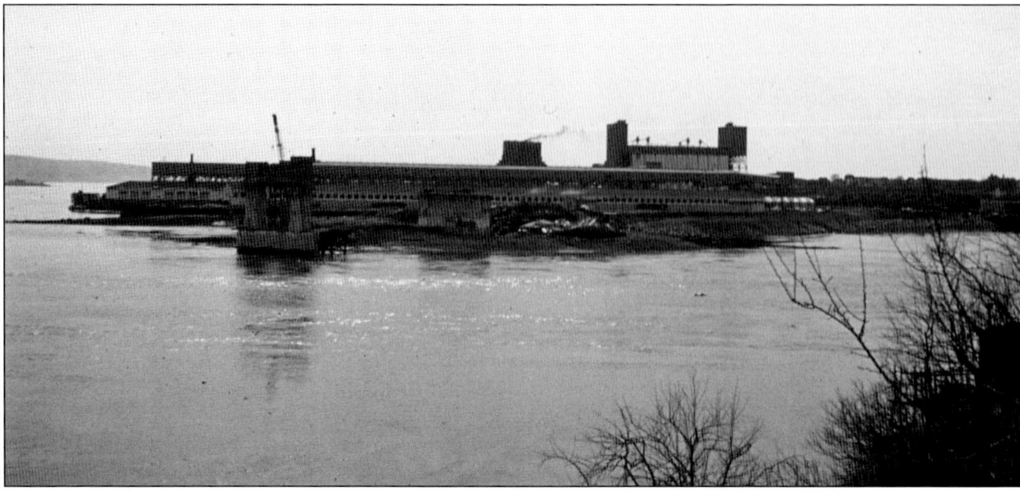

By the 1950s, the harbour ferry system was inefficient and costly, and the cost of building a bridge continued to balloon. The estimated cost was now $4.4 million. Finally, on April 13, 1962, the Saint John Harbour Bridge Authority was constituted by a special act of the New Brunswick Legislature. The authority consisted of seven members, including five from the city, one from the province, and one from the federal government. (Courtesy of Jim Sulis.)

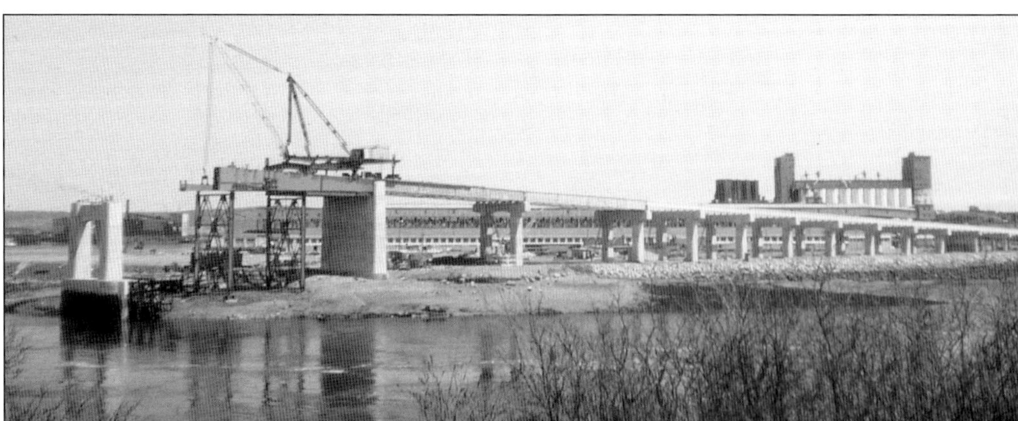

The Saint John Harbour Bridge Authority oversaw the daily operations, repairs, and long-term planning as well as the finances for the bridge. Their first act was to commission a feasibility study to determine the design, location, and cost of a bridge. They needed to build a bridge to not only meet the needs of the day but also to have the capacity to accommodate the city's future transportation needs. (Courtesy of Jim Sulis.)

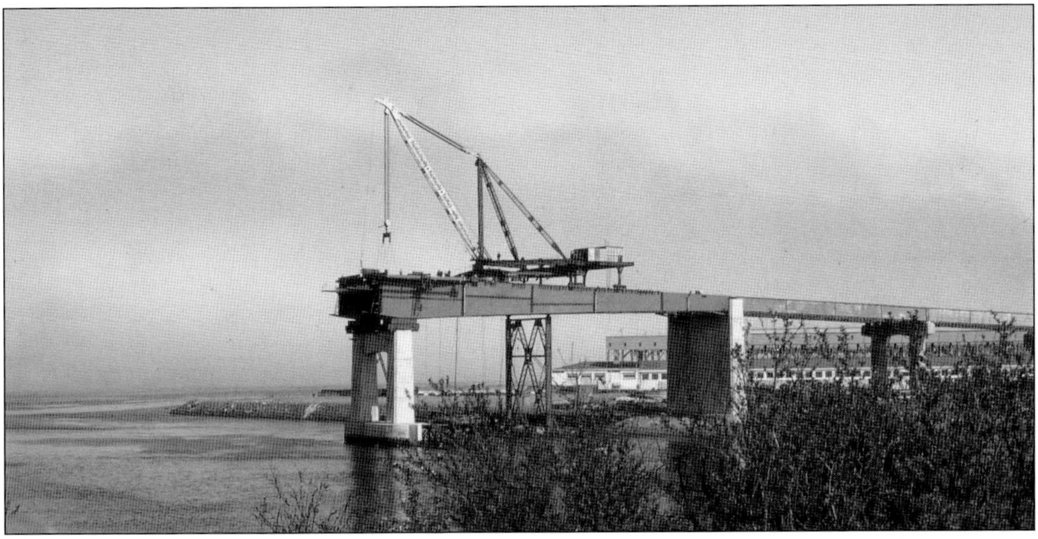

Construction began in July 1965, and by June 1967, most of the flanking spans on the west were in place. Once the north spans were in place, the only piece left to this construction jigsaw was the central orthotropic span, which was 550 feet long. When completed, the bridge had some 45,000 cubic yards of concrete poured. (Courtesy of Jim Sulis.)

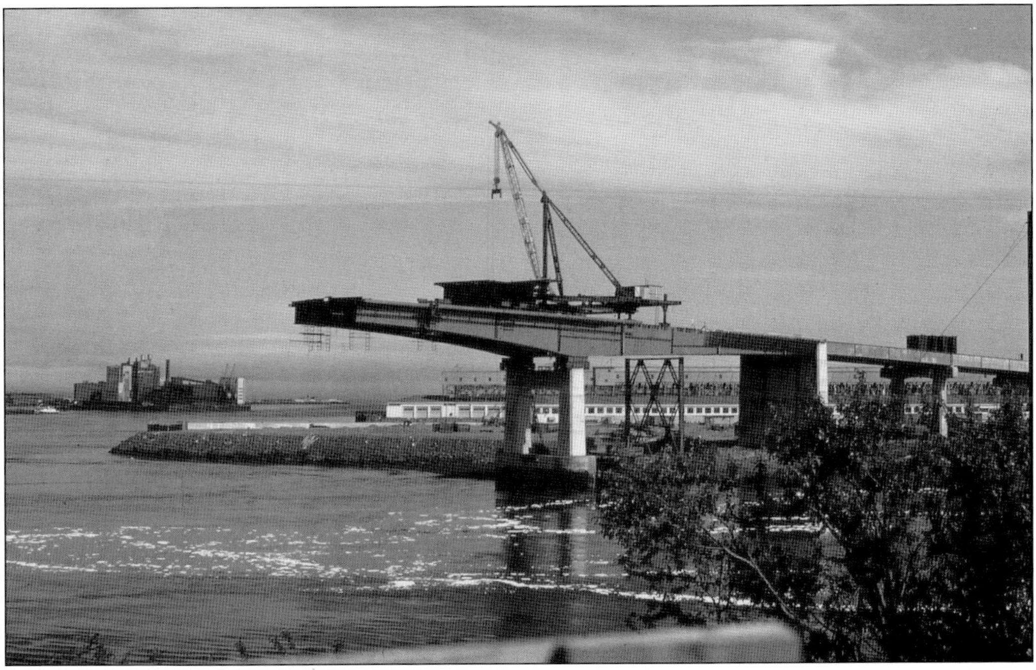

Another span is put in place, inching ever closer to the placement of the central span. There were 8,000 tons of steel used in the bridge over its 1.25-mile length. There were 351 prestressed concrete girders installed. These bridge decks were carried on four massive concrete piers sunk into the hard shale bottom of the harbour. (Courtesy of Jim Sulis.)

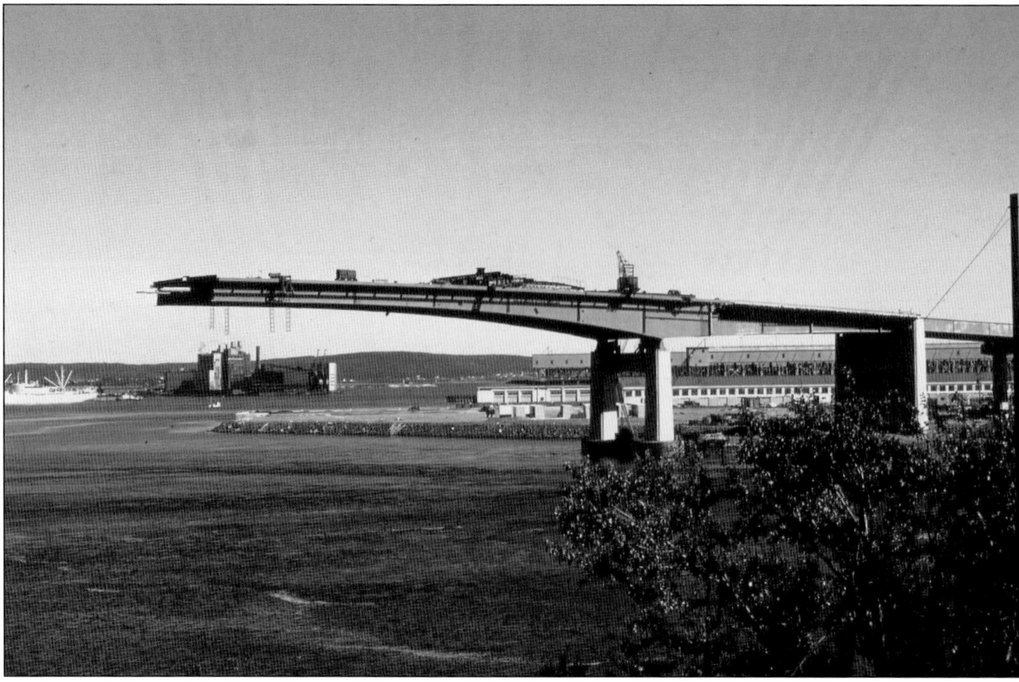

Here, the central span inches closer to the North End. This bridge was quite an engineering feat, considering that the water below ran at 18 feet per second with tides ranging up to 32 feet. The feasibility report concluded that four lanes were needed. The only piece missing was provision for a pedestrian walkway. (Courtesy of Jim Sulis.)

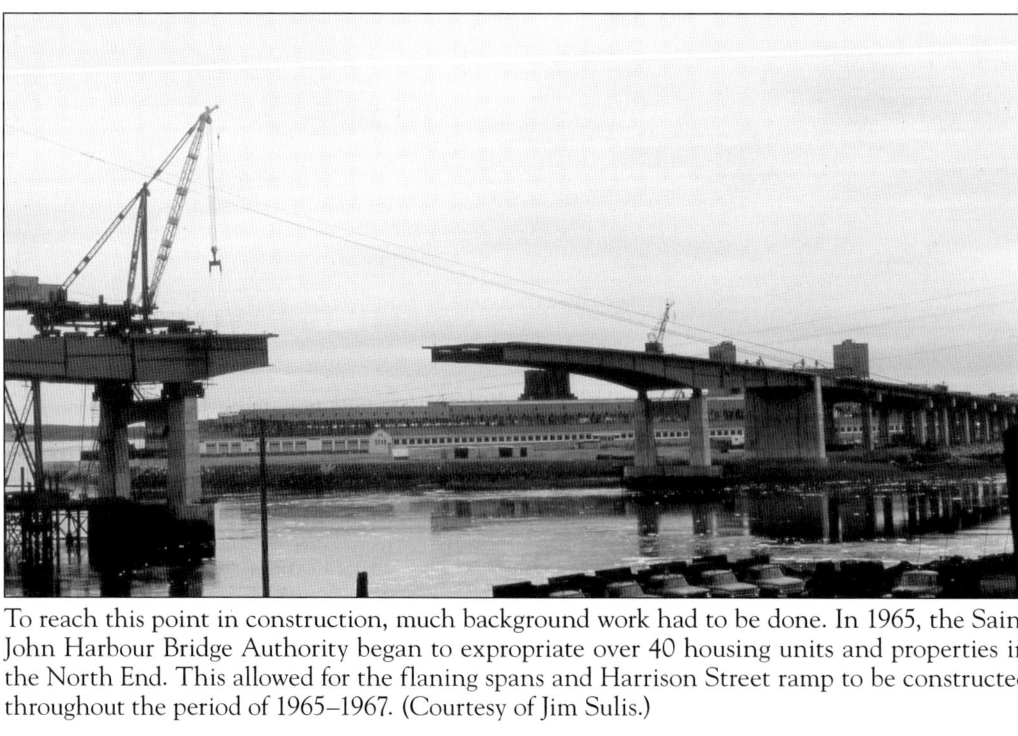

To reach this point in construction, much background work had to be done. In 1965, the Saint John Harbour Bridge Authority began to expropriate over 40 housing units and properties in the North End. This allowed for the flaning spans and Harrison Street ramp to be constructed throughout the period of 1965–1967. (Courtesy of Jim Sulis.)

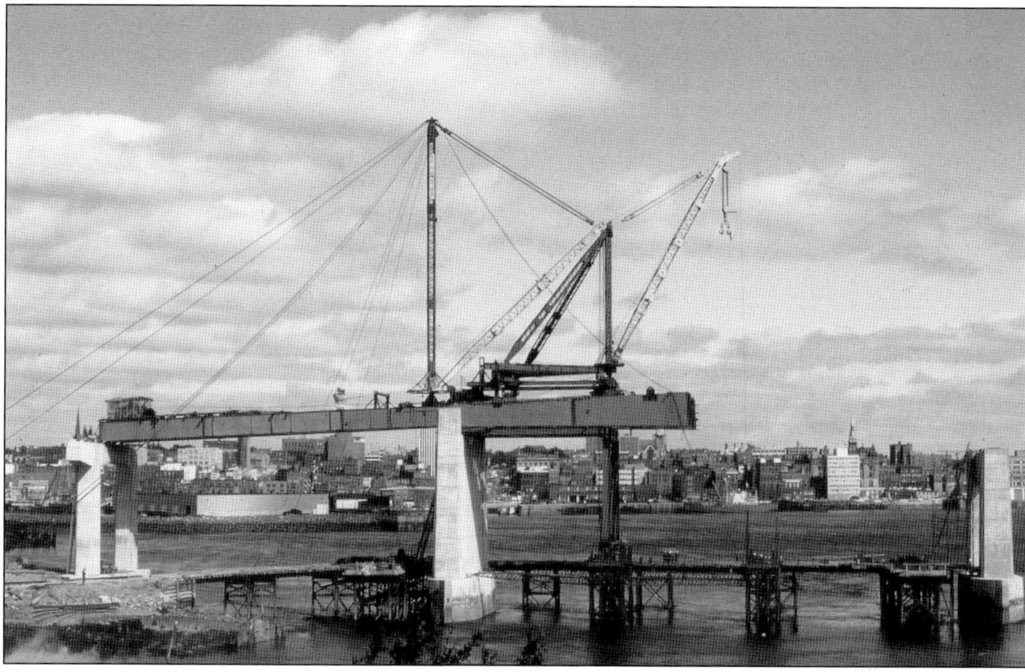

If one was standing on Chesley Drive today and looking at this same location, he or she would not have any idea of the difficulties experienced in putting together the piers and spans and then raising the huge pieces of steel. The concrete pier pedestals shown were anchored by a series of prestressed cables grouted 25 feet into the underlying bedrock. (Courtesy of Jim Sulis.)

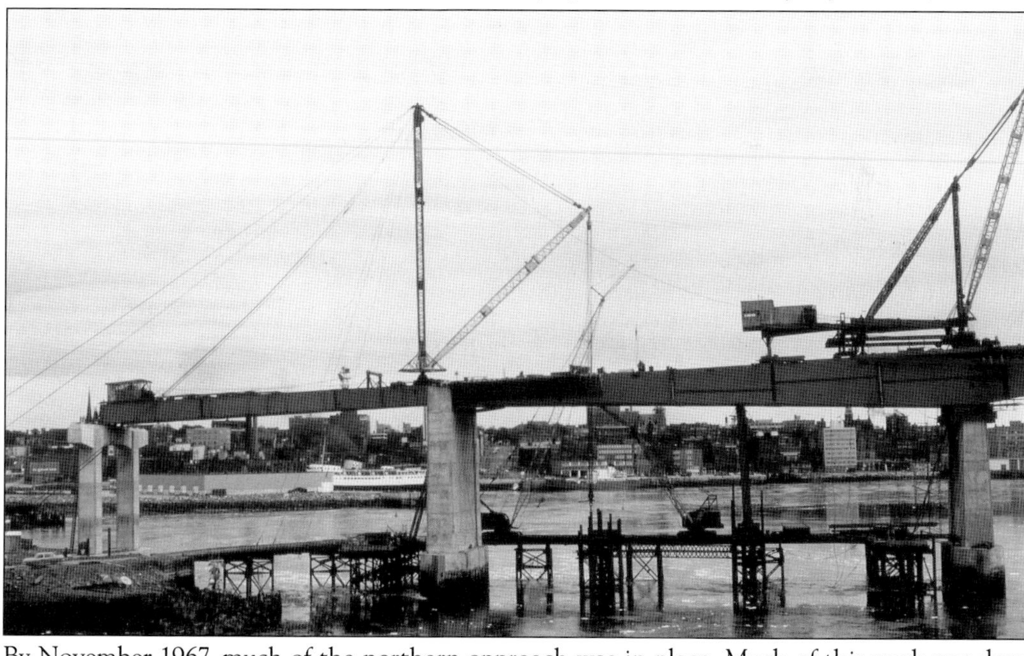

By November 1967, much of the northern approach was in place. Much of this work was done by Steed & Evans, Limited, which had responsibility for this side of the bridge. While difficult to see, there are a few workmen in site. Most are working inside the bridge spans. (Courtesy of Jim Sulis.)

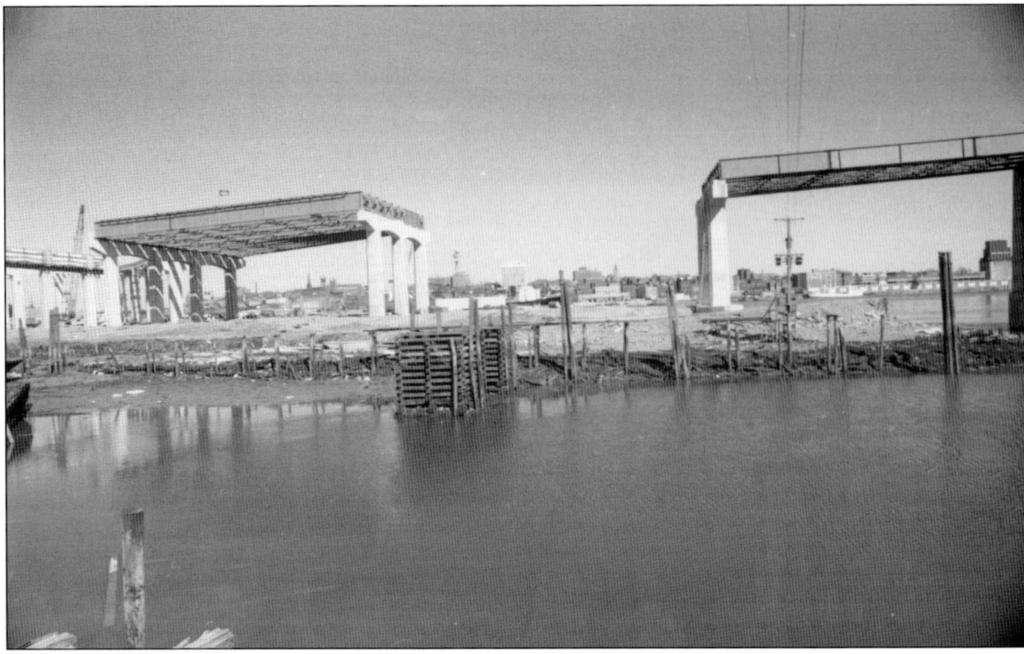

On April 6, 1968, new Saint John resident Bob Boudreau went to Chesley Drive to photograph progress on the bridge. In the foreground are the wood pilings of the former wharf of the Hilyard shipyard. These elevated raps were constructed by Steed & Evans, Limited. (Courtesy of Bob Boudreau.)

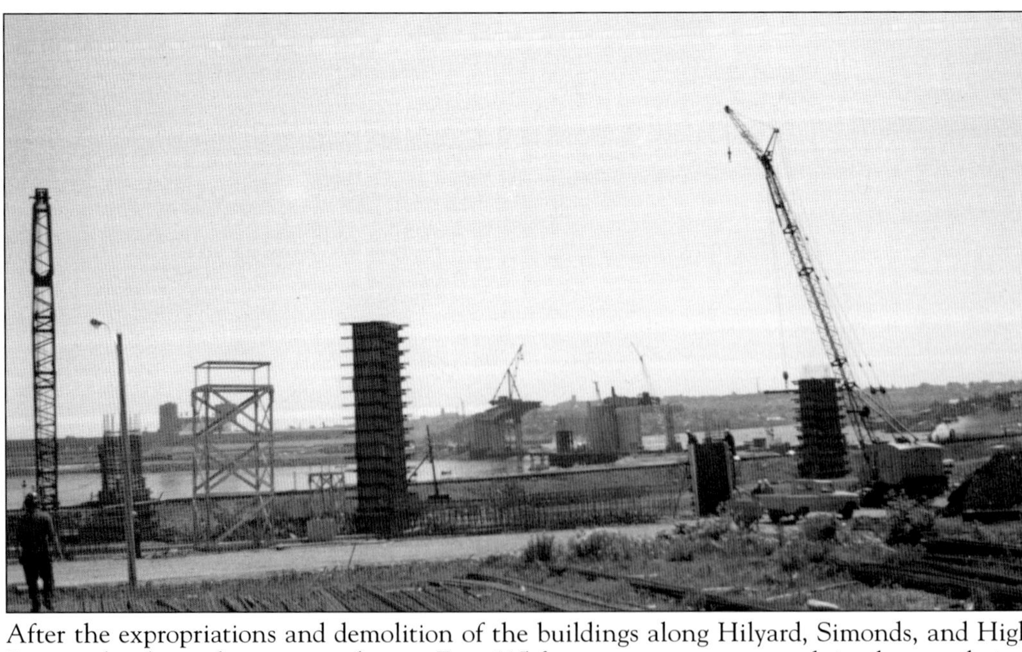

After the expropriations and demolition of the buildings along Hilyard, Simonds, and High Streets, the elevated ramps were begun. Four 115-foot spans were concreted simultaneously in a continuous 48-hour operation.

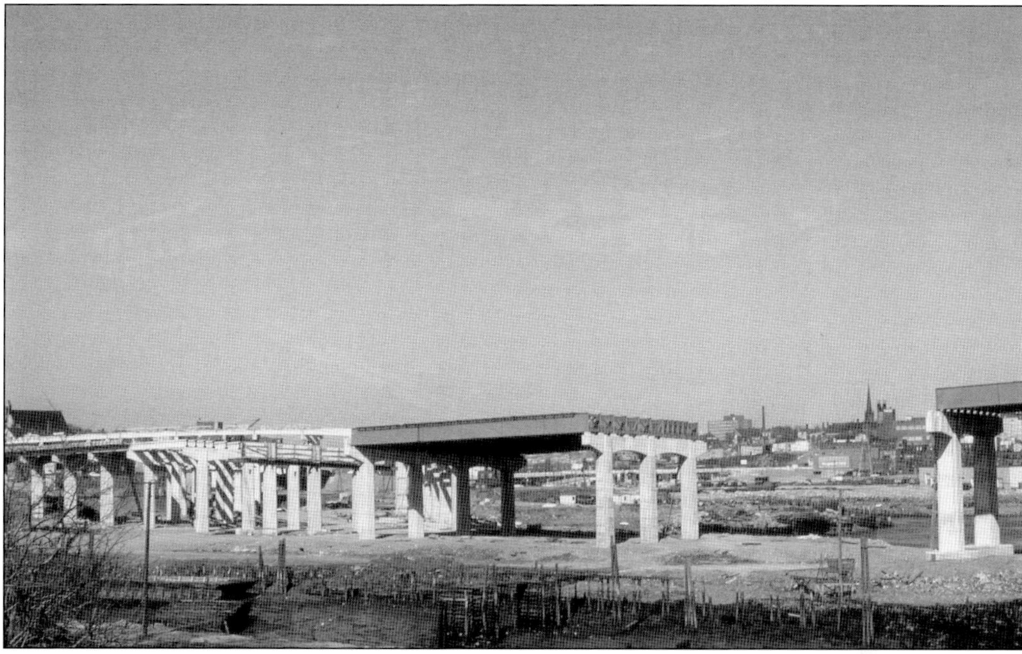

This area under the bridge today is a green space, part of the Harbour Passage walkway. HMCS *Brunswicker* and the Coast Guard are also located there. At the left is the Harrison Street ramp, and in the distance is the Portland United Church. This photograph was one of many slides taken by Jim Sulis in the spring of 1968 to document this dream bridge, which forever changed the appearance of the harbour. (Courtesy of Jim Sulis.)

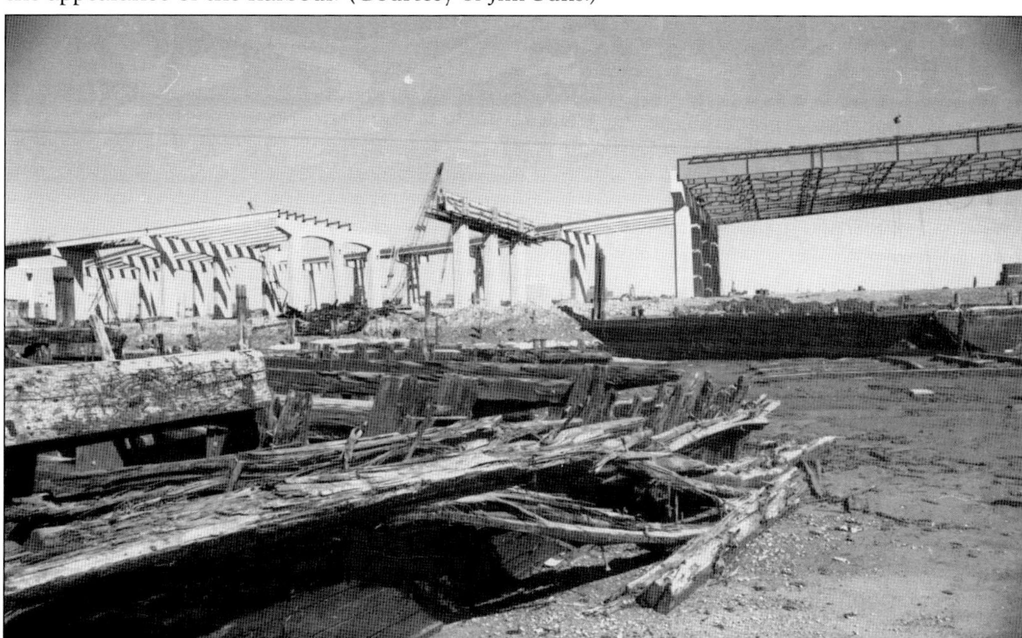

With the new bridge under construction, remnants of the city's marine heritage is evident. Wharf timber is in decay, with a barge sitting high and dry at low tide. The only thing missing here is a salmon fisherman! (Courtesy of Bob Boudreau.)

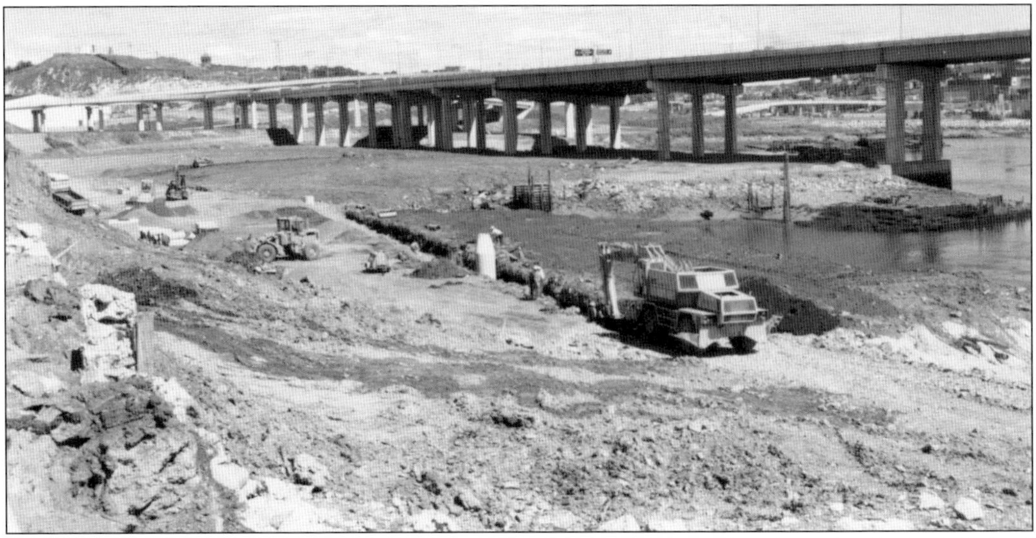

Chesley Drive, formerly called the Straight Shore, was rebuilt and realigned, which dislodged dozens of families and businesses. The drive was to act as a truck route into the uptown, bypassing Douglas Avenue.

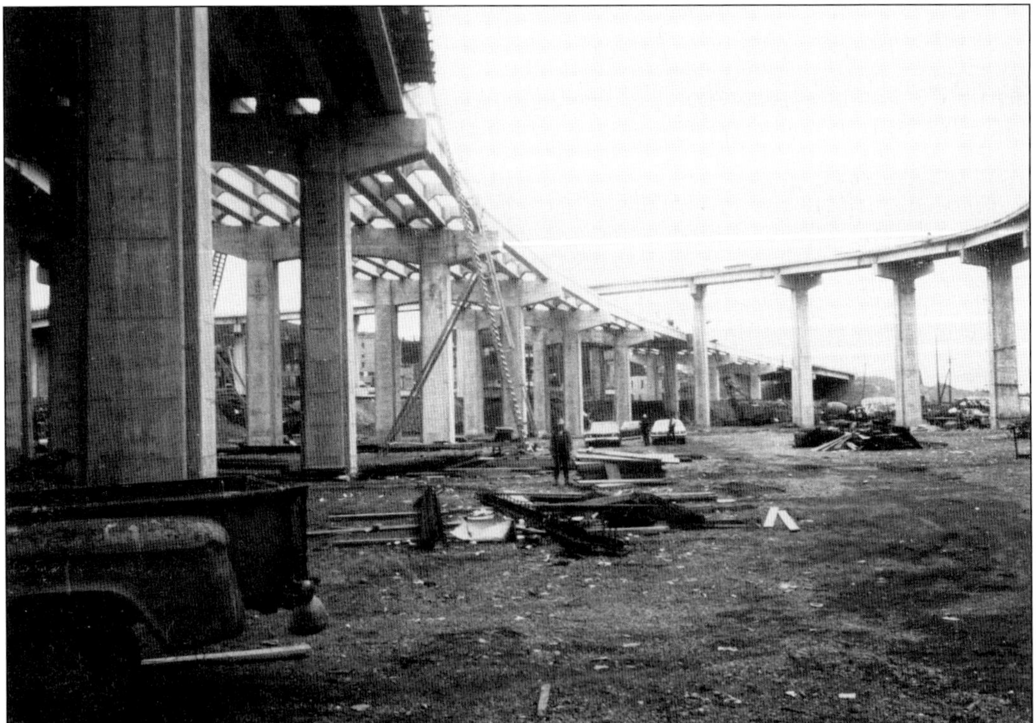

With various phases of construction happening or still in the planning stage, some were thinking of the next phase, the Saint John Throughway or a proposed but not approved urban expressway project and central street system. The latter would see current city streets repaired and widened to allow for quicker access across town. It still did not address the necessity of a second harbour crossing. The urban expressway and central street system would cost $16 million and $26 million, respectively.

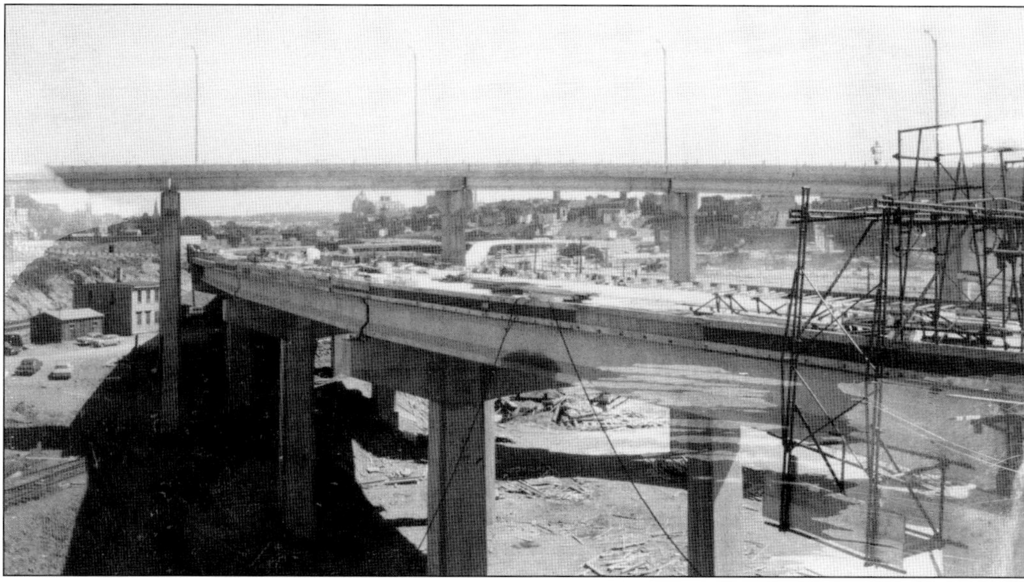

In 1965, the Community Growth Committee supported the central street system. They published hundreds of names supporting that street system. Some of the names included John E. Irving, Norwood Carter, Ken V. Cox, and Wallace P. Macaully. The committee caused such an uproar from its newspaper articles and television and radio broadcasts that Lancaster and Simonds came out in support of the new plan.

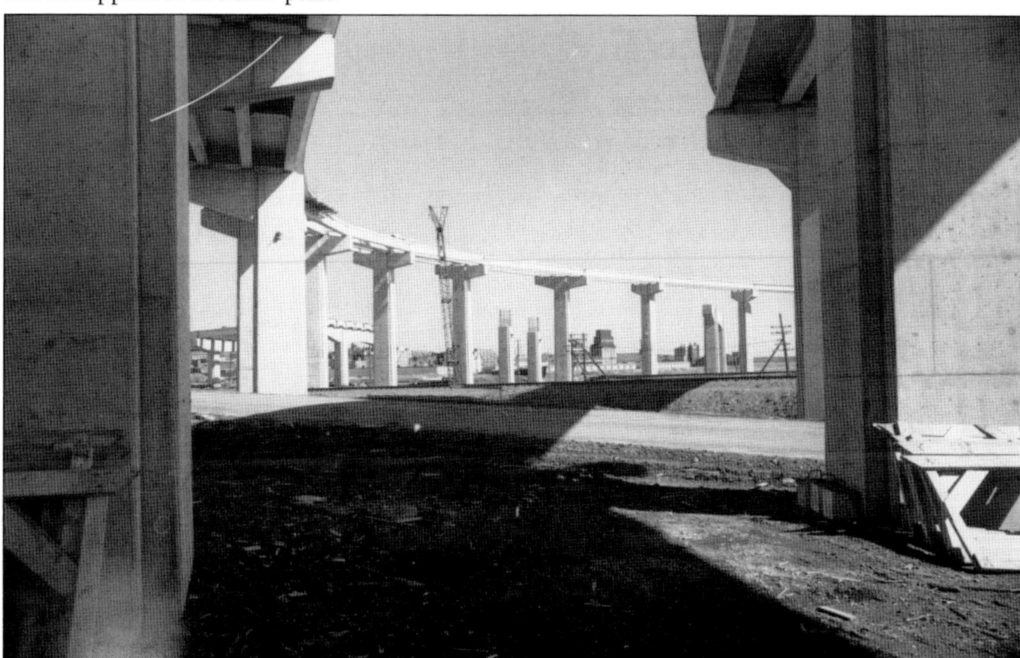

Some citizens believed that the old bridge would soon be inadequate. Tom McGloan, vice chairman for the Saint John Harbour Bridge Authority, confirmed that the estimated cost for the project had risen from $10 to $18 million. There was no planned tax increase, but the issue of a toll was still undecided. This view was taken from Hilyard Street toward the water. (Courtesy of Bob Boudreau.)

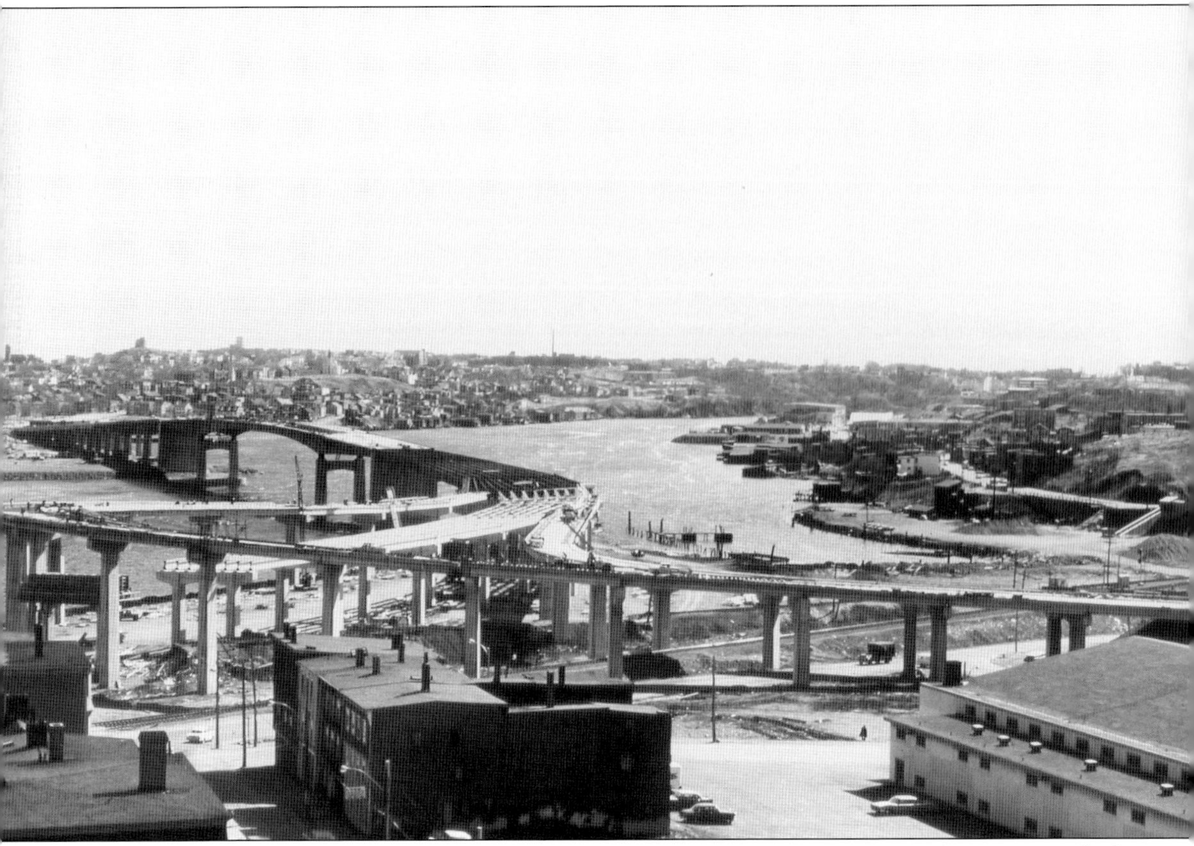

The bridge structure is in place, and the Harrison Street ramp is complete. The concrete deck is being poured in some areas of the bridge. The Lord Beaverbrook Rink is in the foreground. There were a few concerns that the bridge project would balloon to some $45 million. (Courtesy of Jim Sulis.)

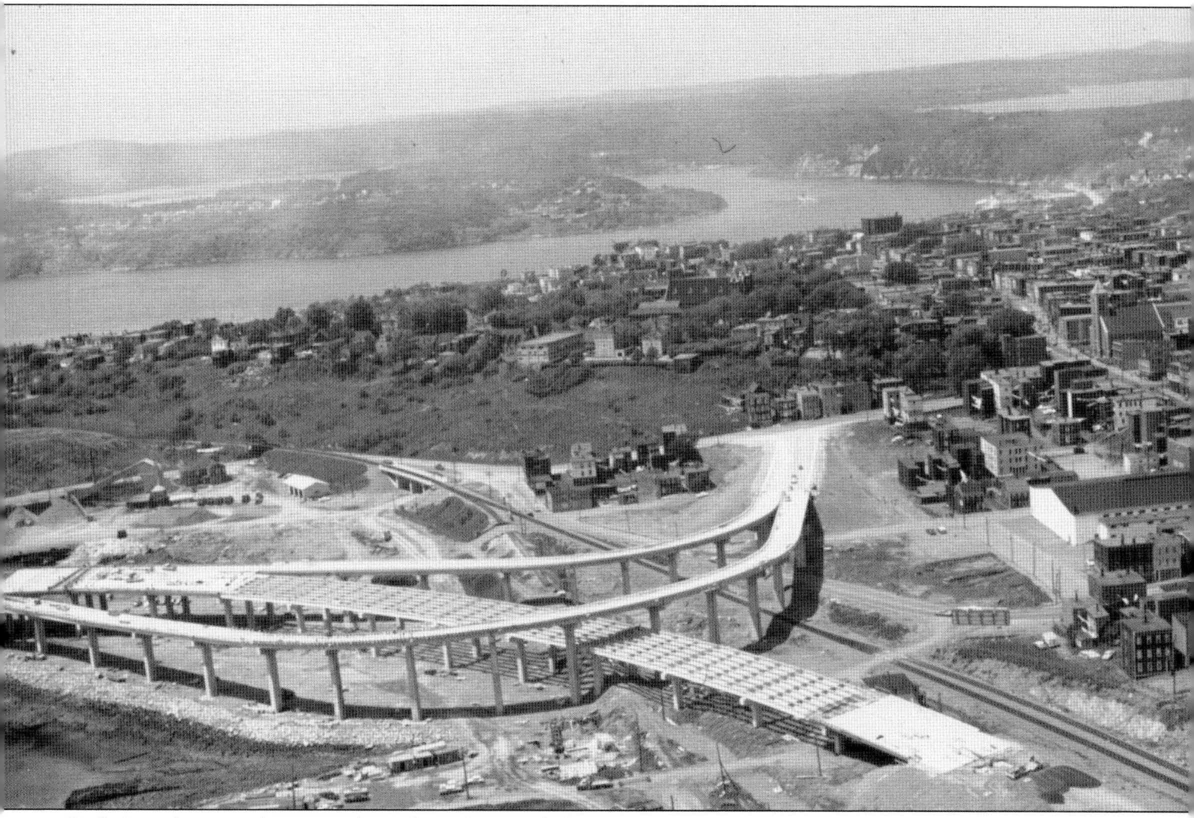

Bob Boudreau's photograph, taken from a helicopter, captures the construction of the bridge decking quite dramatically against the background of Deans Hill, Douglas Avenue, Indiantown, and the Saint John River. (Courtesy of Bob Boudreau.)

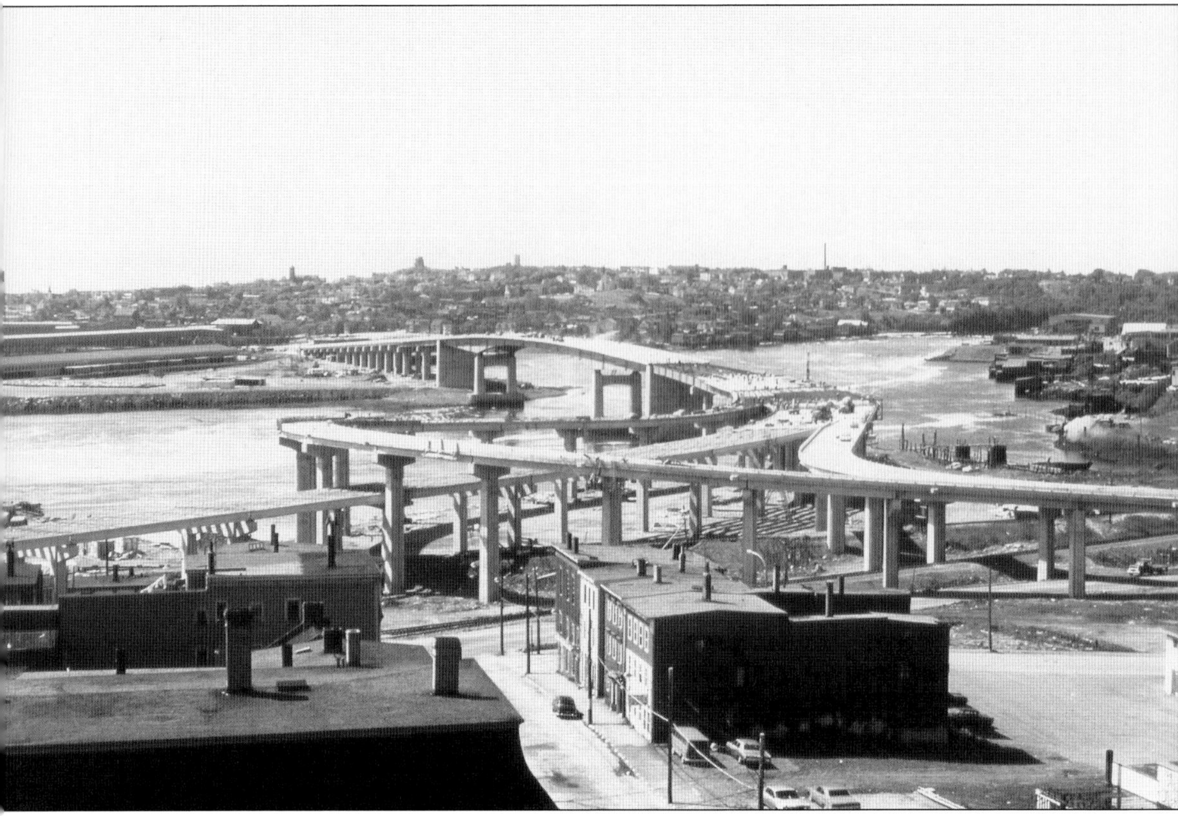

With a few buildings on Simonds Street still standing, the ramps are all in place and a considerable amount of concrete decking is down. Vulcan Asphalt & Supply Company, Limited, was awarded the contract in 1968 to provide the paving and protective systems. The protective application and mastic layer was a technique used for the first time in North America. (Courtesy of Jim Sulis.)

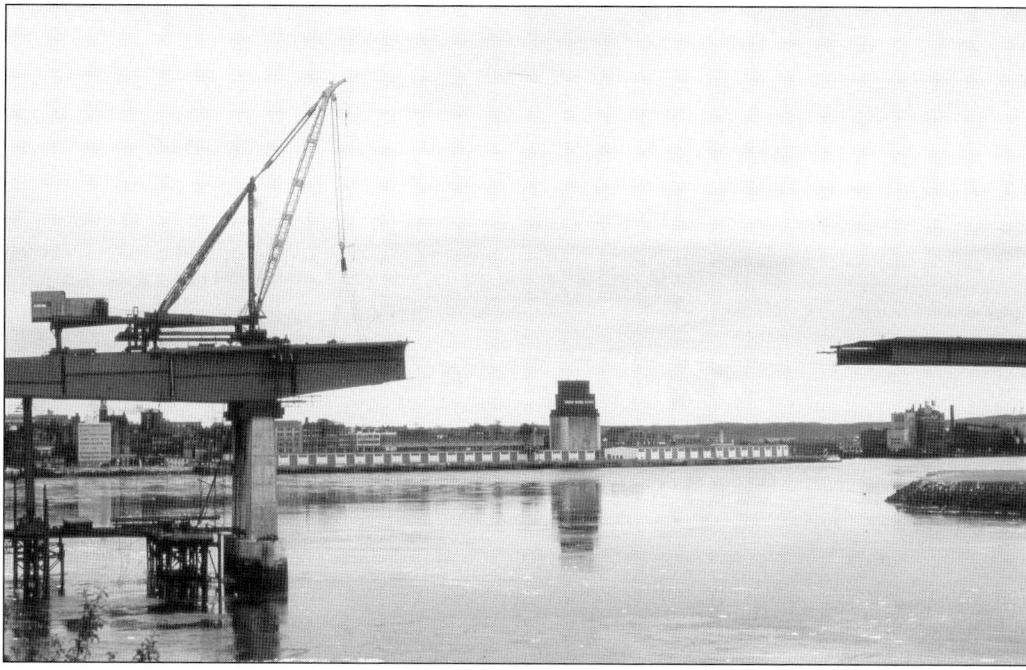

With the CNR grain elevator on Water Street as the focus, there is only a few more feet of steel to place. When the last deck component was put in place in November 1967, at the time this picture was taken, there was almost near-perfect tolerance between the two halves of the bridge. (Courtesy of Jim Sulis.)

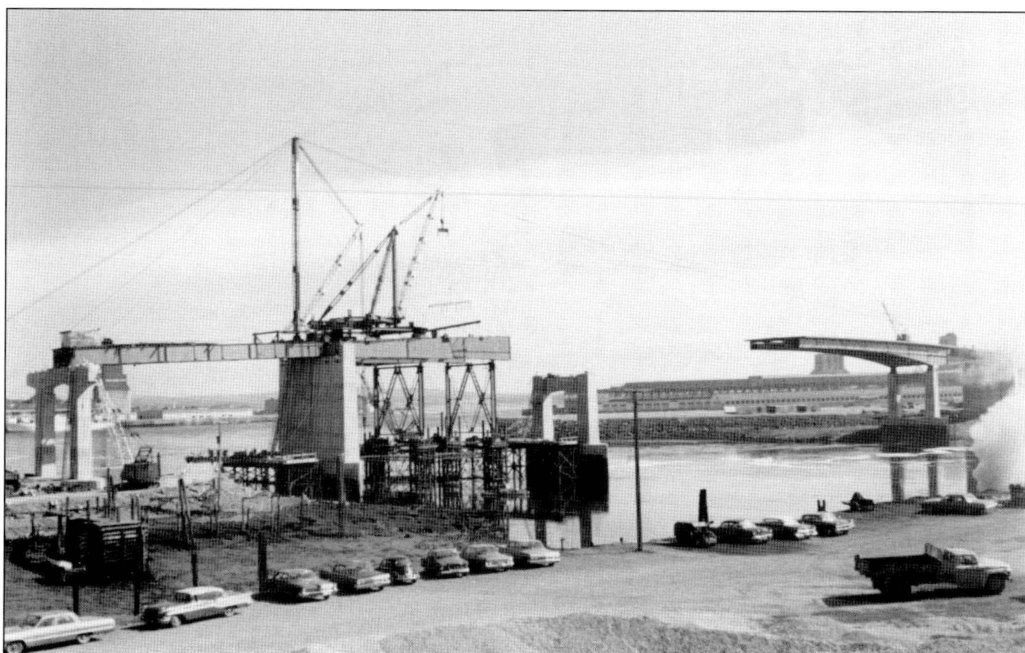

These channel piers were built by Dufresne Construction Company, Limited, of Montreal. In addition to the main bridge structural piers, the firm also built the eastern approaches to the existing Mill Street viaduct.

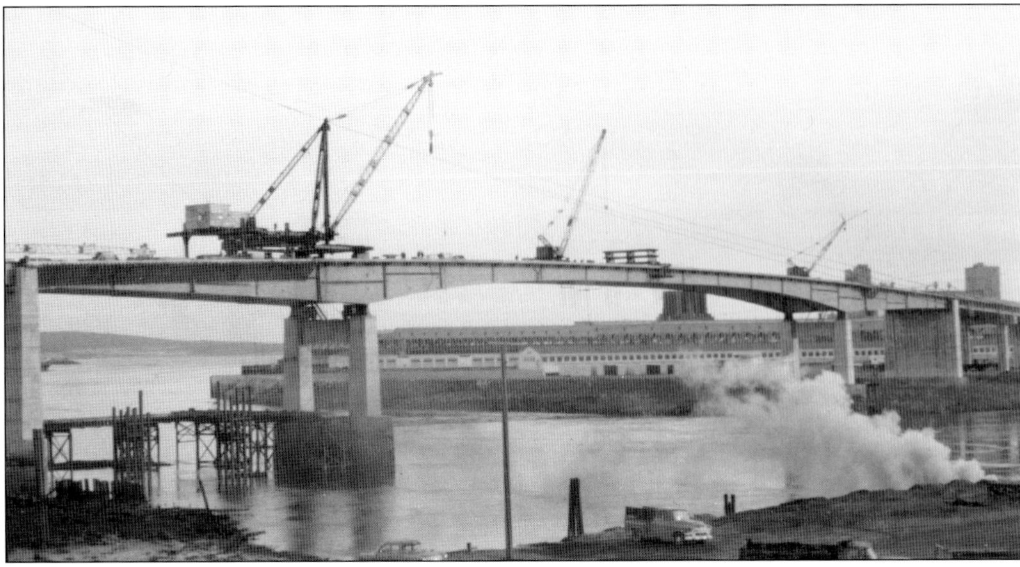

The gap closed on November 20, 1967. Saint John Harbour Bridge Authority chairman Harry Hopkins and Mayor Joseph A. MacDougall watched as workers lowered the final 30-ton section into place and bolted it together, officially closing the gap.

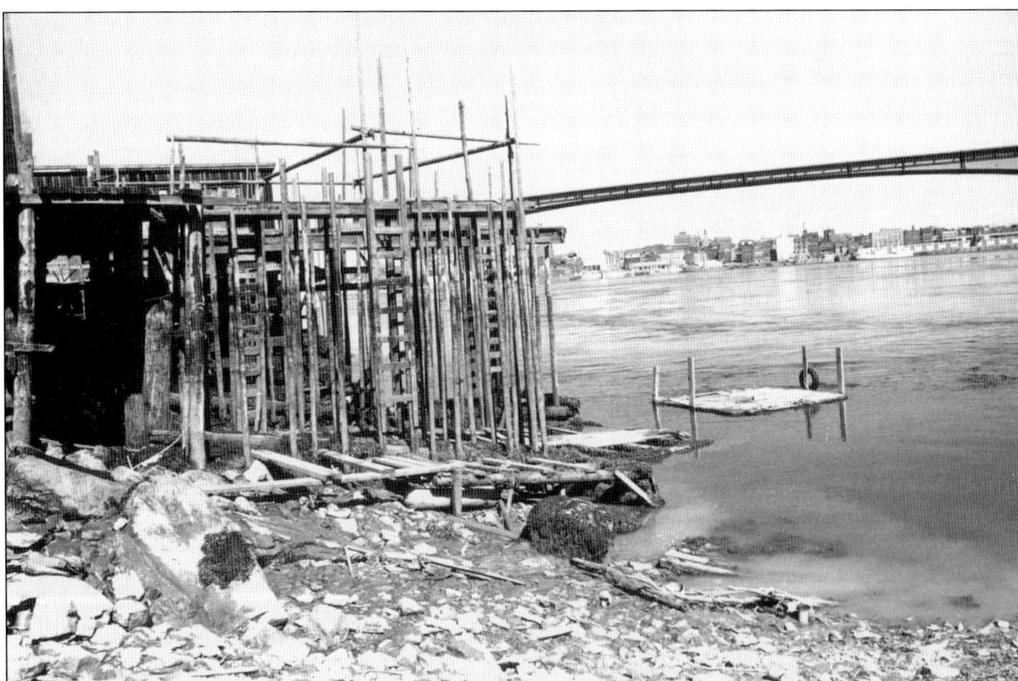

Chesley Drive was, in all reality, a fishing community. Some of the residents, such as the Lords, had relocated here when they were removed from Navy Island in 1930. With the Lords, Logans (another local family), and many others, the men of the community made their living by fishing, selling their catch to McCormack and Zatzman, wholesale fish mongers at 290 Chesley Street. At this point, the bridge was only a few months away from completion. (Courtesy of Bob Boudreau.)

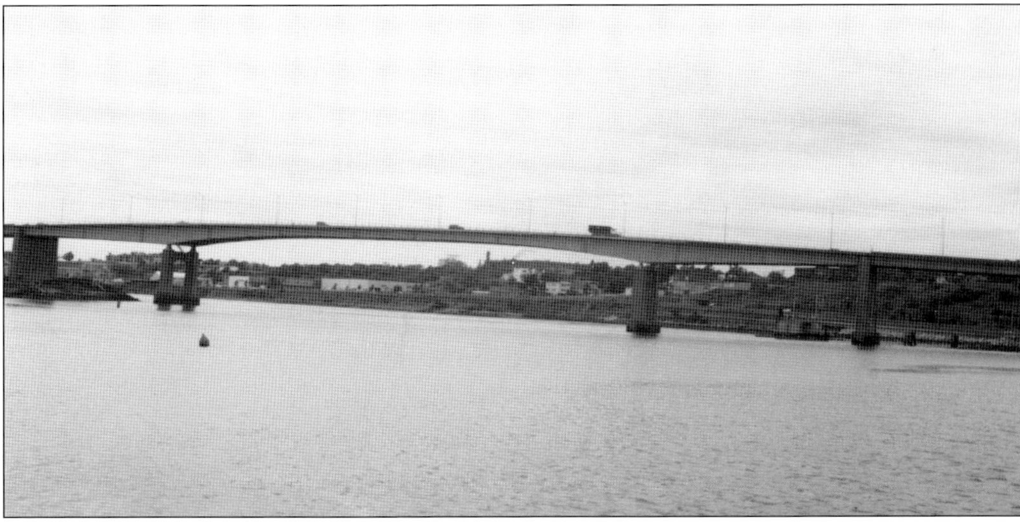

Day or night, the bridge still holds its iconic form. Under the bridge, boats and ships have a 300-foot-wide berth between piers and an additional 80.5-foot-high clearance at high slack tide. This design limited high-clearance ships from heading up the Saint John River. (Courtesy of Bob Boudreau.)

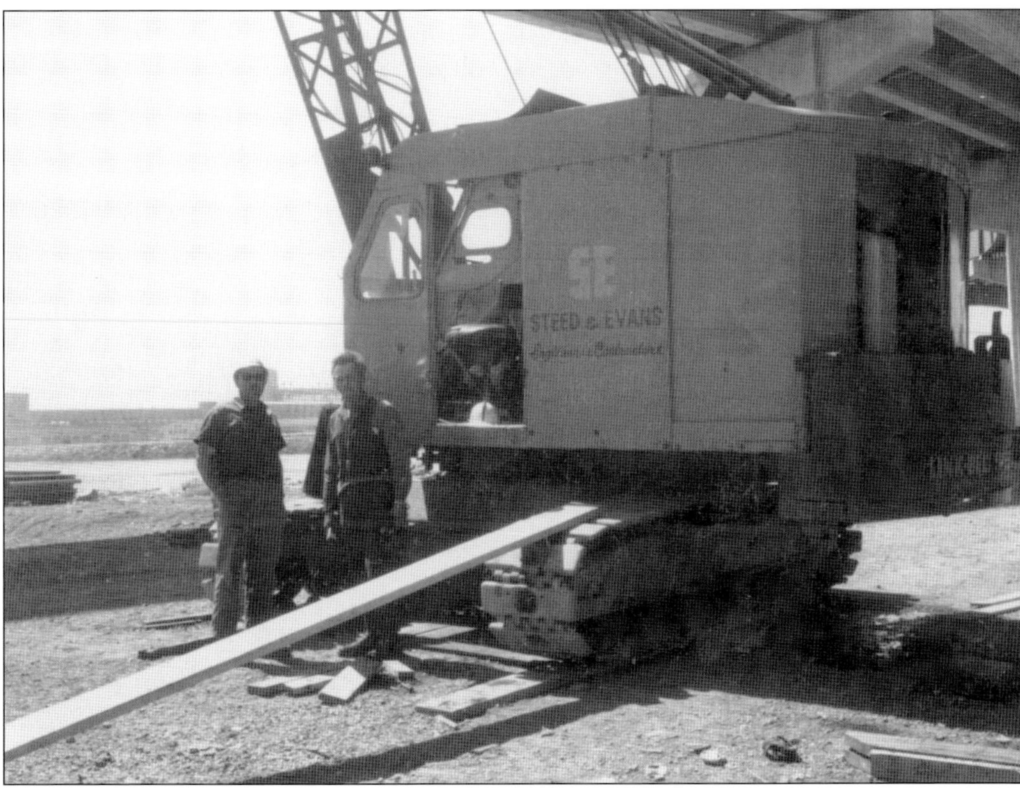

Steed & Evans from Maple, Ontario, were contracted to construct the north approaches and curved ramps. A small man-made marsh on Harbour Passage now lies close to where this photograph was taken. It was quite an engineering feat to have all of the various companies, contractors, and subcontractors working in unison to ensure the bridge was finished on time and on budget.

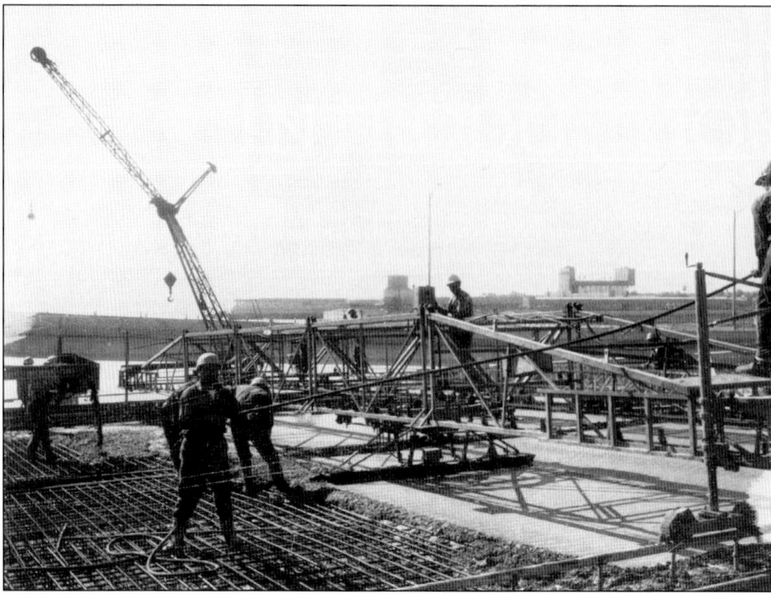

The deck work consisted of the installation of zigzag bars welded to the steel deck plate, sandblasted, and then given the flame spray application of a protective coating. This was followed by a mastic layer and then the normal concrete surface.

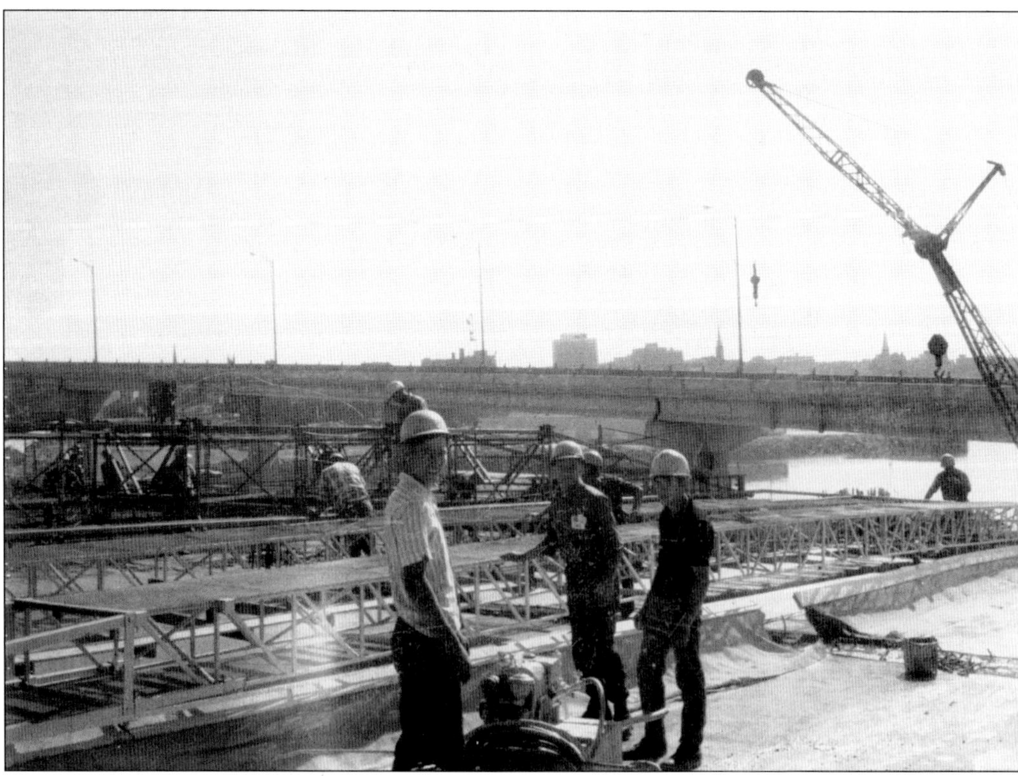

Sgt. Leo Pye of the Saint John Police Force penned a poem titled "Harbour Bridge" in 1972. Part of the third stanza reads as follows: "High high above the racing tide / Atop huge piers, its arches rest / While cars and trucks, like countless toys / Across its spans, roll east and west."

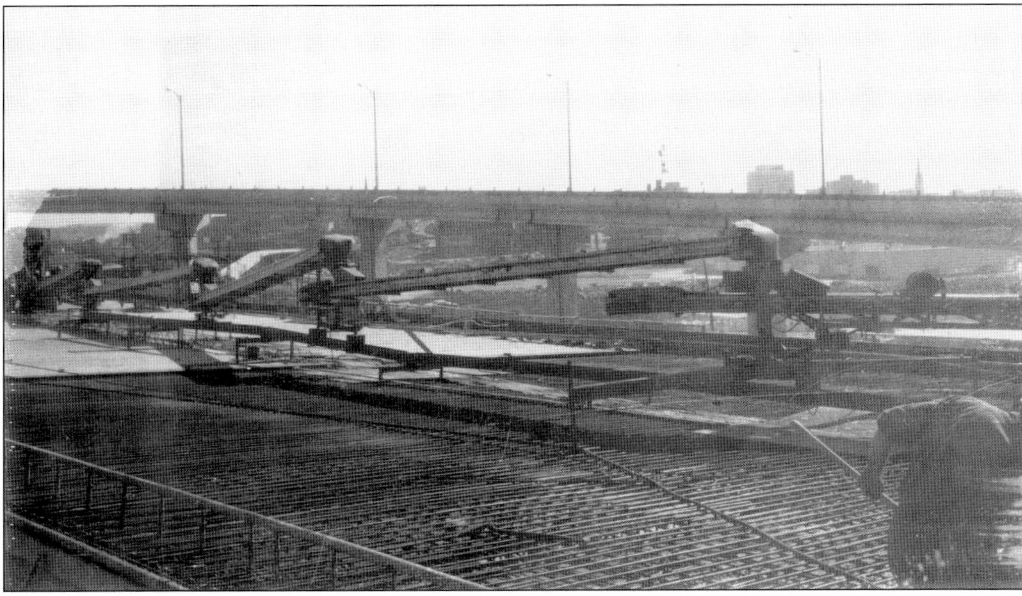

Over the years, these steel rebars have corroded. This has lead to expensive repairs and frustrating delays for the bridge users. Although this was the best technology available in the 1960s, it has led to major bridge repair problems only 40 years later. Perhaps builders should have done what the Romans did—some of their bridges are still standing after 1,000 years.

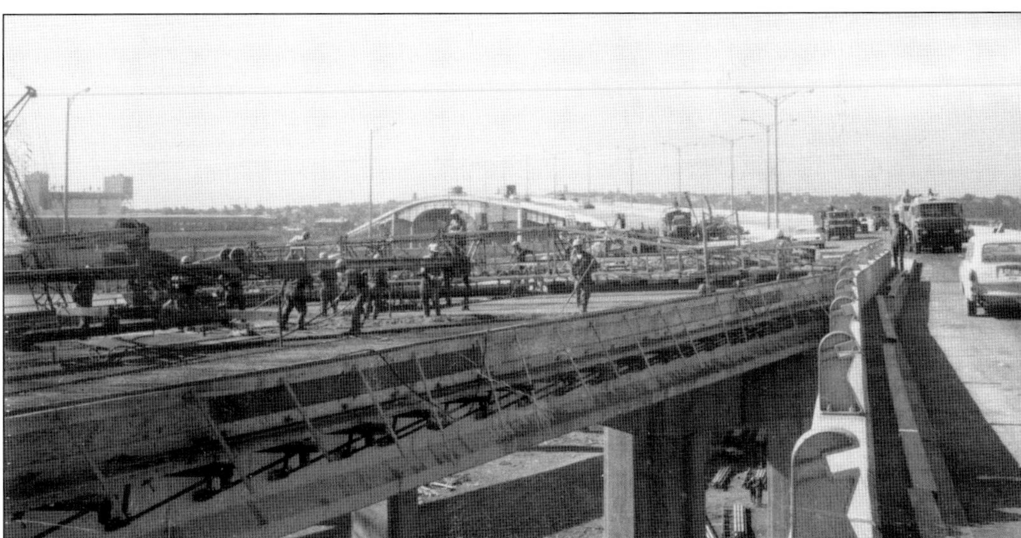

This photograph could have been taken in 2013 as repair work on the same section of the bridge is under way. The street lamps shown were just removed. The Harrison Street ramp is at the right.

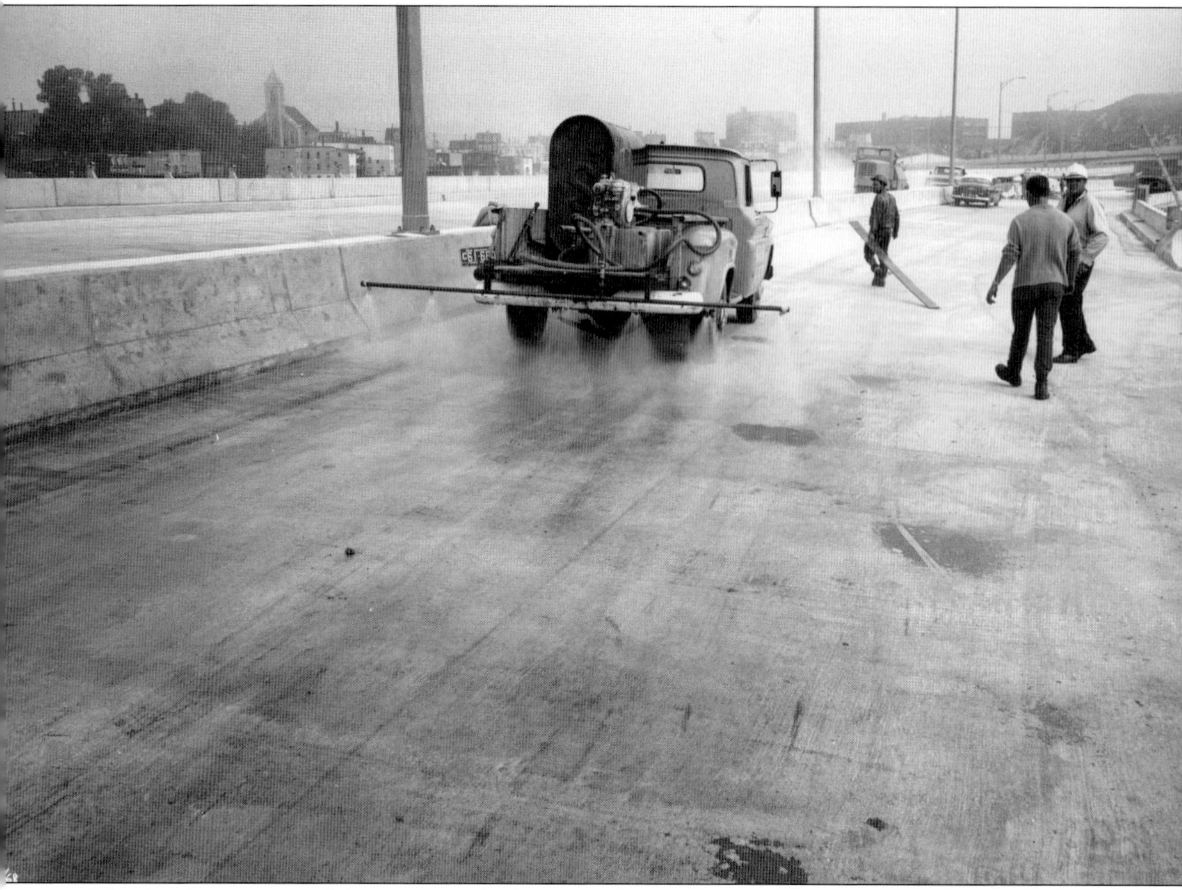

The final treatment of the concrete deck was the flame spray application of a German-patented corrosion protective layer; the placement of a stone, impregnated hot-poured mastic layer; and a layer of normal asphalt concrete wearing surface.

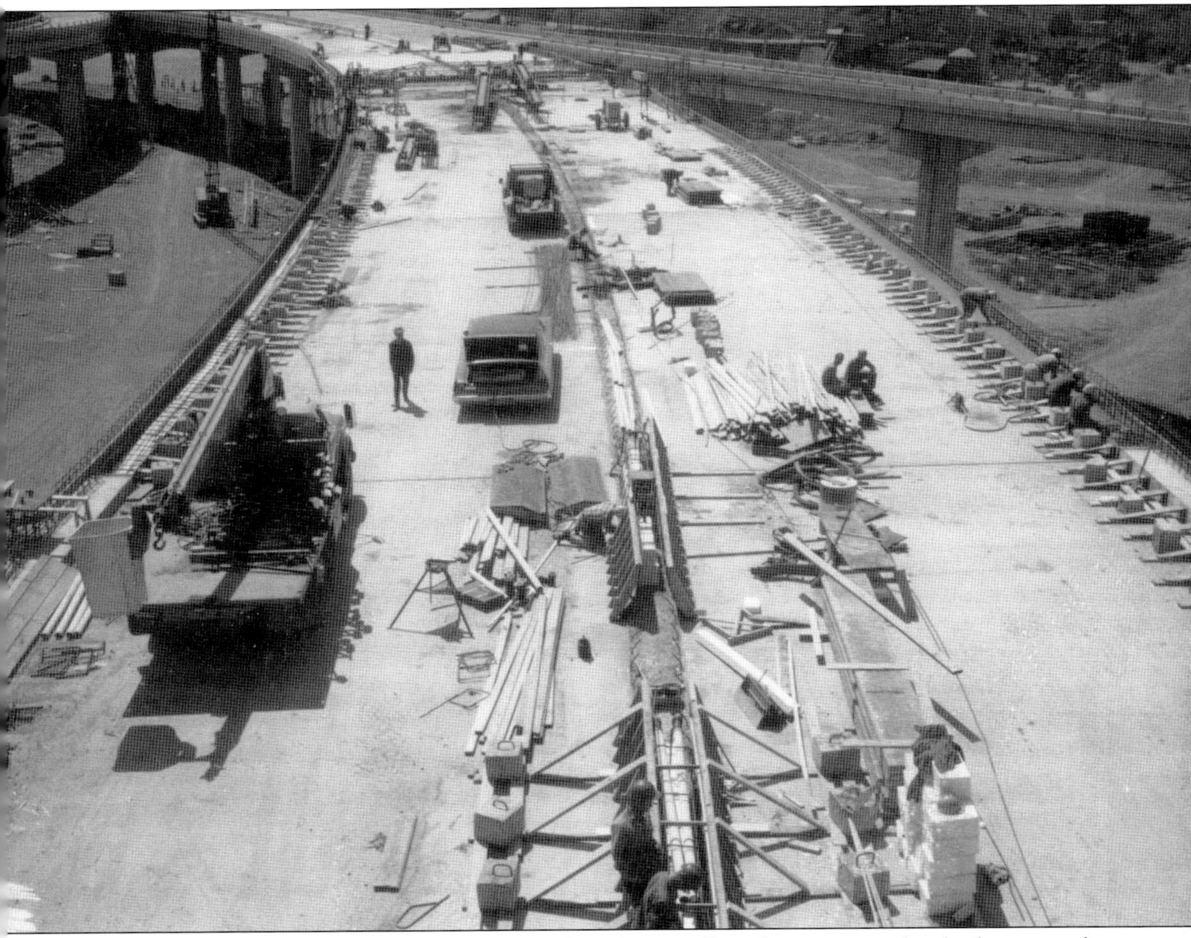

The rebar is being placed for the concrete side rails as well as the concrete divider between the eastbound and westbound lanes. Despite there being several pieces of machinery, there are at least 14 men at work in this image.

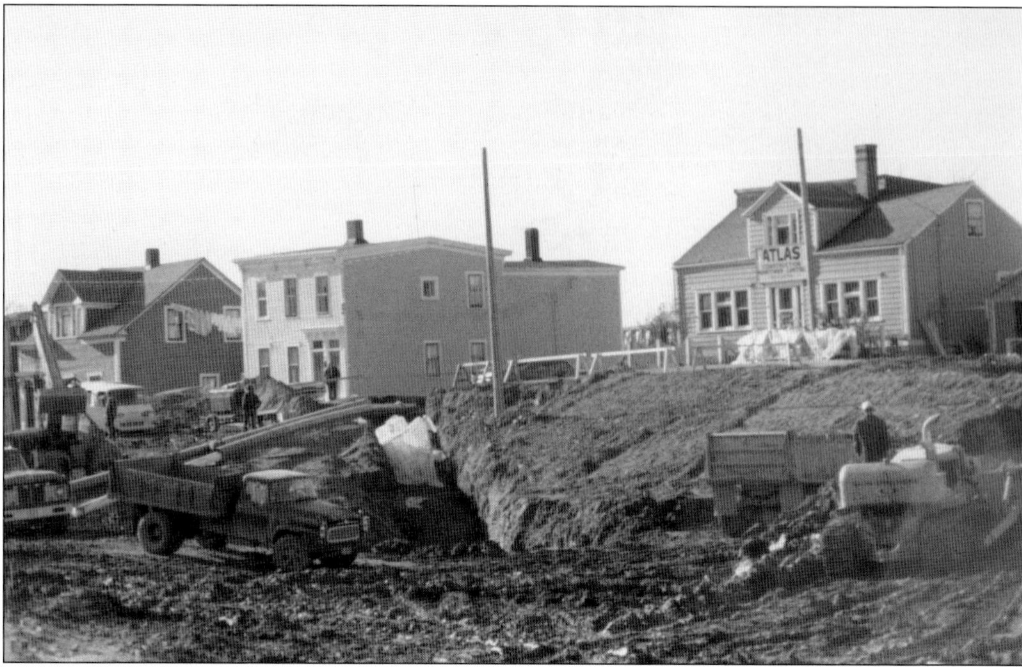

It was FENCO's suggestion to have the bridge as a connector between the Fredericton and Moncton highways. This would make travel between the three cities more accessible and would promote tourism through the summer months. The west side saw a significant portion of housing destroyed to make the throughway project along Riverview Drive a reality.

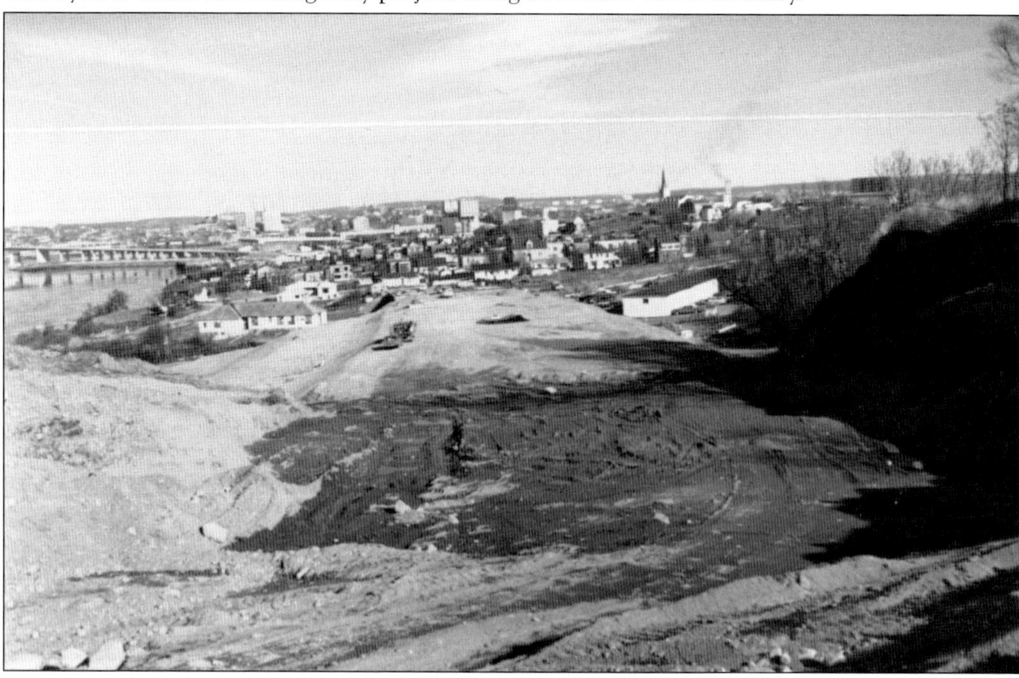

The Saint John Throughway project was just as intensive as the Saint John Harbour Bridge project. This is the western portion of the throughway heading to the toll booth. On either side of the new road are the long white buildings of the DVA Hospital.

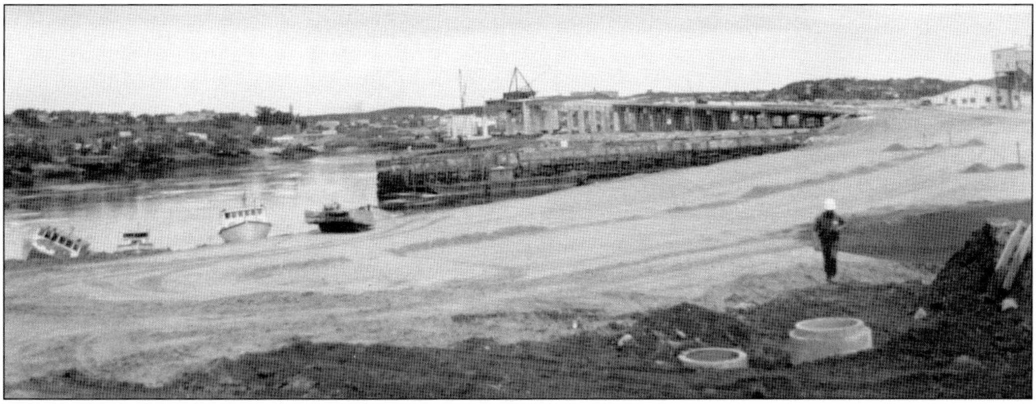

This is the toll plaza area where, due to soft subsoils, H-piles were installed to give the ground a more stable base. The soil here was still settling, so thousands of pounds of fill was dropped and, eventually, removed to accelerate settlement. This was called a surcharge, and the decompression of the soil was constantly monitored until there was no more room for the ground to settle.

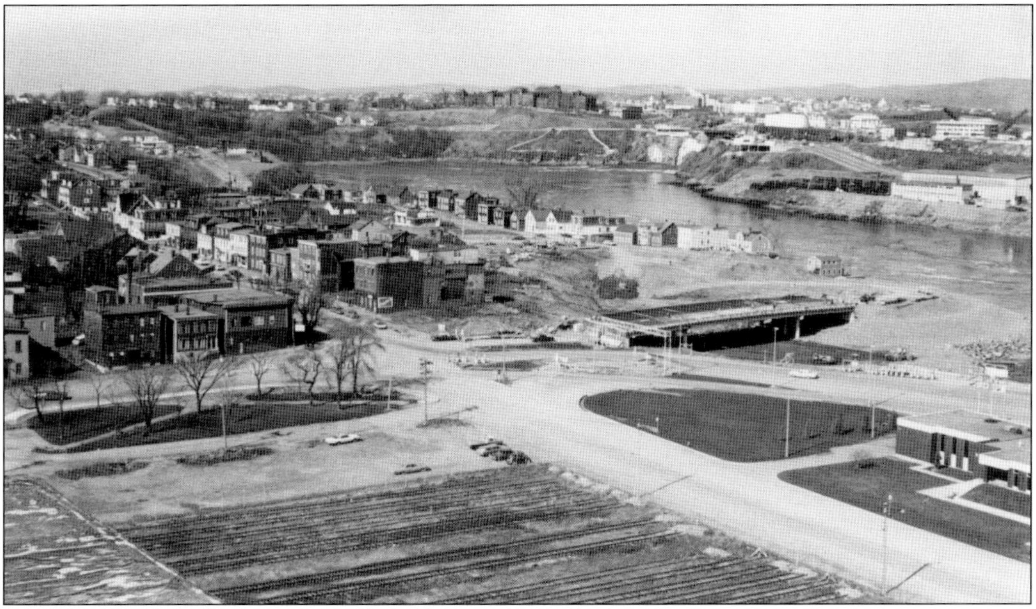

Tilley Square is at the centre while the bottom of the photograph shows land that belongs to the Port of Saint John. The Saint John Harbour Bridge Authority and the Port of Saint John have always had a close relationship. Bridge workers would need to gain access to storage held under the bridge through the port, and the port's large cargo and wide loads would need to pass over the bridge. (Courtesy of David Goss.)

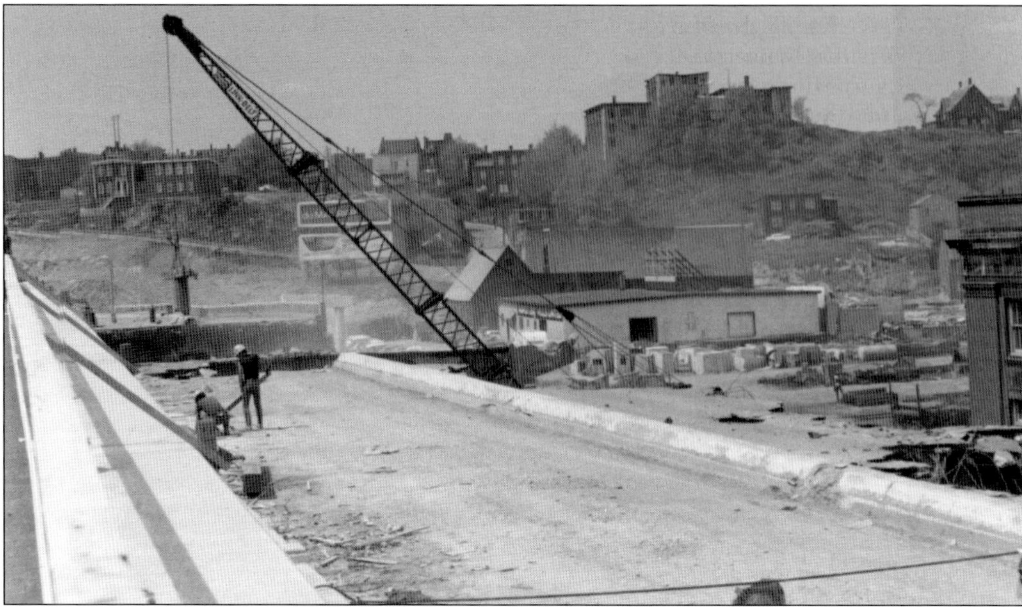

The 1951 viaduct was replaced by a new viaduct that was considered crucial to the Saint John Harbour Bridge and Throughway projects. Before the original viaduct had been paid for, it was demolished in stages to allow for the new viaducts completion in 1970. The Union Station at the right quickly followed in 1974–1975. Harbour Station now sits on the land vacated by the train station.

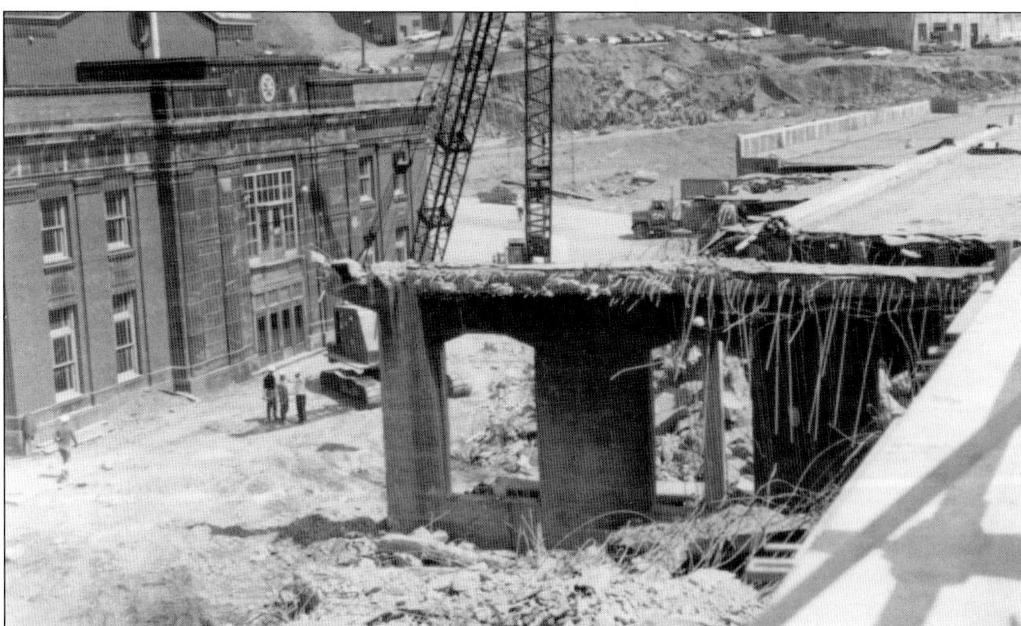

Dufresne Construction of Montreal received the contract to build the new viaduct. When the west side of the six-lane viaduct was complete, demolition began on the east side of the viaduct. The original main entrance into the train station is shown behind the crane.

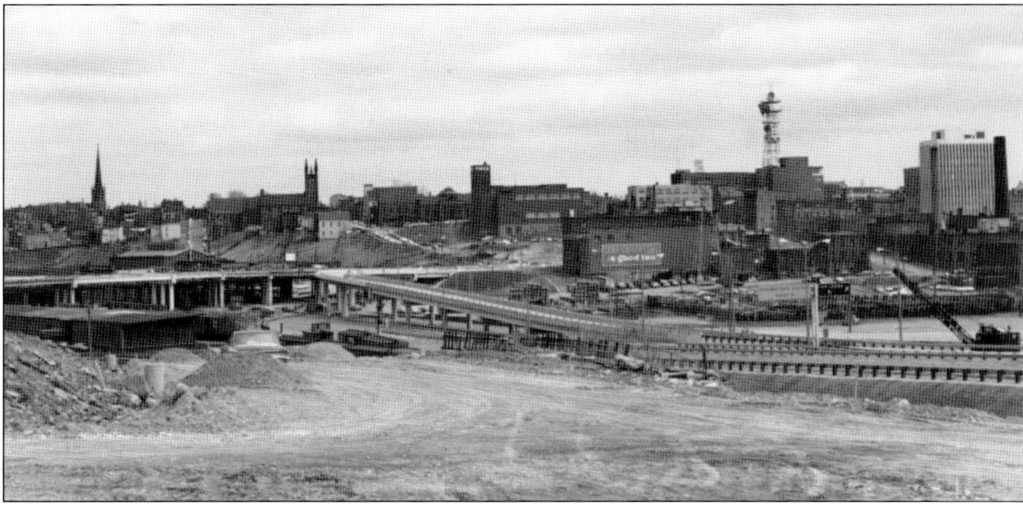

One can see the Mill Street exit from the Saint John Harbour Bridge to the uptown area directly in front of the Red Rose Tea Building. This exit is infamous for its fender-benders, with motorists who rarely yield the right-of-way. The Young Men's Christian Association (YMCA) Building has been replaced by the new Saint John Law Courts.

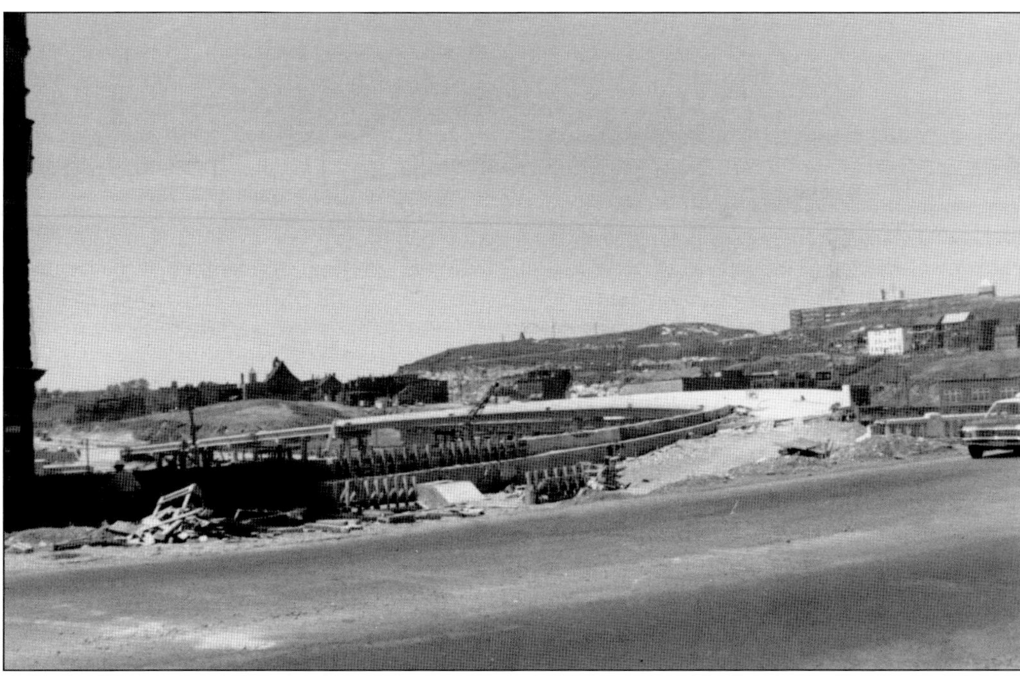

By 1967, all areas were under construction, with work being done at the toll plaza embankment by Galbraith Construction; the Administrative Building by Modern Construction, Limited; the 11-lane toll plaza by Atlas Construction Company, Limited; and the eastern connections by Dufresene Construction, Limited. All work had to be completed by October 1968.

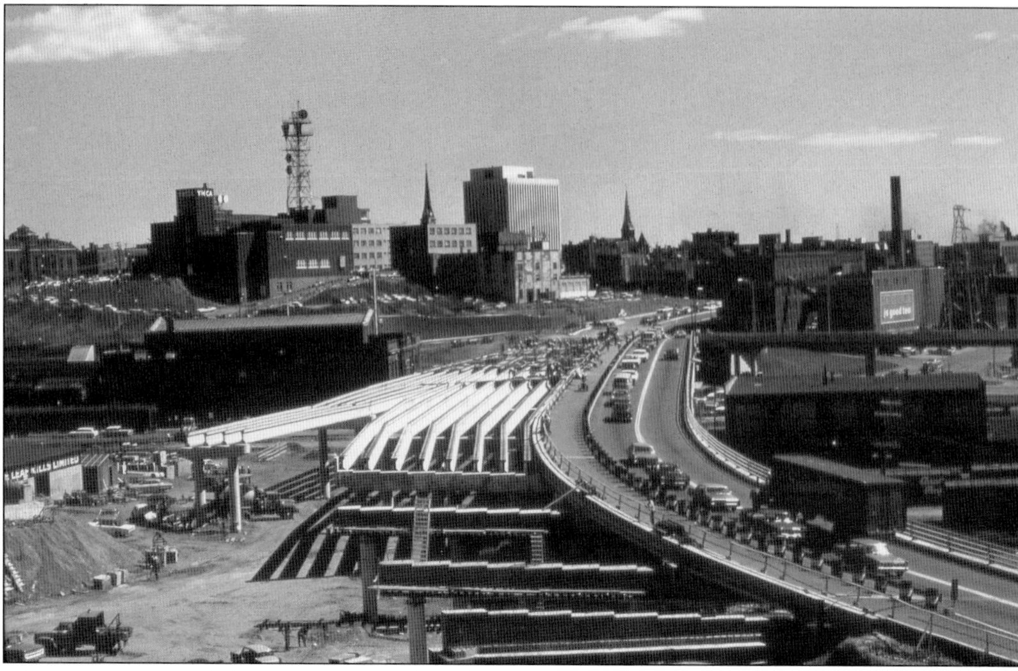

The eastern side of the viaduct is well under way, with the exit onto the Saint John Harbour Bridge taking shape. While this was being built, urban renewal was still happening in the East End and around Main Street. (Courtesy of Jim Sulis.)

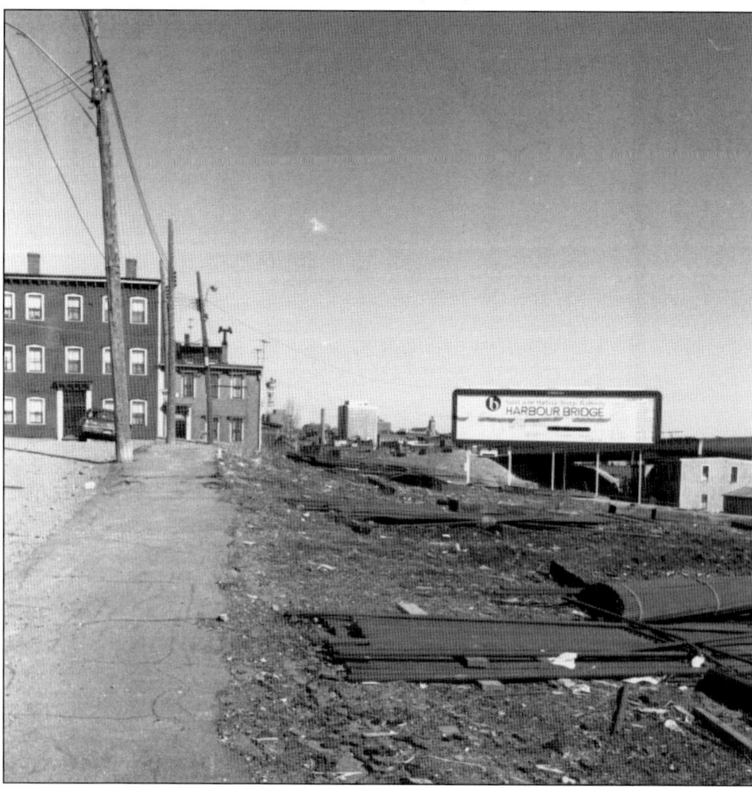

By August 1968, the bridge was completed, including bridge lighting, overhead signs, and railings, by Northern Roofing and Metals Workers of Saint John. Maritime Gardeners, Limited, had also finished the landscaping. Over the course of the bridge project, there were four Saint John mayors in office, Eric L. Teed, Stephen H. Weyman, Arthur L. Gould, and Joseph A. MacDougall. (Courtesy of Bob Boudreau.)

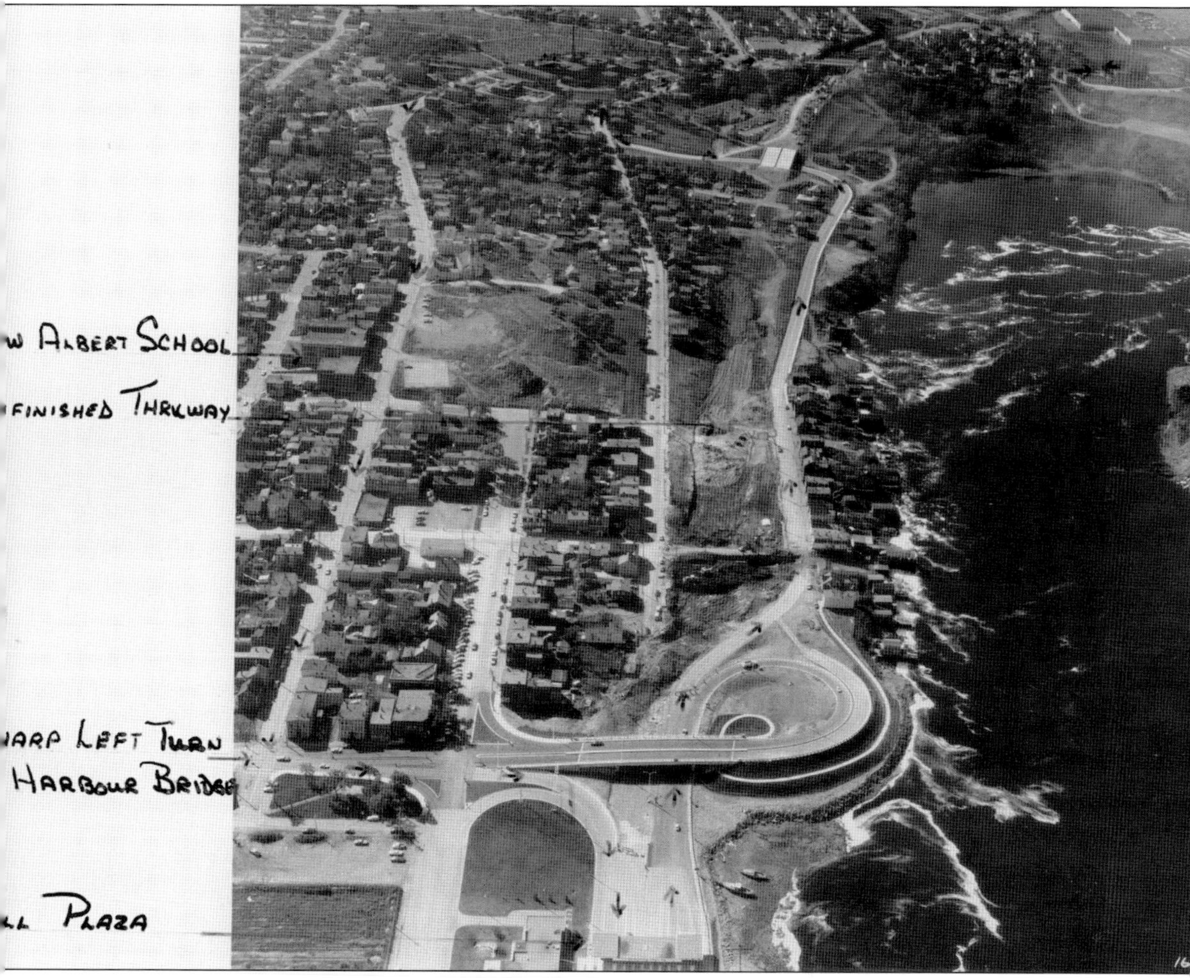

The original opening was supposed to take place in October 1967, but this was delayed due to revised designs to the north approach. On August 17, 1968, the bridge was partially open through to the North End ramps. This lasted until the complete roadway was officially opened in mid-September, which was followed with a full ceremony on September 28, 1968.

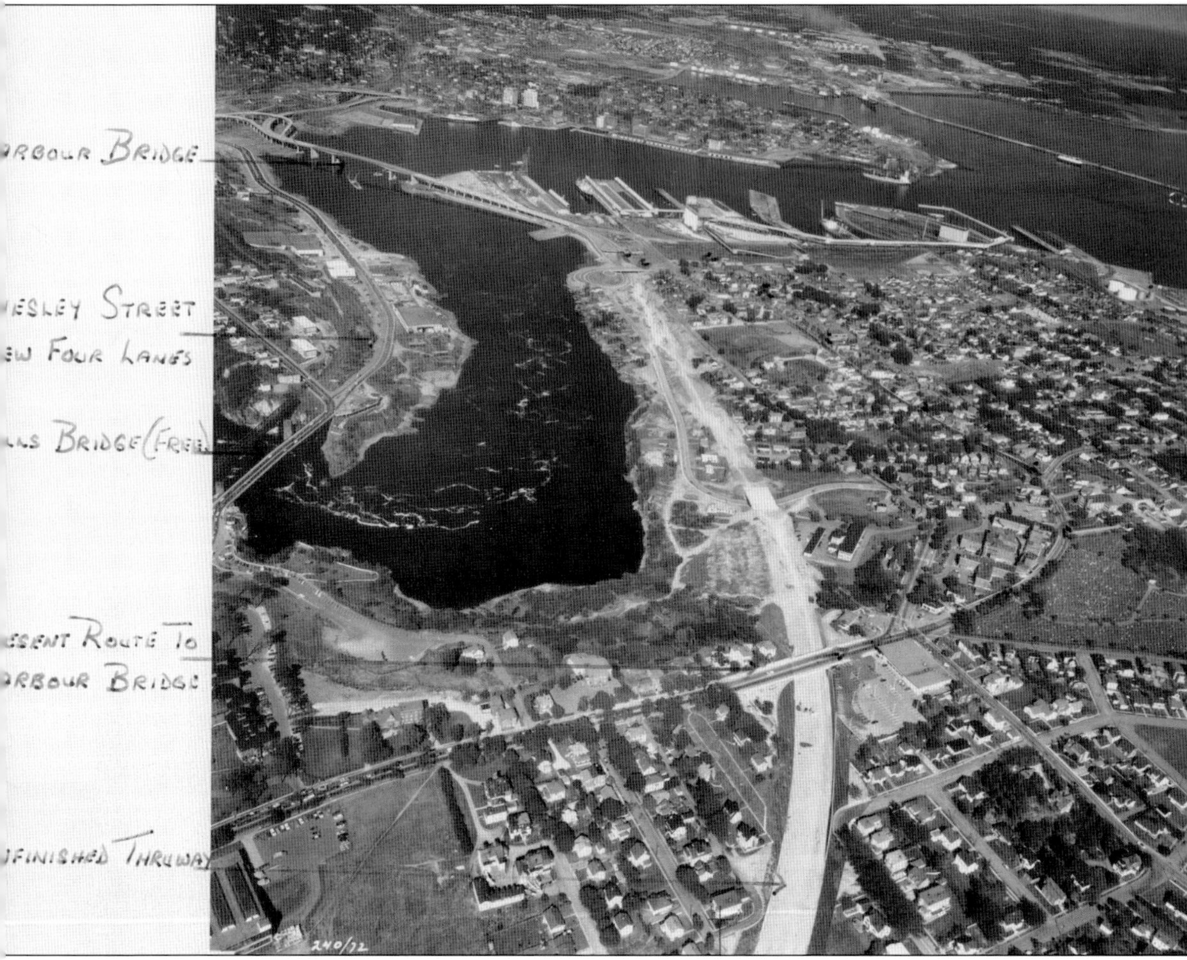

The 100-year dream was finally fulfilled. The only downside to the day's events was the realization that the tolls would be a necessary evil. The battle to remove the tolls began on the day it opened, with Premier Robichaud saying, "We must look forward to the time when our magnificent new bridge will be as it was first conceived to be, a toll-free bridge." The tolls would stay in effect until 4:00 p.m., April 1, 2011, when they were finally removed.

Ten

The Saint John Harbour Bridge Authority

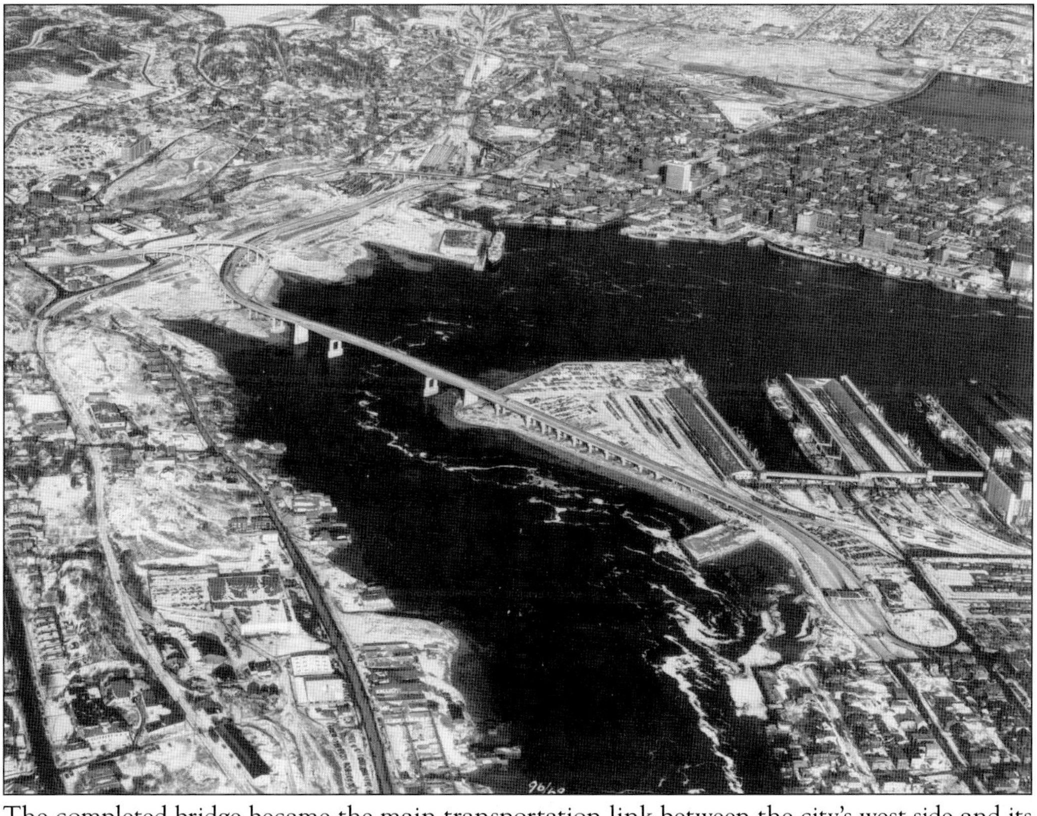

The completed bridge became the main transportation link between the city's west side and its North and South Ends. At the cost of a mere quarter, motorists could save time and gas from having to take the older route at the Reversing Falls. Aside from the ideal location of the bridge, it was also connected to the major highway systems between Fredericton and Moncton and had four lanes instead of two. The throughway would not be completed for a few more years, but traffic congestion would be lessened, even if the public's dislike for the toll was not.

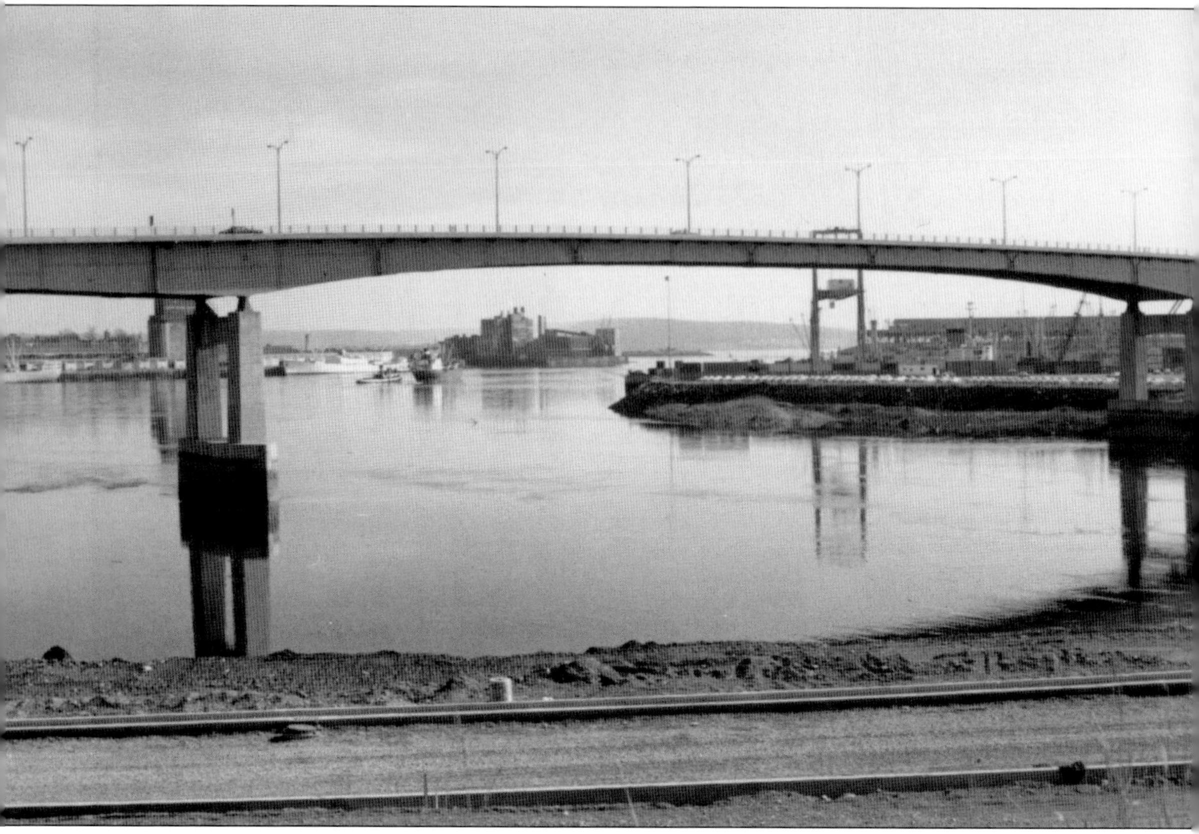

The bridge's size did not disrupt much of the fishing activity in the harbour or any of the usual shipping movement that came from the pleasure craft on the Saint John River. The green orthotropic span was now a part of the city's identity and offered the best view of the uptown as one approached from the west side. For years, boaters could float about the harbour with the only concerns being the tides, the spring freshshet, and other harbour boating activities. With the bridge in place, they needed to pay attention to the concrete piers.

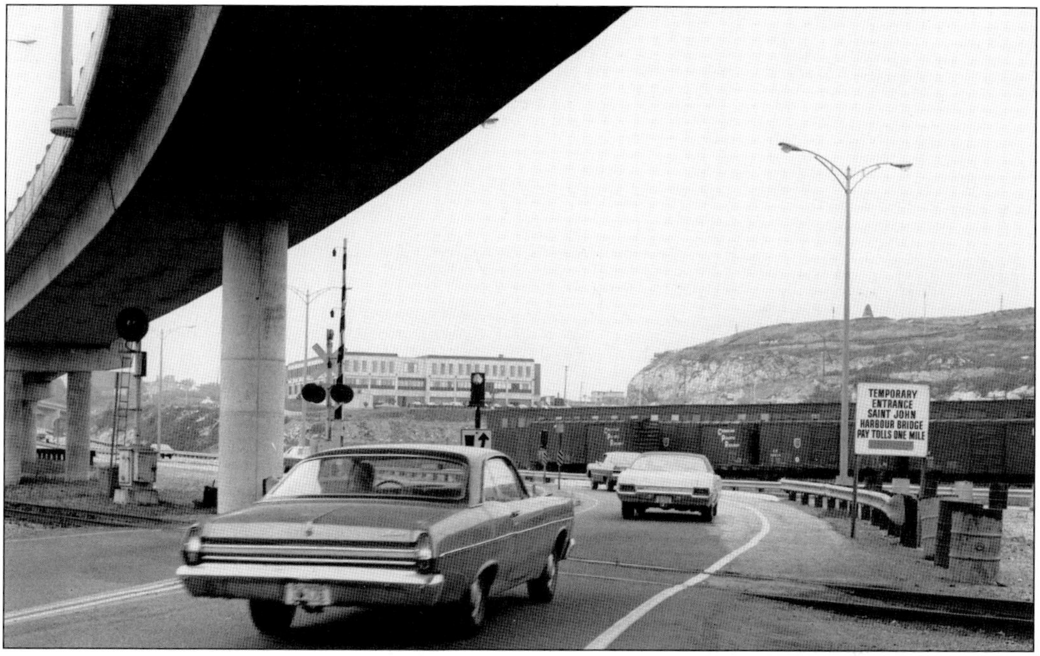

This is the temporary Mill Street approach; it was used until the throughway was completed. The rail line is still intact, and the Harbour Passage walkway skirts the train line to Chesley Drive and HMCS *Brunswicker*. In the distance is Fort Howe where the current "SAINT JOHN" neon sign is located.

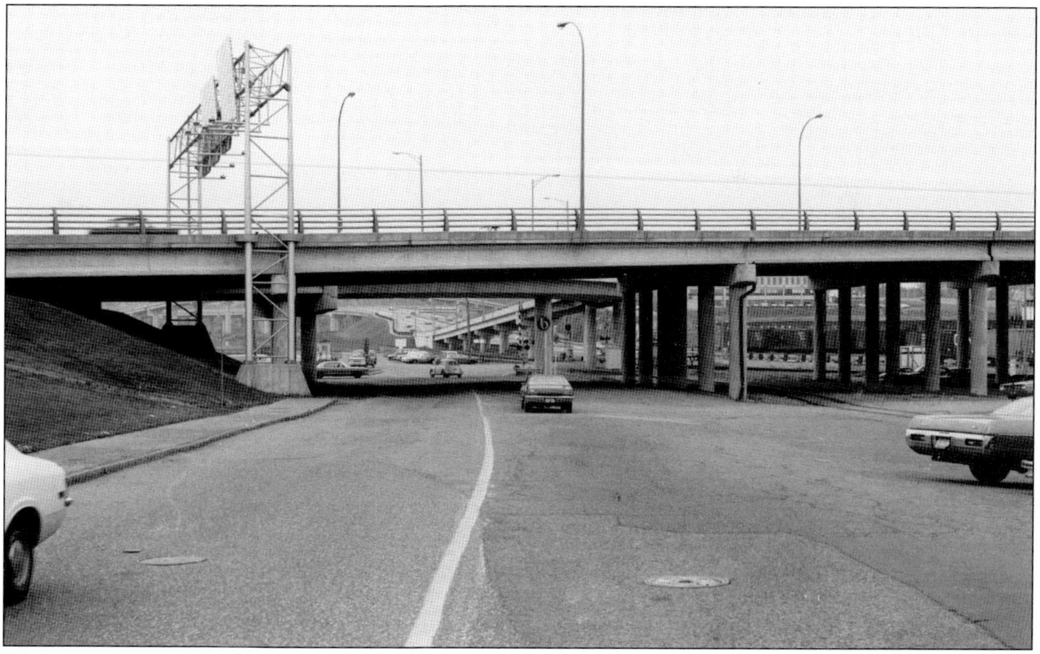

This was the approach to the Mill Street on-ramp that curves to the right under the bridge. Note the Saint John Harbour Bridge arrow sign on the concrete post. For a few years, this was the only way onto the bridge from the uptown area. Today, the skateboard park and parking for Harbour Station are at the right under the viaduct.

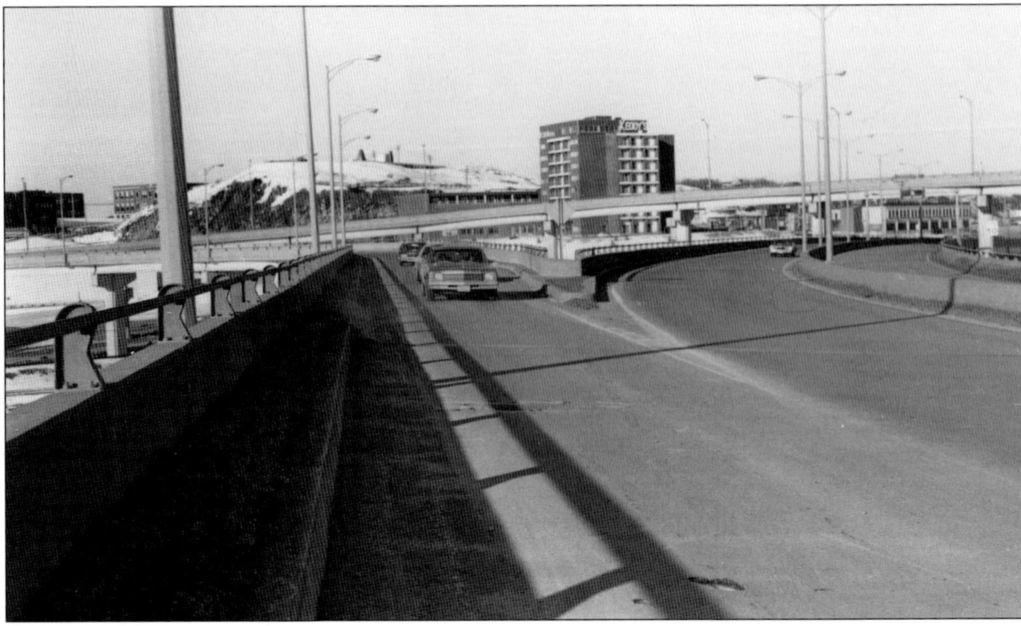

The Harrison Street ramp collects traffic from the North End heading west. Every spring, the dirt acquired from the winter's snowplows and traffic is removed. Each of the bridge's rubber joints are blown clean of debris with an air compressor, and any deck repairs that are needed are identified. This process usually takes place over April and May and can slow traffic down during the daytime between peak operational hours.

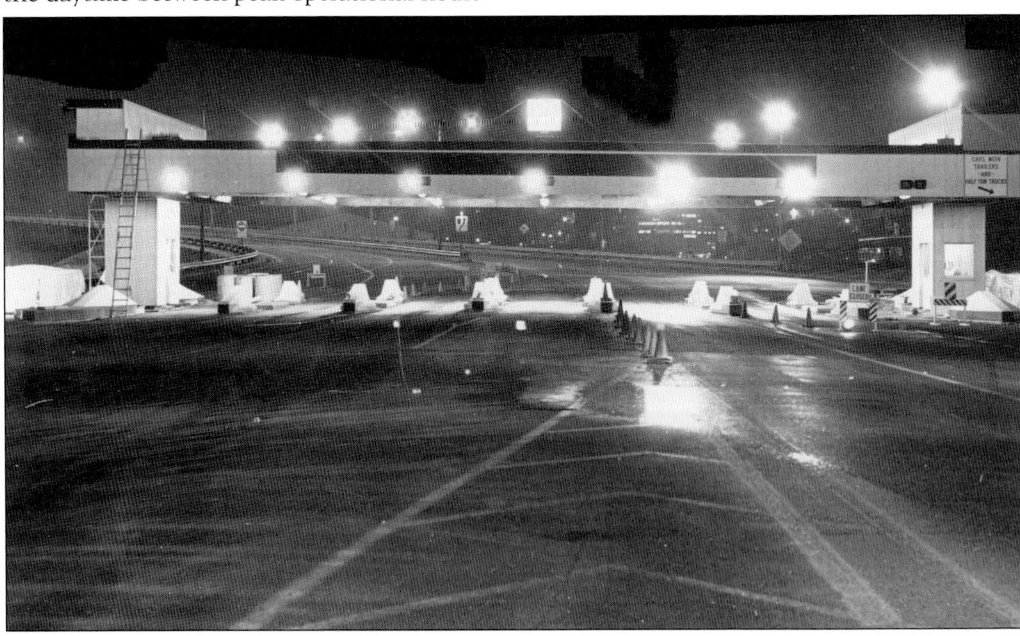

The toll plaza consists of four large outside lanes for transport trucks, two inner eastbound and three inner westbound lanes, and one break down lane on each side. This shows the plaza under construction and without the four toll booths, which shielded the staff collectors from the elements and traffic. Typical maintenance at the toll plaza included daily maintenance of the coin machines and any damage caused by traffic.

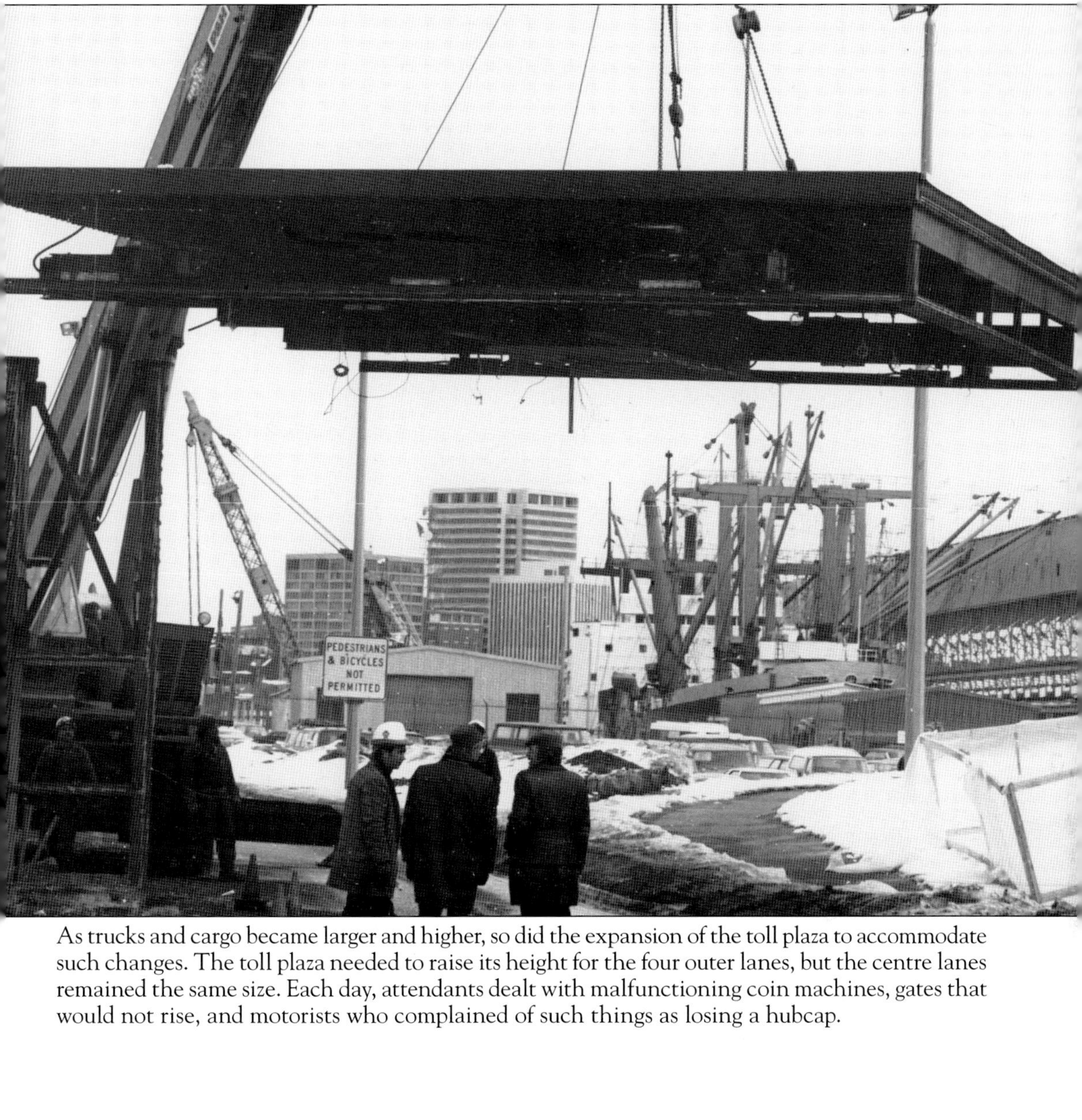

As trucks and cargo became larger and higher, so did the expansion of the toll plaza to accommodate such changes. The toll plaza needed to raise its height for the four outer lanes, but the centre lanes remained the same size. Each day, attendants dealt with malfunctioning coin machines, gates that would not rise, and motorists who complained of such things as losing a hubcap.

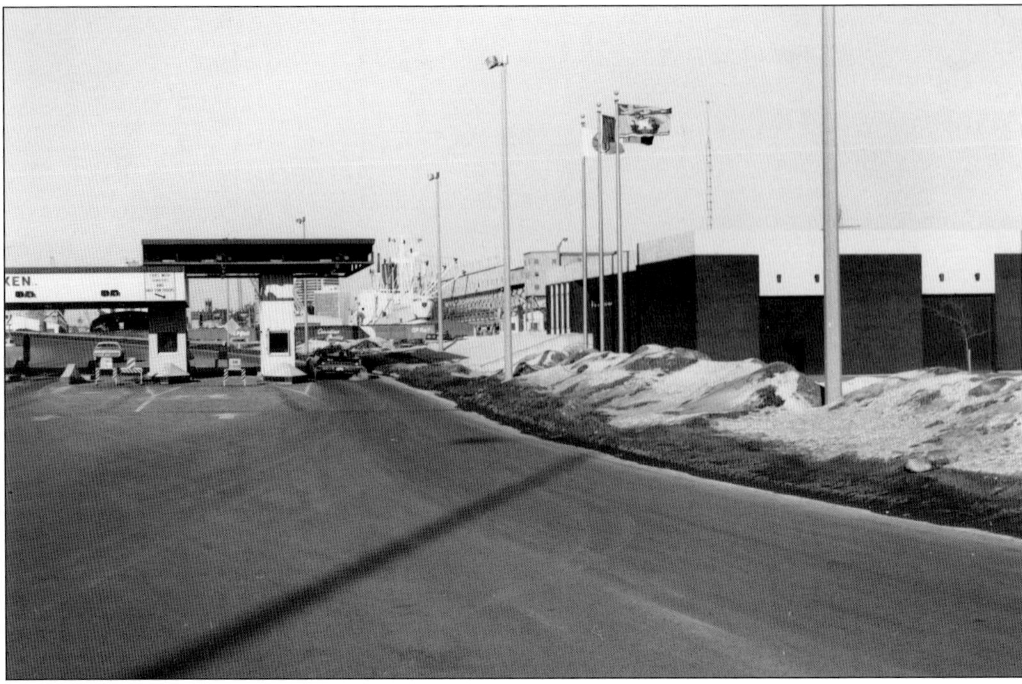

This is the toll plaza as viewed from entering the bridge from the west side. The maintenance and office buildings are at the right. This is the home base for coin collectors, maintenance workers, and office staff. From this base, staff did everything—road plowing, guard rail repairs, maintenance of the lawns and flower beds, and painting. In 2007, a video camera system was installed to catch "runners," those who would try and get through the tolls without paying.

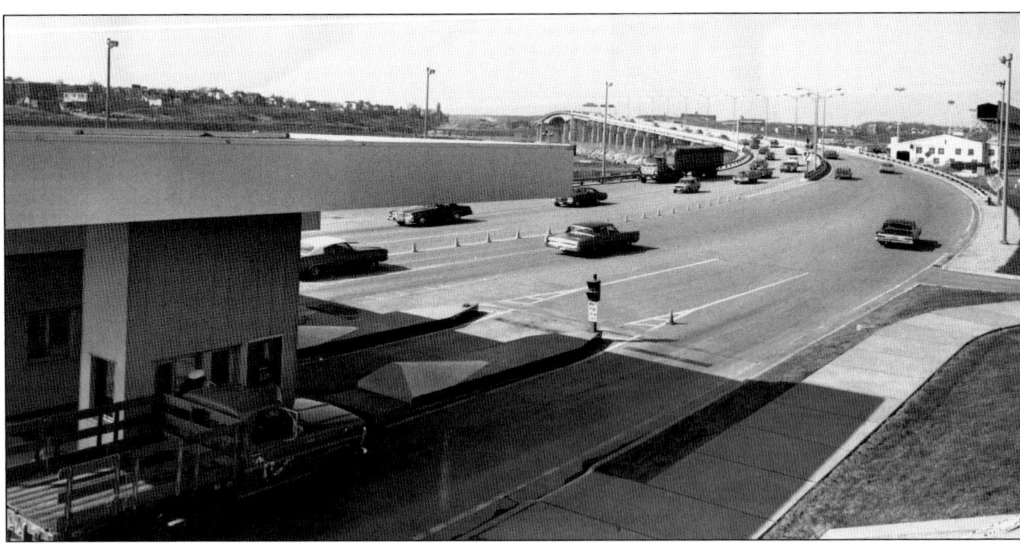

Cars heading east needed to be aware that there were four lanes leaving the plaza merging into two on the bridge itself. The morning rush hour, between 7:00 a.m. and 8:30 a.m., was usually a slow affair, with bottlenecking occurring at this spot. Daily shutdown of lanes would only occur between peaks traffic times to lessen public outcry and the potential for accidents on the bridge.

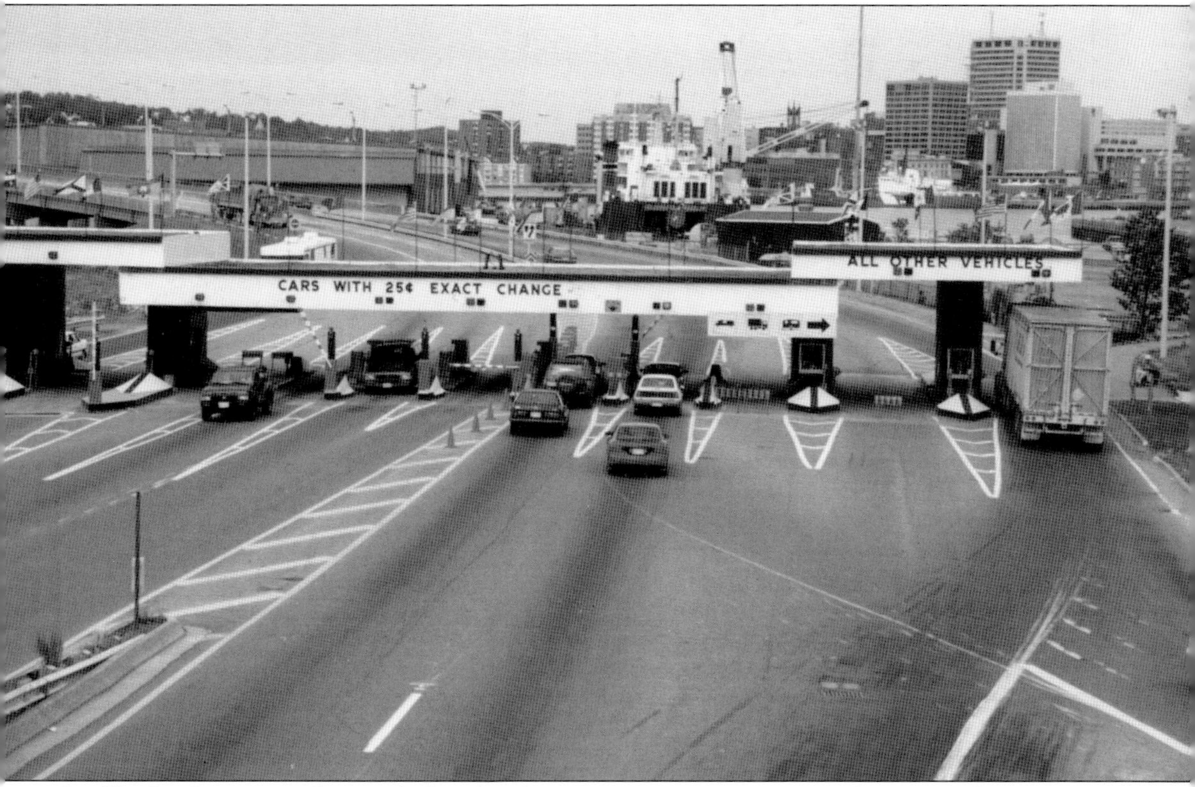

Staff had to be ever vigilant with their heads up to stop someone trying to bring a trailer, camper trailer, or even a one-ton truck through the centre lanes. If there was an accident, breakdown, or spill, attendants put up a barricade and directed traffic to the other lanes.

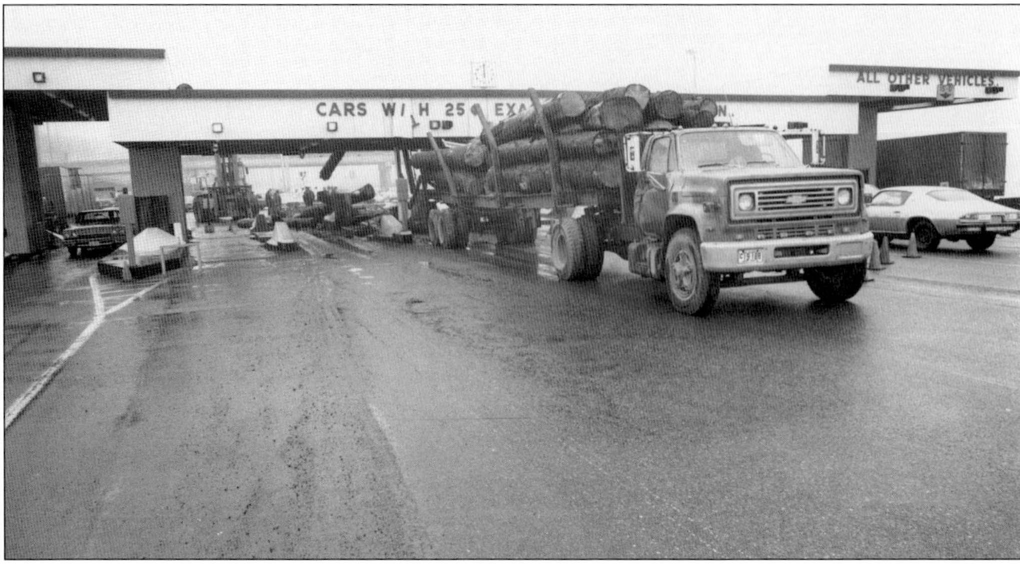

The bridge could be a dangerous spot to work. On February 1976, a wood truck heading east did not adhere to the signs and went through one of the centre lanes. Luckily, no one was injured, and there was no severe structural damage except for the steel panels on the western side of the plaza. Aside from the physical clean up, there were the necessary repairs to the siding, electrical, and coin collecting machines. Over the years, more signage was put up, but it does not always prevent accidents in the lanes.

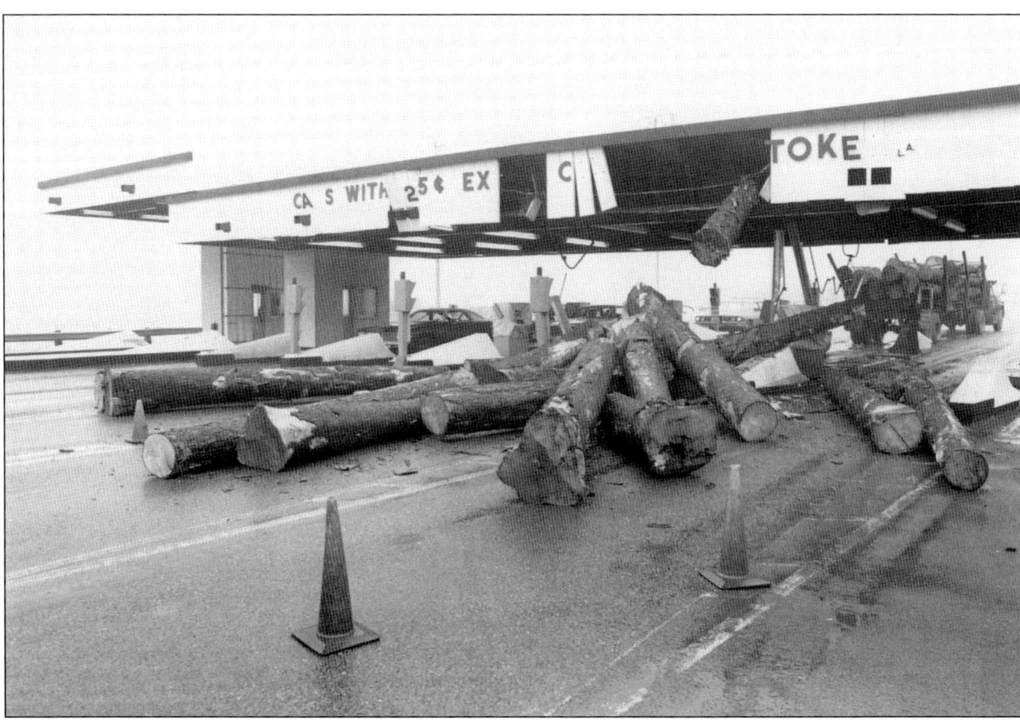

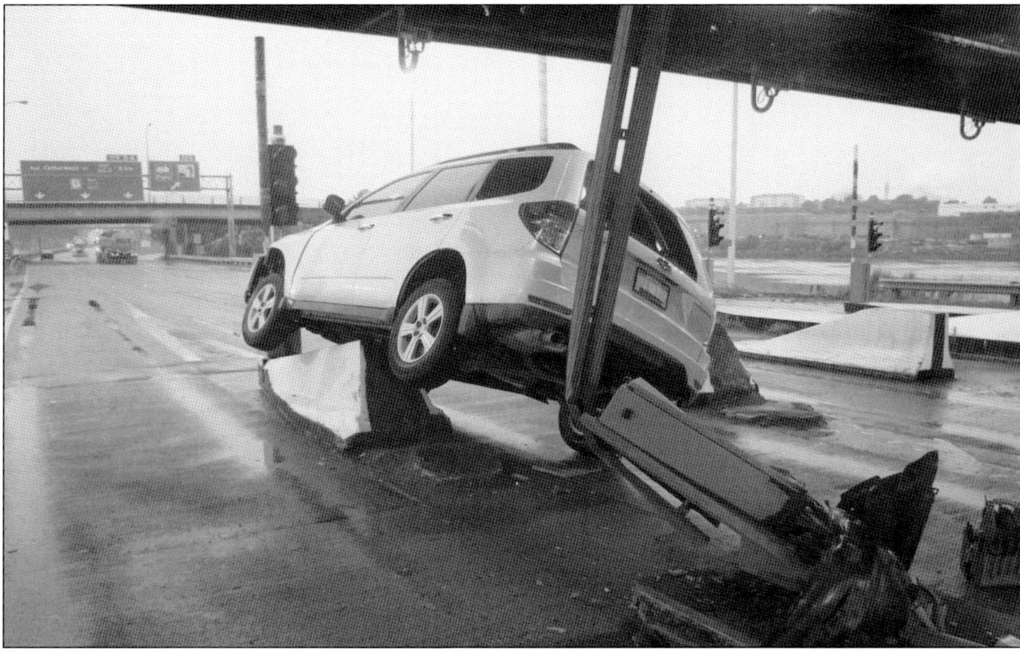

The lanes were sometimes a scary spot for the attendants and workers alike. The drive through was so narrow that if a car hit one side of the medians, the car could be projected through the air or could bounce around destroying coin machines or electrical boxes. There are countless stories regarding the excessive speed, accidents, or inattentive drivers. (Courtesy of Joseph Goguen.)

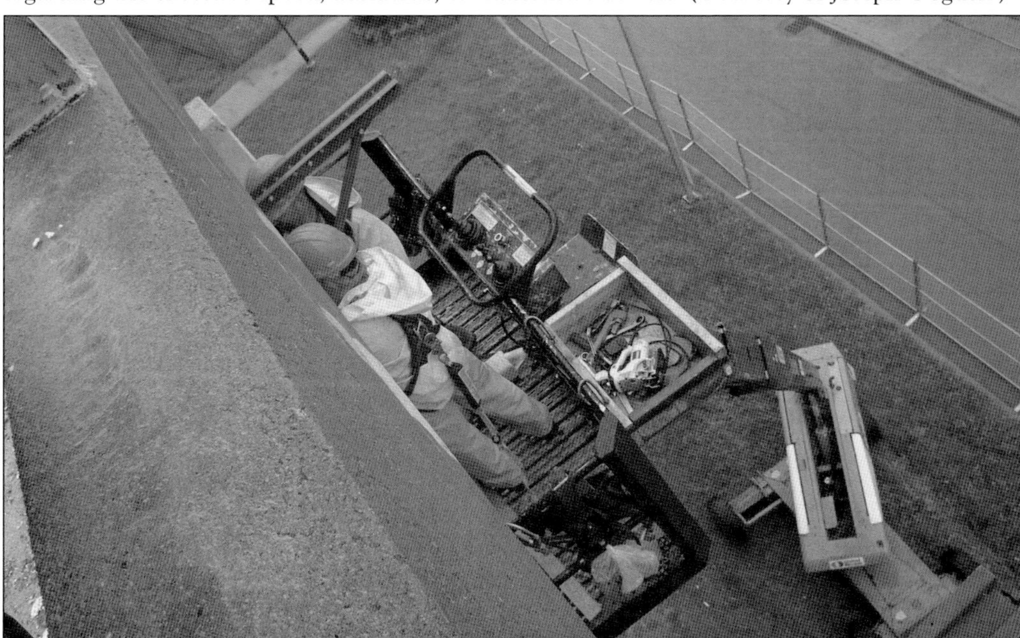

Over the years, there have been significant upgrades to the bridge, including a new paint job, pier repairs, re-decking, and removal of the old lighting system. The steel rails were replaced with new concrete walls. These repairs were long overdue but have caused numerous back-to-back summer traffic problems. (Courtesy of Joseph Goguen.)

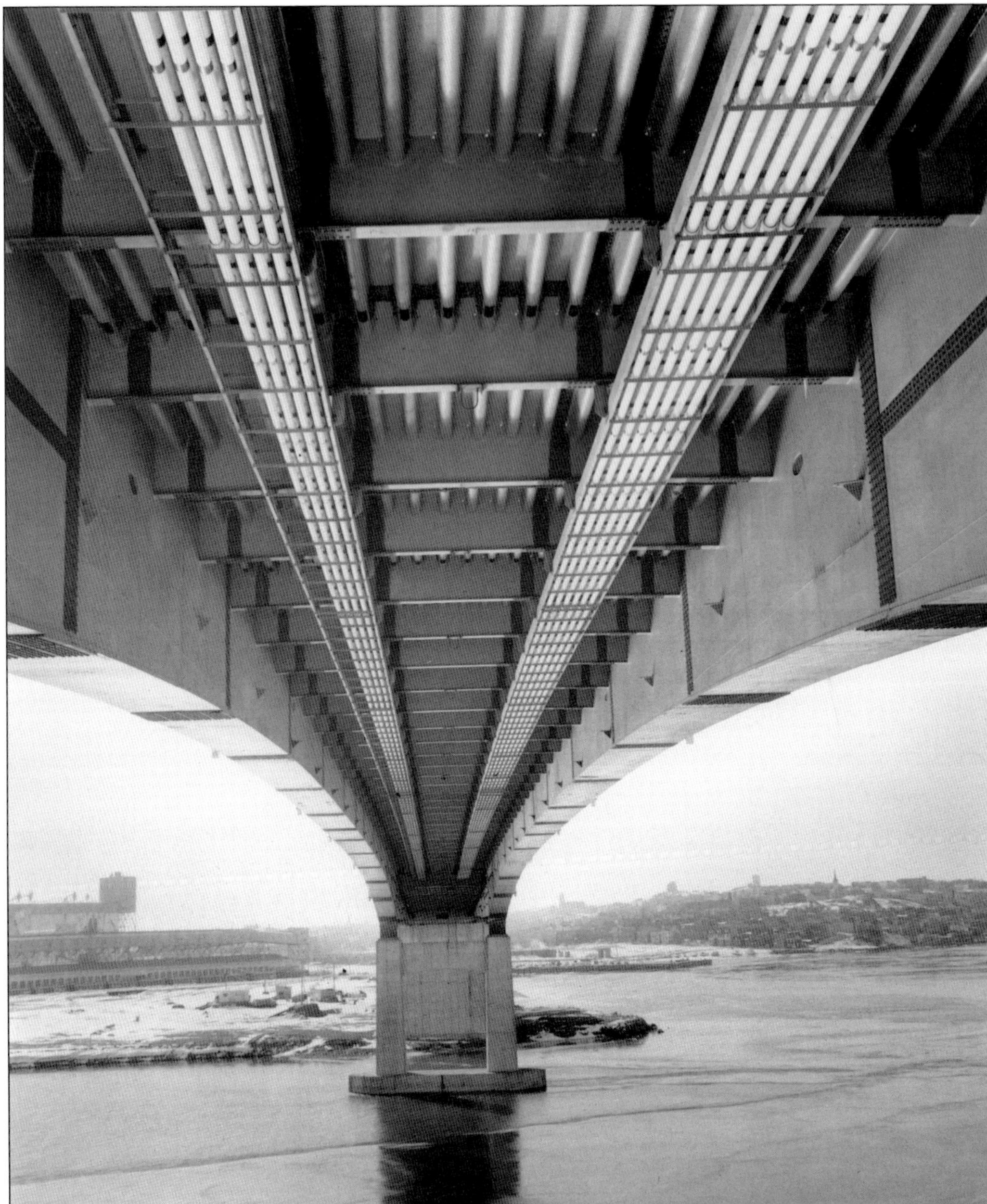

The 970-foot orthotropic span (550 feet main, two 210 feet side flanks) is hollow within, like a submarine. The span interiors are dark and only lit by light bulbs strung from one end to the other and powered by a gasoline generator. There have been racoons and countless pigeons found in the structure. To access the inner parts of the span, one needs to go down an enclosed steel ladder that drops over each side of the bridge and then crawl under the concrete on one's knees until reaching a metal hatch that keeps out the animals and weather. The centre span holds a series of pipes and power and telephone lines.

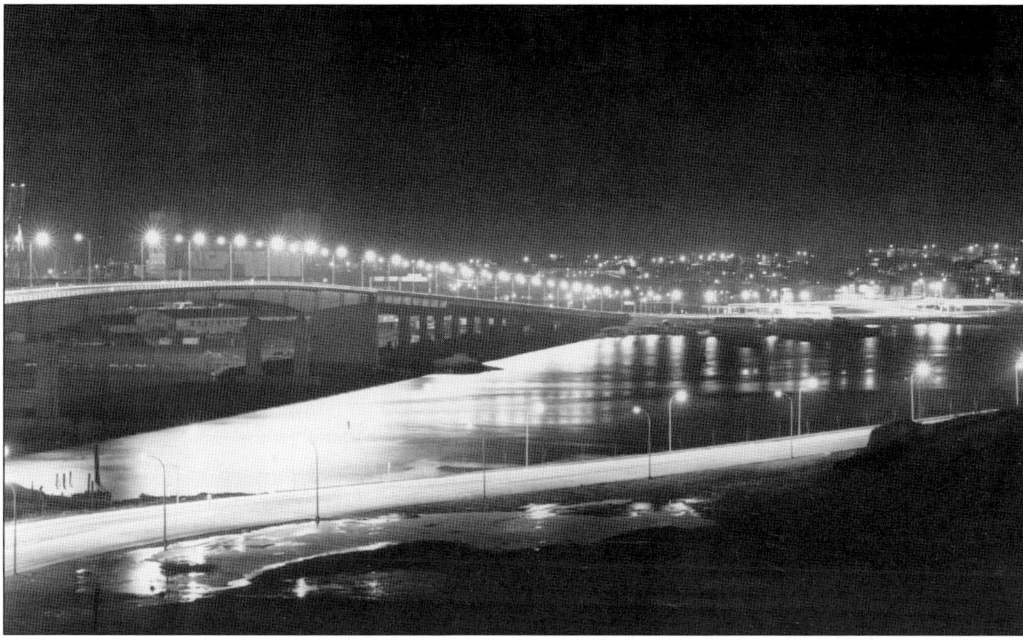

For over 45 years, the harbour has been silhouetted by the bridge. Some motorists may take the bridge for granted, but its importance is always felt when the Reversing Falls Bridge is closed for repairs or when the Saint John Harbour Bridge is down to one lane in each direction. Innovations in construction have allowed the bridge to stay partially open during the past few summers while repairs have been completed.

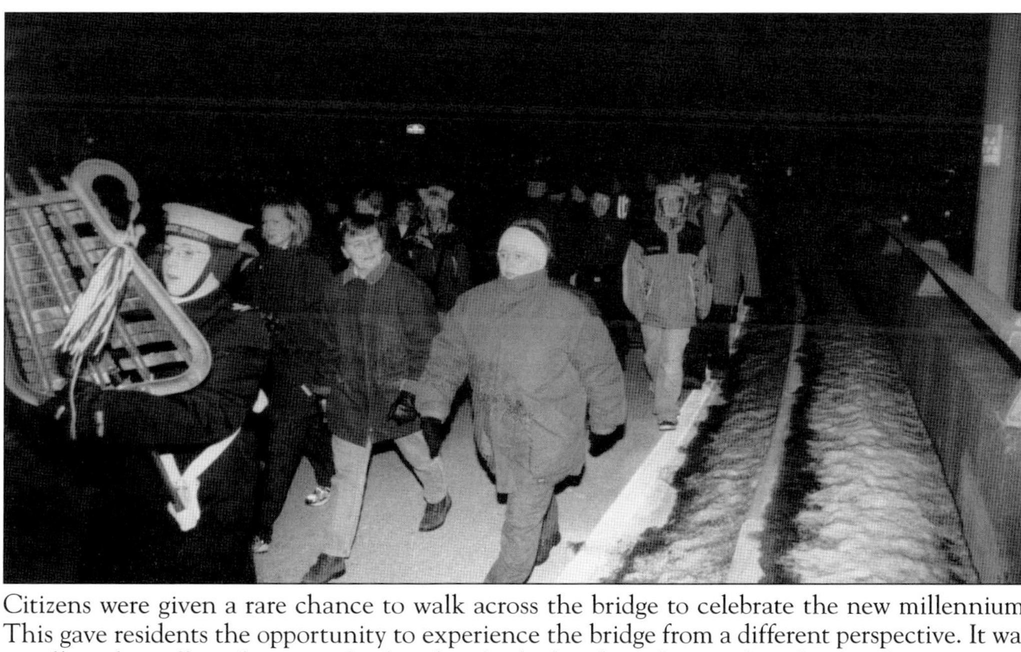

Citizens were given a rare chance to walk across the bridge to celebrate the new millennium. This gave residents the opportunity to experience the bridge from a different perspective. It was usually only staff, or those involved with a fender-bender, who got this close to the pavement. Any other time of the year, it is illegal to walk the bridge.

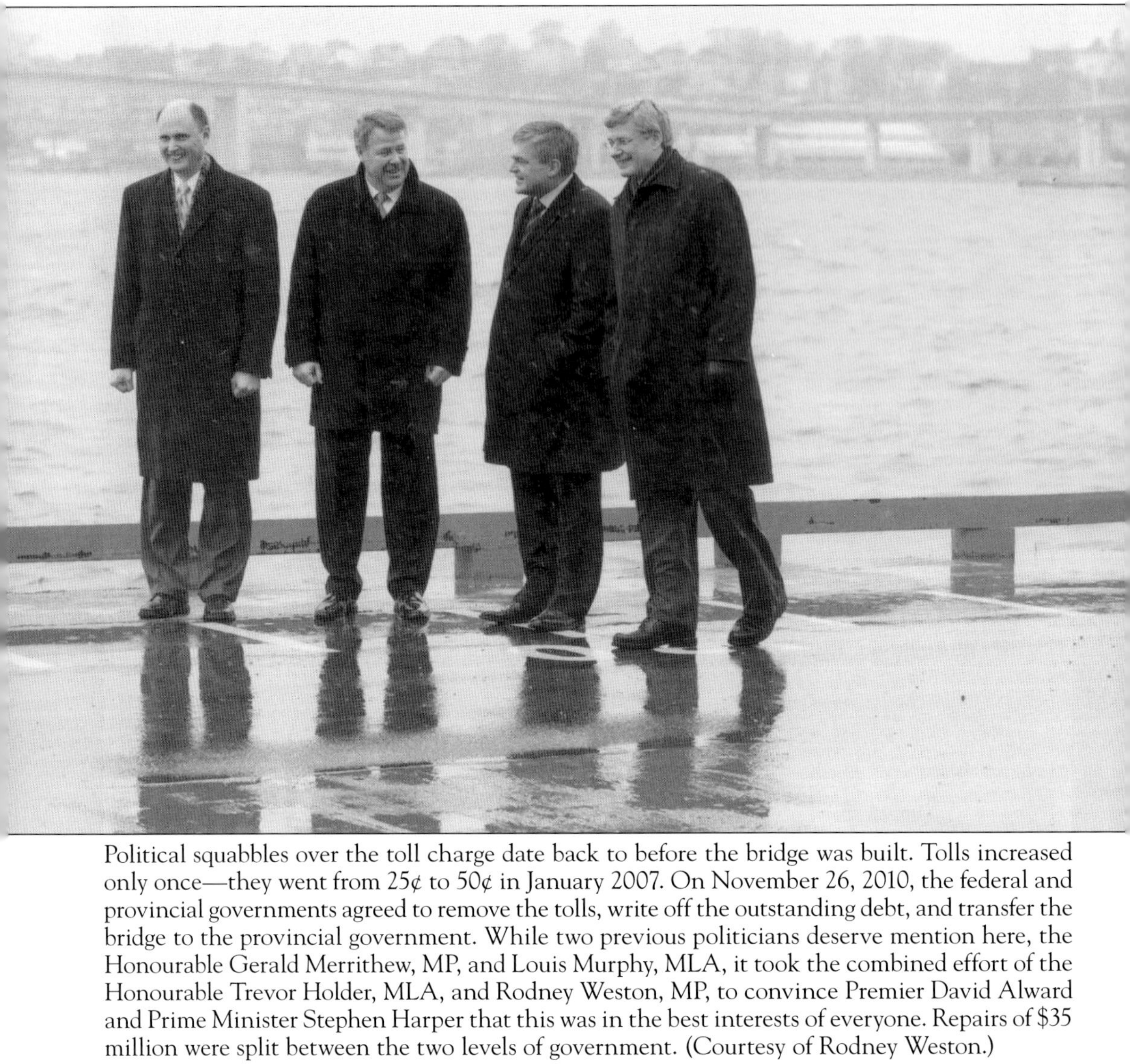

Political squabbles over the toll charge date back to before the bridge was built. Tolls increased only once—they went from 25¢ to 50¢ in January 2007. On November 26, 2010, the federal and provincial governments agreed to remove the tolls, write off the outstanding debt, and transfer the bridge to the provincial government. While two previous politicians deserve mention here, the Honourable Gerald Merrithew, MP, and Louis Murphy, MLA, it took the combined effort of the Honourable Trevor Holder, MLA, and Rodney Weston, MP, to convince Premier David Alward and Prime Minister Stephen Harper that this was in the best interests of everyone. Repairs of $35 million were split between the two levels of government. (Courtesy of Rodney Weston.)

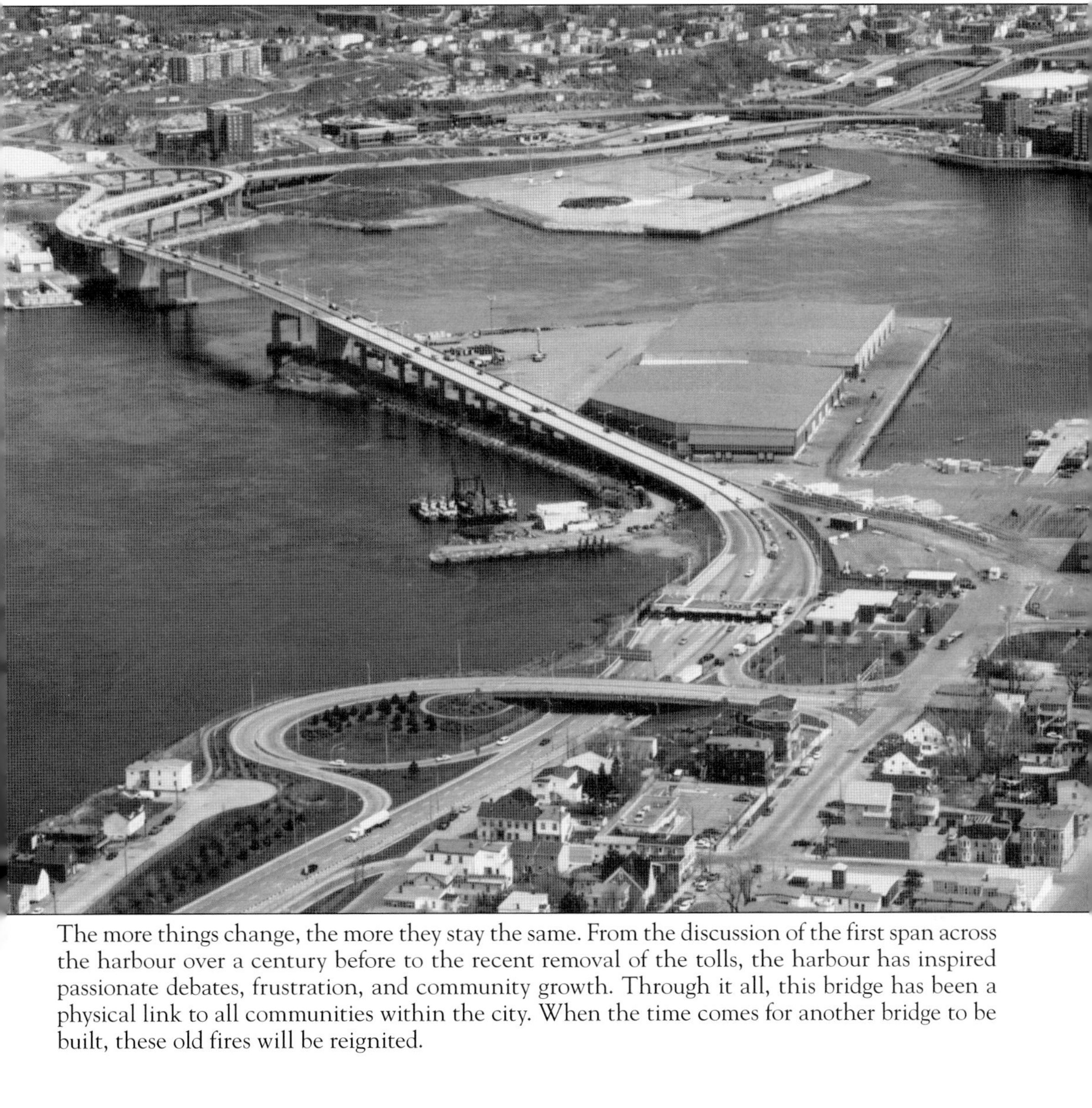

The more things change, the more they stay the same. From the discussion of the first span across the harbour over a century before to the recent removal of the tolls, the harbour has inspired passionate debates, frustration, and community growth. Through it all, this bridge has been a physical link to all communities within the city. When the time comes for another bridge to be built, these old fires will be reignited.